Troubling Muslim Youth Identities: Nation, Religion, Gender

"A richly detailed cross-national study of the diversity of Muslim youth, which sheds light on the complexity of their attitudes towards national and gender, as well as religious, identities. An extremely valuable resource for anyone seeking to go beyond well-worn clichés about global Islam."

—**Cécile Laborde,** *Nuffield Professor of Political Theory, University of Oxford*

"A timely work that needs to be read and discussed widely."

—**Shahnaz Rouse,** *Professor of Sociology, Sarah Lawrence College, Bronxville, N.Y. 10708, USA*

"By exploring the pluralities of Muslim youth identity formations in three different regions - South Asia, Middle East and West Africa, and in four contrasting national contexts – Pakistan, Lebanon, Senegal and Nigeria, the authors of this book expose the deep fault lines in collective histories, challenge reified identities, and reflect on what accounts for the "untroubling" of representations of gender in its intersections with other axes of belonging. This book is a must-read for scholars, students and practitioners committed to understanding agency in a dynamic and nuanced manner, from the ground up."

—**Professor Mariz Tadros,** *Institute of Development Studies, University of Sussex, UK*

"In the context of ever escalating stereotypes in public discourse that depict Muslim youths one dimensionally as posing a security problem, this book makes a powerful case for the relevance of more nuanced and grounded assessments of the of the issues faced by young Muslims in particular settings. Its carefully chosen range of case studies and clear style assure that the book holds critical relevance for students, scholars and policy makers seeking to better understand the pressing concerns faced by young men and women across the Muslim world."

—**Magnus Marsden,** *Professor of Social Anthropology, Director of Sussex Asia Centre, School of Global Studies, University of Sussex*

"Amid widespread increases in extreme violence globally, we are witnessing an uncritical acceptance of dominant narratives about young Muslims and their identity, which homogenise Muslim youth and presents them all as active or potential agents of terror rather than as agents of change.

"Troubling Muslim Youth Identities: Nation, Religion, Gender" by Máiréad Dunne, Naureen Durrani, Kathleen Fincham and Barbara Crossouard comes as a welcome antidote to a narrative that continues to fuel popular misconceptions about Muslim youth. Based on 4 diverse country contexts - Pakistan, Lebanon, Nigeria and Senegal, they illustrate the localness of Muslim youth identity formation but that it also involves "a complex interweaving of the local and the global, as well as the historical and the contemporaneous".

The authors "multi-layered analysis of the heterogeneous ways that national and local cultures, societies and their education systems represent and produce social identities" is particularly relevant as various actors in the education community grapple with the issue of global citizenship education that is a core element not only of SDG4-Education 2030 and its target 4.7 but of the Transforming our World: 2030 Agenda for Sustainable Development as whole. The book and its focus on "nation, religion and gender and the intersections in their constructions of 'us' and 'others'" is most opportune as it will help challenge the current discourse around global citizenship education that has a tendency towards simplistic prescriptions linked to curriculum, measurement and indicators."

—**Dr Jordan Naidoo, Director,** *Division of Education 2030*
Support and Coordination, UNESCO, Paris, France

Máiréad Dunne · Naureen Durrani
Kathleen Fincham · Barbara Crossouard

Troubling Muslim Youth Identities

Nation, Religion, Gender

Máiréad Dunne
Centre for International Education
University of Sussex
Brighton, UK

Naureen Durrani
Centre for International Education
University of Sussex
Brighton, UK

Kathleen Fincham
St Mary's University
London, UK

Barbara Crossouard
Centre for International Education
University of Sussex
Brighton, UK

ISBN 978-0-230-34837-0   ISBN 978-1-137-31279-2   (eBook)
DOI 10.1057/978-1-137-31279-2

Library of Congress Control Number: 2017934059

© The Editor(s) (if applicable) and The Author(s) 2017
The author(s) has/have asserted their right(s) to be identified as the author(s) of this work in accordance with the Copyright, Designs and Patents Act 1988.
This work is subject to copyright. All rights are solely and exclusively licensed by the Publisher, whether the whole or part of the material is concerned, specifically the rights of translation, reprinting, reuse of illustrations, recitation, broadcasting, reproduction on microfilms or in any other physical way, and transmission or information storage and retrieval, electronic adaptation, computer software, or by similar or dissimilar methodology now known or hereafter developed.
The use of general descriptive names, registered names, trademarks, service marks, etc. in this publication does not imply, even in the absence of a specific statement, that such names are exempt from the relevant protective laws and regulations and therefore free for general use.
The publisher, the authors and the editors are safe to assume that the advice and information in this book are believed to be true and accurate at the date of publication. Neither the publisher nor the authors or the editors give a warranty, express or implied, with respect to the material contained herein or for any errors or omissions that may have been made. The publisher remains neutral with regard to jurisdictional claims in published maps and institutional affiliations.

Cover credit: © Anthony Haigh/Alamy Stock Photo

Printed on acid-free paper

This Palgrave Macmillan imprint is published by Springer Nature
The registered company is Macmillan Publishers Ltd.
The registered company address is: The Campus, 4 Crinan Street, London, N1 9XW, United Kingdom

For Understanding

Acknowledgements

We extend our thanks firstly to all the focus group participants in Pakistan, Senegal, Nigeria and Lebanon. Their willingness to give up their time to participate, their interest and engagement in the discussions were crucial to the research. We also owe tremendous thanks to all the gatekeepers who facilitated access to youth, to others who generously provided the spaces for the focus group discussions and to those who translated and transcribed the interviews. Special thanks go to the in-country researchers who organised and conducted the interviews, and their support and insights were indispensable. Finally, we acknowledge the particular and highly valued contribution of those individuals and organisations listed below who have in different ways supported the research in at least one of the country contexts. They include Adedoyin Adesina; Prof. Oladele Akogun; Prof. Arshad Ali; Dr. Salihu Bakari; Dr. Moses Dauda; Maimouna Djitte; Latsouck Gueye; Mandy Healy; Dr. Sara Humphreys; Jeunes Volontaires pour l'Environnement (JVE) in Fadia; Dr. Laila Kadiwal; Jiddere Kaibo; M23 in Dakar; Babacar Mbaye; Sani Njobdi; Diatou Sonka; Rinmicit Temlong; and Muhammad Zubair.

About This Book

Provoked by contemporary concerns about youth alienation and radicalisation, particularly in the Global South, the central interest of this book is the production of Muslim youth identities. In particular, it explores the construction of youth narratives of identity with respect to nation, religion and gender in the four different national contexts of Pakistan, Senegal, Nigeria and Lebanon. As Muslim-majority, post-colonial states with significant youth populations, these offered critical case studies for the exploration of the different grammars of youth identities. The uniqueness of this book lies in its rigorous and detailed attention to the local, situated and contingent ways in which youth articulate their identities and sense of belonging. This provides a counter to the pervasive homogenisation and decontextualisation that typifies many representations of 'youth' within global discourses.

Based on empirical investigations with youth, we trace how youth narratives use difference and the notion of the 'other' in framing their identities. Informed by post-structural and post-colonial theories of discourse and identity production, we explore how youth articulations of difference involve both external and internal 'others'. In each country case we highlight the complex ways that the history of the nation-state and its imagined community continue to inform social formations and remain significant within youth identity narratives. Importantly, we consider the relationships between national and religious belongings. We highlight how religion, in this case Islam, is used as a significant marker of identity and an axis of difference. However, in our explorations of the intersection of nation and religion, we also show how religious belongings can be recruited to consolidate national and ethnic affiliations in ways that challenge many Western understandings of 'secular' modernity. In each country case, we return to the ways these narratives of identity are persistently inflected by gender. Although largely rendered invisible in hegemonic representations of citizenship, we trace how symbolic representations of the nation and of religious ideals are bound up with particular forms of subordinated, docile femininities. Our analysis traces gender as a key axis of difference in the active production and contestation of female and male youth citizenship identities.

We conclude by reflecting on the importance of affect, belonging and affiliation in the construction of youth narratives of identity as well as highlighting their political and contested nature. In the face of globalising discourses of cosmopolitan citizenship and religious identifications, we illustrate the significance of the local and how this makes particular discourses available for the production of youth identities. Through our four case studies, we demonstrate the continued relevance of the nation to youth as a key structuring influence on their discourses of identity. We further show the ways in which youth's national affiliations are articulated with their religious affiliations, and finally how youth's discourses of nation and religion are consistently and pervasively gendered.

Contents

1	**Introduction**	1
	1.1 Overview	2
	1.2 Structure of this Book	4
2	**Geographies of Identity**	15
	2.1 Introduction	16
	2.2 Troubling 'Youth'?	17
	2.3 Troubling Identities?	21
	2.4 Citizen Identities, National Belongings and State Formation	30
	2.5 Religion	38
	2.6 Intersections of Gender, Nation, Religion	49
	2.7 Conclusion	53
	Note	55
	References	55
3	**The Research**	61
	3.1 Research Rationale	62
	3.2 Research Contexts	63

	3.3 Research Approach and Research Methods	68
	References	74

4 Pakistan: Converging Imaginaries in an Islamic State — 77
- 4.1 Introduction and Context — 78
- 4.2 The Research — 90
- 4.3 Constructing the Nation — 92
- 4.4 Religion, Unity and Divisions — 97
- 4.5 Constructing the 'Ideal' Pakistani Citizen: Gendering the Nation — 106
- 4.6 Gendering the Nation Through the External 'Other' — 111
- 4.7 Conclusions — 116
- **Notes** — 119
- **References** — 121

5 Senegal: Muslim Youth Identities in a Secular Nation — 127
- 5.1 Introduction and Context — 128
- 5.2 The Senegalese Context — 129
- 5.3 The Research in Senegal — 135
- 5.4 Imagining the Nation: New Formations of the Secular — 140
- 5.5 Being a Young Senegalese Muslim: Rejection of the External Other — 149
- 5.6 Gender as Trouble: Impossible Positions? — 159
- 5.7 Conclusion — 168
- **Note** — 170
- **References** — 171

6 Nigeria: Muslim Youth and Internal Others in a Multi-religious Nation — 175
- 6.1 Introduction and Context — 176
- 6.2 The Research in Nigeria — 184
- 6.3 Youth Identities—Initial Views — 187
- 6.4 Nation and External Others — 190
- 6.5 Religion and Internal Others — 196
- 6.6 Gender — 211

	6.7 Conclusions	217
	Note	220
	References	220
7	**Lebanon: National Imaginaries, State Fragilities and the Shi'a Other**	**225**
	7.1 Introduction and Context	226
	7.2 The Research	234
	7.3 Nation and External Others	236
	7.4 Religion, Ethnicity and External Others	240
	7.5 Gender and External Others	248
	7.6 Conclusion	255
	Notes	258
	References	260
8	**Conclusions: Intersecting Nation, Religion and Gender**	**263**
	8.1 Introduction	264
	8.2 Identities	264
	8.3 Troubling the Nation—Muslim Youth's National Belongings	266
	8.4 Troubling Religion?	270
	8.5 Gender Untroubled?	274
	References	278

Appendix A: Generic Bio-data Sheet — 281

Appendix B: Generic Focus Group Discussion Pro-forma — 283

Author Biographies — 285

Index — 289

List of Figures

Fig. 5.1　Map of Senegal　129
Fig. 6.1　Map of Nigeria　179

List of Tables

Table 3.1	Case study country statistical comparisons	66
Table 3.2	Sample across country cases	70
Table 4.1	The Pakistan sample	89
Table 5.1	The Senegal sample	136
Table 6.1	The Nigerian sample	186
Table 6.2	Initial youth identifications by region in Nigeria	188
Table 6.3	Initial youth identifications by religion in Nigeria	189
Table 6.4	Initial youth identifications by gender in Nigeria	190
Table 7.1	The Lebanon sample	235

1

Introduction

Abstract This chapter provides the rationale and outline for research and analysis on Muslim youth in four different national contexts. In a global scenario of social uncertainty and increasing fear, youth and Muslim youth in particular have been the focus of intensified attention. Our aim within the research has been to 'trouble' universalised and homogenised constructions of Muslim youth through investigations of the diverse ways in which they produce, articulate and perform their identities within the local contexts of their everyday lives. This introductory chapter sets out how our poststructural and postcolonial understandings inform the theoretical and methodological approaches to the research in four contrasting national contexts—Pakistan, Senegal, Nigeria and Lebanon. As a precursor to in-depth theoretical discussion later in the book, we provide an initial elaboration of identity as fluid and dynamic, replete with histories of place and claims of belonging. Our research involved nuanced engagements with youth in face-to-face encounters with each other. The fine-grained, multi-layered analyses of these diverse youth narratives focused on nation, religion, ethnicity and gender as intersecting axes of belonging. Overall, this chapter outlines the ways this book is offered to 'trouble' the universalistic and homogenised ways that youth and Muslim youth are often (mis-) represented and (mis-) understood.

1.1 Overview

Youth as the inheritors of our world are critical to its future sociality and environment, and within the increasing social uncertainties of the early decades of the twenty-first century, they have become a focus of concern globally. This attention has been intensified for Muslim youth in a period when fears about Islam are highlighted in the West and religious-based tensions and conflicts proliferate especially in parts of the Global South. At the same time, much of the debate and discussion has tended to homogenise both youth and Muslim youth in ways that decontextualised them from the very context in which they learn who they are and how they are positioned socially in the globe, in their nation and in their community and family. Consistent with the theme of this book, here we report on research that set out to 'trouble' universalistic constructions of Muslim youth and to investigate the diverse ways in which they produce, articulate and perform their identities within the porous local contexts of their everyday lives.

The analysis in this text embraces understandings of identity as fluid and dynamic and constructed through difference. From these perspectives, identity is constantly (re-)fabricated through the selective articulations of available discourses within specific localities. These discourses are replete with umbilical referents; the traces of particular histories of place are symbolically represented in identity claims of belonging and distinction. This identity work involves constant reiteration of the inclusions and attachments of 'us' as well as the exclusion, distancing and often the denigration of the 'other'. These processes are neither singular nor absolute but rather accomplished along different boundaries and across multiple intersecting axes of belonging. Through research with youth in four Muslim-majority countries in the Global South, in this book we have brought poststructural and postcolonial understandings together in analyses of Muslim youth identities along the axes of nation, religion, ethnicity and gender.

The intention of our research was to explore the pluralities of Muslim youth identity formations in three different regions—South Asia, Middle East and West Africa, and in four contrasting national contexts—Pakistan, Lebanon, Senegal and Nigeria. We explicitly sought to provide nuanced engagements with the diverse accounts of identity developed with youth in face-to-face encounters with each other. Our contribution lies in the ways that we have illustrated the unique localness of identity discourses of Muslim youth in different contexts, even though these may draw on discursive threads from much further afield. We show how youth's identity discourses are produced through a complex interweaving of the local and the global, as well as the historical and the contemporaneous. Youth weave these together in the ways that root their identities within sustainable interpretative frameworks of intelligibility. In the midst of the hopes and fears associated with youth and especially Muslim youth, this kind of empirical, fine-grained analytical engagement is startlingly rare. Given this background, the critically and theoretically informed work in this book is offered to 'trouble' the universalistic and homogenised ways that youth and Muslim youth are often (mis-)represented and (mis-)understood.

This book provides a highly original contribution to the field through comparative study of social identity formations and different 'becomings' within contrasting configurations of nation, state, religion, ethnicity and gender in four 'southern', predominantly Muslim contexts. This book presents comparative research with a multi-layered analysis of the heterogeneous ways that national and local cultures, societies and their education systems represent and produce social identities. More specifically, based on the accounts of youth, we provide nuanced analyses of the complexities of the relationship between 'nation' and 'state', the dynamics of ethnicity, the ways that Islam in its different variations is implicated in these constructions and how 'Islamic/Islamist' national narratives are mediated through discourses and performances of gender. The inclusion of particular cohorts of youth across different contexts opened the space for us to consider how young people, and Muslim youth in particular, appropriate, perform and/or resist dominant discourses of nation, religion and gender and the intersections in their constructions of 'us' and 'others' in their expressions of belonging. This research work has implications for social relations and social cohesion at local, national and supranational levels. With all four country cases in the top half of the fragile states ranking, two in the top 15 and three suffering ongoing or chronic conflict, this research has direct relevance for understanding local and global relations in the post-9/11 world of the early twenty-first century.

1.2 Structure of this Book

Following this introductory chapter, we outline the key theoretical constructs that have shaped the research as a whole, the data collection processes, the data analysis and our writing. Entitled 'Geographies of Identity', Chap. 2 first attends to the key concepts of youth and identity and then elaborates upon each of the three axes of nation, religion and gender, as well as the multiple ways in which these intersect in different social contexts. This is an extensive chapter that provides the core structure and framework for our analysis.

We begin with a review of the ways that 'youth' have been defined by various national and international agencies and the ambivalent ways that they have been portrayed in terms of both hope and fear. We then outline and 'trouble' the central concept of identity to disrupt modern understandings of the self, to elaborate our poststructural and postcolonial theorisations and to emphasise the significance of belonging, affiliation and affect in the production of identities. Through reference to gender, we illustrate identities as multiple and fluid, always in process and constantly brought into being in performative ways. In the rest of the chapter, we expand on the main axes of identity that frame our analysis. We first consider 'nation' and problematise the Western origins of the nation-state and its relevance within a globalised world. We explore the complexities of citizen identities which are of highlighted importance in our country cases, all of which are relatively newly constituted and fragile nations with Muslim-majority populations. Each has emerged in different and particular geo-political contexts that remain influential in the production of the imagined community of the nation. We also reflect on the historical arbitrariness of nation-state boundaries and how this produces fragmented national affiliations and belongings, as well as raising questions about possibilities for post-national forms of citizenship.

This leads us to religion as another important axis of identity in our case studies. We question the claims of secular modernity to separate religion from politics and argue that Western notions of the secular are bound up with and instantiated through religious affiliation. Flowing from this, we critique suggestions that Islam is in some way 'incompatible' with modernity and modern state formation. As part of this critique, we shift focus from global structures of affiliation and their universalising discourses to the local social contexts within which youth construct, produce and perform their identities. This is the crucible in which youth appropriate different available discourses of identity and constantly informs how these intersect, coalesce, solidify and liquefy. This theoretical attention to the local particularities of the invocations of discourses of nation and religion is crucial to our analyses of youth accounts of identity in each country case. The final part of this chapter returns to gender, engaging with feminist and postcolonial literature to highlight the ways that youth's national and religious affiliations are consistently and pervasively inflected by gender.

The theoretical space for our analysis provided in Chap. 2 is followed by details of our research in Chap. 3. We begin by providing a rationale for the research that contrasts a widespread policy concern for youth with the limited in-depth research that has incorporated their voices and perspectives. We link these widespread policy interests in youth to contemporary fears in the West about Islam, the global ummah and youth radicalisation in order to contextualise our research, which centred on exploring the pluralities of youth identity formations in the four different predominantly Muslim national contexts of Pakistan, Senegal, Nigeria and Lebanon. With their particular histories, these countries represent different configurations of relations between state, nation and religion that provided opportunities for a deeper comparative study of youth social identities. Based on the research team experience in each country context, our intention was to 'trouble' and disrupt homogenised representations of Muslim youth identities by listening to the multiple different ways in which youth themselves construct and perform their identities through their engagement with nation, religion, ethnicity and gender within their local contexts. We outline our research approach, which was mainly through focus group discussions supported by local and/or youth researchers, provide details of the sample and refer to the collaborative and ethical processes of data collection and analysis by the research team.

More specific details of the research in each context are included in the next four chapters, each of which focuses in turn on one of the country case studies. These chapters have a uniform structure in which each case starts with the respective social, historic and demographic context and continues with the country-specific details of the research sample and processes. This is followed by the analysis of the youth identity narratives with respect to the axes of nation, ethnicity, religion and gender, highlighting the ways these mark both the external and internal 'others'. Each chapter concludes with an overview of the key issues identified within the case.

Chapter 4 introduces the first country case of the Islamic Republic of Pakistan. With a predominant majority of Sunni Muslims, it is the second largest Muslim-majority country in the world and the only nuclear-armed Muslim state. It was established through the partition of British India at the end of British colonial rule; despite the separation along religious lines, it was led by secular-modernist leaders. Religion, however, remains a key marker of national identity within the ethnically, linguistically and socio-economically diverse population. Details of the Pakistan youth sample provided in this chapter indicate a predominance of Sunni Muslims and Pakhtuns with slightly more males than females. Following an outline of the research methods, the context is further elaborated as a means to situate the youth narratives of identity with respect to nation, religion and gender. The analysis shows that Pakistani youth articulate an explicit sense of national identity that is intrinsically interwoven with (Sunni) Islam, which provides the locus of national unity and boundary from external 'others'. The Pakhtuns, who are the majority in the sample, subsume their ethnic identity within these unifying discourses of nation and religion. This shared identity within a Muslim nation reciprocally constructs difference from the external 'other' in a discursive thread that is sustained through reference to historical and contemporary conflicts, including the 'War on Terror'.

The dominant youth articulations of a unifying Muslim nation, however, were also riven by exclusions on religious, ethnic and gender grounds which worked to produce the internal 'others' of Pakistan. The divisive question of what constitutes 'proper' Islam implied a hierarchy that penetrated the construction of national and religious imaginaries and reverberated in ethnic and gender identity narratives. The wideranging discussions in focus groups, however, often left youth positioning themselves in apparently contradictory ways. The aspiration to compliance with 'proper' Islam sat alongside discursive commitments to secular democracy, citizenship and equal rights that were also accompanied by critiques of political leadership and government accountability. Integral to this, the majority of youth expressed and performed highly gendered subjectivities. The external threat to the Pakistani nation was an important symbolic spine for the accumulation of highly militarised masculinities in the defence of the nation, Islam and women. The portrayal of subordinated and fragile femininity was used symbolically to further valorise strong masculinities in ways that made the oppression and control of women an imperative. Female youth continued to be subjected to disciplinary regimes that restricted the spaces accessible to them, their embodiments and their voice. While there was acknowledgement within the youth discourses of the local and global influences on the dynamics of national and religious identities and difference, gender position and relations were largely assumed to be stable, essentialised and naturalised.

Chapter 5 presents the case of Senegal which with a predominantly Muslim population has certain similarities with Pakistan. Its differences, however, are significant. In contrast to the formation of the Islamic state of Pakistan in the aftermath of British colonisation, Senegal was a French colony and at independence declared itself to be a secular republican democracy based on the French model. It has witnessed relatively little political instability and is the least fragile country within the research sample. The youth participants in Senegal were drawn from the urban setting of the capital city Dakar. The sample was ethnically diverse and included Muslims and Christians. Youth narratives underlined the importance to them of national belonging and produced a distinctive national identity that located Senegal as superior to other African nations. They also drew in contradictory ways on its shared history with France, on the one hand, recruiting it as a marker of positive distinction, and on the other, in opposition to their subordination under French colonial rule. The unity of the nation against the colonial other was a dominant discursive thread in which the national secular imaginary sat harmoniously with religious values, which for Muslim youth were bound up with their religious affiliations to Senegal's Sufist brotherhoods. Their importance in Senegal's struggle for independence contributed to a flattening of both ethnic differences and those between these Sufist brotherhoods. As such, the Senegal youth trouble any assumptions that see Islam as being incompatible with a modern, secular nation-state.

In terms of religion, the youth legitimated their local, African forms of Islam, including syncretic versions that were interwoven with ethnic customs and beliefs. They emphasised that Islam was a religion of peace and framed their practice in opposition to the '*jihadist*' Islam practised in other contexts including countries in Asia, the Middle East and other African nations, specifically Mali and Nigeria. For these youth, local attachments were always more important than transnational associations with others of the same religion. Similar to Pakistan, gender was a locus of significant inequalities and female subordination was entrenched and stabilised through discourses of nation, ethnicity and religion. While challenges to gender inequalities were evident in some focus group discussions, especially by women in higher education, these could readily be condemned as an alien intrusion from the external others of the Global North.

Staying in West Africa, Chap. 6 presents the case study of Northern Nigeria. This provides a distinctive context within which to explore Muslim youth discourses of identity. Nigeria as a secular democratic state with a multi-religious population of enormous ethnic and linguistic diversity offers a particular set of social circumstances that contrast with the very high Muslim populations in the Islamic state of Pakistan and the secular state of Senegal. Nigerian Sunni Muslims are concentrated in the larger and poorer northern regions of the country.

In common with the previous case studies, the state emerged from a period of colonial rule and like Pakistan it was under a British administration. The focus groups were conducted with Muslims and Christians in Northern Nigeria although the focus here is on Muslim youth. Across both religious groups, youth asserted strong affective attachments to their nation as the 'lion' of Africa; despite acknowledging its poor external reputation, they underlined its importance to their narratives of identity. In common with the Pakistan and Senegalese case, the Nigerian youth expressed dissatisfaction and disappointment with successive national governments, the electoral system and local governance processes. The failures of the state, especially with respect to youth, were offered by some in explanation for the emergence of the Islamic extremism of Boko Haram which had led to the declaration of a state of emergency in their state in 2013. This explanation by the youth did not shift into sympathy for extremist causes or strategies; in contrast, they sought to distance themselves from terrorism and defend themselves against such accusations.

As discussions turned to identity and difference within Nigeria, regional belonging emerged as a prominent symbolic structure of internal 'othering'. A region–religion dyad of Northern Muslim and Southern Christian was a dominant discursive axis taken up by the youth to frame and confirm their identities. As in wider state politics, region and religion were constantly used by youth to 'trouble' the nation in ways that referred back to the very beginnings of the Nigerian state. The regional and religious fracturing of the nation was used by the Northern Muslim youth to highlight the importance of religion, to point out the sometimes fragile alliances within the state and to underline the political might of the North within these. Interestingly, the conflation of region and religion that worked to flatten ethnic difference within the multi-ethnic North was used to further vilify ethnic groups and Muslims originating in the South. The religious rift between Northern and Southern Muslims was rationalised on the basis of a 'proper' Islamic practice in the North and opposed to the syncretic forms of the Southerners. Access through ICT to principled forms of practice beyond the national landscape had informed and bolstered the religious identity of Northern Muslim youth. However, although animating a discourse of religious universalism, this was articulated and performed within the specific social geography of their locality to re-invoke internal regional distinctions from Nigerian others. The fraught complexities of interweaving national, regional and religious imaginings into distinct identity narratives often led to exaggerated assertions of position expressed in authoritative masculinist ways. As observed in Pakistan and Senegal, although gender was largely invisible within the youth identity narratives, their everyday life was highly gendered and projections of subordinate and modest femininity were vital to the masculinist images of strength, control and superiority in Northern Nigeria. As a critically important symbol of religious identity, it was again used to resist gender equality and to denigrate Southerners as both Western and colonial.

The final country case in Chap. 7 is Lebanon, which like Nigeria is a secular democratic state with a multi-religious population and a small Muslim majority. The country situated on the Eastern Mediterranean lies at the crossroads between east and west. It includes Christians as well as Sunni and Shi'a Muslims and has often been at the centre of Middle Eastern conflicts. Distinct from the previous country cases, however, here we concentrate on Shi'a Muslim youth in the south of the country where they are the majority population. At the same time within the region dominated by Sunni Islam, they are the Muslim minority 'others'. The complex religious composition of Lebanon, its location within a region of contemporary conflicts, as well as its political fragility presented a particularly difficult context for the articulation of a clear or singular nationalist narrative. Nevertheless, it was in this context that youth constructed a distinct and unifying Lebanese identity based on both pluralism and 'shared suffering' as a result of the ongoing conflict with the common enemy, Israel. For the Shi'a youth, however, discourses of identity also drew on their particular sectarian historical narratives that animated distinctions within the nation. These provided a discursive connection with Shi'a beyond the national borders in ways that challenge a unified Lebanese national imaginary and make visible the sutures in the formation of Lebanon as a nation-state.

Notwithstanding the historical tensions between Muslim and Christian communities in Lebanon, it is relations between Sunni and

Shi'a Muslims that are the current nexus of national and regional conflict. It is in this context that the Lebanese Shi'a youth navigate significant ethnicity–religion axes of difference in the amalgam of their unique identity narrative. As Shi'a Muslims, they are one of the most significant groups within their country although perhaps the least powerful in terms of governance positions. On the other hand, they are ethnic Arabs who share much with Arabs within Lebanon and beyond the national borders. However, most Arabs are Sunni Muslims and most Shi'a Muslims are not Arab. This leaves the south Lebanese Shi'a youth navigating multiple and intersecting axes of identity that have been agitated most recently by the war in neighbouring Syria. This conflict has invoked contradictory claims of allegiance that cut across the religious, ethnic and national belongings of the Shi'a youth. Specifically, Shi'a Muslims are called upon to defend their Syrian co-religionists against the Sunni with whom they otherwise identify in ethnic and national terms. At the same time as they share space, culture and politics with 'others' in their geographical locality, these south Lebanese Shi'a youth claim their unique identity by 'troubling' dominant national, regional, ethnic and religious belongings. It is the work of these narratives that normalises the performances of identity, especially within unstable and changing social and political contexts.

In common with the other country case studies, gender remains rather uncontested or untroubled. The restricted gender scripts for females are framed through reference to an Arab culture and made imperative through discourses of religion. The ubiquitous masculine imaginary of heroic men as providers and defenders had redoubled significance in a context of conflict and armed resistance and was complemented by the construction of Lebanese Shi'a women as wives, mothers and protectors of the family's 'honour'. These were discursively installed through religion; godly authority and religious duty were invoked to prevent any contestation of the sustained gender inequalities.

The final chapter returns to the key theoretical themes of this book that were highlighted in Chap. 2 and illustrated and elaborated in the four country case studies. Our intention was to 'trouble' the homogeneous depictions of Muslims in local and global imaginaries and, through the case studies, to illustrate the complex configurations of identity with specific reference to nation, religion and gender. In particular, we exemplified the ways that the historical formation of each nation-state remains a significant motif in national narratives of identity. We have also used the production of independent, postcolonial and affective national belongings within these relatively new state formations in a critique of a singular imagining of a modern secular nation, with all its attendant assumptions of a gendered division of public and private spheres, and an equally gendered understanding of the modern self as a unitary, rational and transparent entity.

Taking up our conceptualisation of identity as fluid and performative, we have illustrated the ways that, notwithstanding supranational connections and communications, youth identity narratives are produced and performed within the social and political nexus of the local. In these complex scenarios, in which culture, ethnicity, gender, religion and politics intersect, in sometimes convoluted or contradictory ways, youth learn, navigate and perform their identities. Our case studies offer rich examples of these processes for particular groups of Muslim youth in four very different country settings. Our country cases highlight the importance of 'othering' and the framing of 'us' and 'them' in the production of identities. They elaborate how it is within the everyday contexts of the local that identities are almost silently produced through the revivification of historical differences (them) and allegiances (us) which are then animated, expressed and performed in their specific tropes of identity. In this final chapter, we return in turn to the three main axes of nation, religion and gender to illustrate the complex contingencies in which Muslim youth work to construct themselves as intelligible subjects.

Turning first to nation, we illustrated the sustained importance of national pride and belonging and the ways that this was used to demarcate the external 'other'. We also explored how the national imaginary was troubled by different youth fractions in all the country cases in ways that produced internal 'others' along ethnic, religious and geographic lines. The injuries of colonial history were invoked in expressions of resistance to Westernisation as the 'other' of local culture and incorporated in a claim to a unique postcolonial nation. This resistance to

Westernisation, particularly visible in reference to gender equality, was also used to produce internal distinction from compatriots and to denigrate them as internal others.

Moving on to religion, we firstly deconstruct its imagining in binary opposition to both modernity and secularism, illustrating how it has been recruited in support of political and social reform, rather than necessarily sitting in antithetical relation to modernity. We then point to the multiple forms of Islam and the ways that these were often integral to a unique national imaginary articulated by Muslim youth. In both Pakistan and Nigeria, a notion of a 'proper' universal Islam haunted the identity narratives of male youth in particular. In some cases, religious identity narratives were used to challenge local cultural practices and to trouble nation and ethnic belongings, as illustrated by the Shi'a youth in Lebanon. Nevertheless in all country cases, Muslim youth managed to interweave feasible narratives of identity that incorporated both national and religious belongings, even where significant proportions of religious 'others' were incorporated within the national boundaries.

Finally, we turn to gender. As suggested in the subheading of the last chapter, we illuminate the ways that traditional gender positions and possibilities remain largely untroubled across all the country case studies. Indeed gender inequalities and male domination are used as a symbolic marker of both nation and religion. Gender is the key axis of identity through which differences from the West are re-stated. It is the pedestal upon which the substance and tone of the claims to unique religious nationhood are voiced with masculinist vigour and a certainty that at the same time reveals its vulnerability.

2

Geographies of Identity

Abstract This chapter introduces the key concepts of the research and the theoretical frameworks we draw on to analyse our four country case studies. After addressing the concept of youth, we use poststructural and postcolonial theories to elaborate our understandings of identities as being multiple and fluid, always in process. These perspectives are again drawn upon to understand gender, as constantly brought into being in performative ways. We conclude this section by emphasising the significance of belonging and affiliation in the production of identities. As part of our concern with youth's national belongings, we explore the complexities of citizen identities, probing the imagined community of the nation, and how national affiliations may, or may not, coincide with modern nation-state boundaries. We problematise the Western origins of the nation-state and the implications for states emerging from coloniality. We then consider the relevance of the nation-state within a globalised world and related questions about post-national or more cosmopolitan forms of citizenship. Pursuing our interest in different axes of youth identities, we turn to religion, interrogating the supposed separation of religion and politics in secular modernity, as well as the putative incompatibility of Islam with modernity and modern state formation.

We return to cosmopolitanism to critique its modern, Eurocentric origins and the implications for 'Muslim cosmopolitanism'. We conclude this chapter by engaging with feminist and postcolonial literature which demonstrates how national and religious affiliations are consistently and pervasively inflected by gender.

2.1 Introduction

This chapter introduces the key concepts of the research and the associated theoretical frameworks that we used in the analyses of the four country case studies that follow. We first address the concept of youth, problematising the different ways it is defined and the constellations of contemporary concerns that surround youth, particularly in the Global South. We then turn to our understandings of 'identity' itself, taking up poststructural and postcolonial theories that disrupt modern understandings of the self as a disembodied, autonomous being and instead discuss how we understand identities as being multiple and fluid, always in process. This section also addresses gender, and how this is similarly understood as constantly brought into being, in performative ways. We conclude this section by re-emphasising the significance of belonging and affiliation in the production of our identities.

We then explore the complexities of citizen identities, probing the imagined community of the nation, and how national affiliations and belongings may, or may not, coincide with modern nation-state formations. We problematise the Western origins of the nation-state and the implications of the imaginings of the nation for those nation-states emerging from colonial rule. We also consider recent questions about the relevance of the nation-state within a globalised world, including arguments for post-national or more cosmopolitan forms of citizenship.

We next turn to religious affiliations, questioning the supposed separation of religion and politics in secular modernity, arguing instead with Butler (2011) that religious affiliations are deeply rooted within Western notions of the secular. This also leads us to critique the supposed incompatibility of Islam with modernity and modern state formation. We return to the concept of cosmopolitanism at the end of this section to explore its intersection with religion and, more particularly, with different understandings of Muslim cosmopolitanism. Here, we position our study within descriptive rather than normative understandings of cosmopolitanism. This requires us to pay sustained attention to the local social relations which inform youth identity constructions. We finally return to gender, engaging with feminist and postcolonial literature which points to the ways national and religious affiliations are consistently and pervasively inflected by gender.

2.2 Troubling 'Youth'?

In addition to troubling the category of youth itself and problematising its work of social construction, we explore in this section the rise of 'youth' as a category of concern in the discourses of international and national policy makers and non-governmental organisations. As a category, youth is typically defined in terms of an age range, although definitions vary considerably. For example, the United Nations (UN) (1995) defines youth as those aged between 15 and 24, while the African Youth Charter (African Union 2006) construes youth to be those aged 15–35. In providing its definition, the UN recognises how the category overlaps with those of the child (defined in Article 1 of the UN Convention on the Rights of the Child as persons up to the age of 18) and of adulthood or 'age of majority', this being 18 years in many state legislations. Sitting astride these different overlapping definitions, 'youth' as a category would seem to benefit neither from the 'innocence' associated with Western notions of childhood nor from the 'maturity' that is assumed of the adult. Importantly however, it cannot be assumed that age relations are the same across different contexts. When we further consider how these age-related definitions are gender-blind, and misrecognise how age relations differ between male and female youth, their assumptions become increasingly problematic. Indeed, the very notion of youth has been questioned as a Western concept, holding Western age-related norms that may be quite irrelevant in the Global South (Cole 2011; Evans and Lo Forte 2012; Sommers 2006). However, we can readily identify international policy documents on youth, such as World Bank (2006), which are nevertheless premised on the transition of an individual from being a child to a youth, and finally to adulthood, as if such life stages could be assumed to be discrete and universal. This supposed linearity also conceals the different ways that 'youth' as a life stage is understood. For example, while youth can be constructed as agents of change and looked to for their potential demographic dividend (see for example UNESCO 2013a), they can also be associated with risk-taking, rebellion, alienation and radicalisation. Overall therefore, the concept of youth reverberates with ambivalence and hybridity (Bhabha 2004).

The contemporary salience of youth as a social category is also related to their socio-demographic prominence, particularly in the Global South, whose youthful populations contrast starkly with the ageing and diminishing populations of many countries of the Global North. Even if the youth population is now projected to fall as an overall percentage of the world total, in absolute numbers youth are still projected to increase massively in the Global South. When launching the World Programme of Action for Youth in 1995, the UN noted that the majority of the world's youth (84% in 1995) lived in the Global South and projected this to increase to 89% by 2025 to 1.2 billion. More recently, UNESCO (2013b) reported that 89.7% of people under 30 live in emerging and developing economies, particularly in the Middle East and Africa.

However, it is the particular conjuncture of this youth 'bulge' with other factors that have made youth's socio-demographic salience a particularly troublesome phenomenon to many policy makers. High levels of youth unemployment are a key issue in a range of different contexts, including many countries of the Global South. After signalling youth as whole to be a 'generation at risk' in 2013, the International Labour Office (ILO) (2014) suggests that youth around the world remain particularly vulnerable. They estimate that 74.5 million young people—aged 15–24—were unemployed in 2013, an increase of one million from the previous year, with global youth unemployment rates at a historical peak of just over 13%, almost three times as high as the adult unemployment rate. The participation of females in the formal labour market also trails that of males in all regions of the world. While globally youth unemployment has stabilised (ILO 2015), it continues to rise in the Middle East, which currently has the world's highest youth unemployment rate and the largest gender differential in youth unemployment. Importantly however, ILO (2013) also acknowledges the great insensitivity of these statistics to employment conditions in developing economies and suggests that as many as two-thirds of young people there may be 'underutilized', meaning that they are unemployed, in irregular, often informal employment, or not in education and training. ILO (2014, 2015) acknowledges the lack of progress in tackling informal employment, which it sees as a major barrier to poverty reduction. It also singles out developing economies, youth and women as all being especially implicated in such kinds of work.

Policy concerns about youth unemployment have been aggravated by the concentration of unemployed youth in the Global South, and in some cases because of the numbers of youth who follow Islam across many of its countries. Although the Pew Forum on Religion and Public Life (2011) show that the 'youth bulge' across Muslim-majority countries peaked in 2000, by 2010 the overall percentage of those who were under 30 remained at 60% in these countries. With two exceptions, all of the Muslim-majority countries are classified as 'developing countries', following UN definitions. Overall, the number of Muslims in the world is also projected to rise at a faster rate than other religious groups, increasing by about 35% in the next 20 years, from 1.6 billion in 2010 to 2.2 billion by 2030. Nigeria is also predicted to become the 50th Muslim-majority state by 2030 (Lebanon, Pakistan and Senegal are already Muslim-majority countries).

The conjuncture of significant sections of the population in the Global South being unemployed has therefore come together with fears about the development of Islamic 'fundamentalist' beliefs among youth who are marginalised, who may have little to lose, and who are at a risk of becoming alienated and disaffected from society. Such fears have been intensified by the wider geo-political turbulence surrounding the role of Islam in the contemporary world. This has seen a rise in Islamophobia in the USA and in Europe, particularly in the aftermath of 9/11 and the subsequent wars waged in Iraq and Afghanistan, under the banner of the 'War on Terror', later followed by uprisings and political protests across the Middle East, in Tunisia, Bahrain, Libya, Yemen, Turkey, Egypt and Syria. In today's media, radical Islamic groups that feature regularly include Boko Haram in Nigeria and those fighting under the banner of Islamic state in the conflicts besetting Syria and the wider region. The racialisation of Islam within Europe has also contributed to the polarisation of debate, so that Islamic beliefs come to be constructed in opposition to the right to free speech within 'secular' democracies and the wearing of Islamic dress (such as the *hijab* or *burka*) as an affront to secular principles (Laborde 2008). We critique many of the assumptions surrounding Western forms of secularism in the sections below, particularly when discussing religion (Asad 2003; Butler et al. 2011).

This fear and indeed demonisation of Islam can also be discerned in connections made between fragile states and the presence of a 'youth bulge'. Political science theorists in the USA have posited a correlation with 'burgeoning youth populations' and countries that are prone to conflict. Beehner (2007) sees the main concern being for 'large pools of disaffected youths who are more susceptible to recruitment into rebel or terrorist groups' and who are 'especially prone to virulent strands of Islam as an alternative force for social mobility'. Of 67 states experiencing youth bulges, 60 are claimed to be experiencing conflict and instability (Beehner 2007). Reporting to the UN, Urdal (2012) claims that the presence of youth bulges increases the risk of conflict outbreak significantly, such that for every percentage point increase in the youth population, the risk of conflict increases by more than 4%. Other writers (for example Amin 2013) resist the deficit constructions of youth that are relayed through such correlations, pointing to the 'democratic dividend' that some countries have been able to accrue from a youthful population and highlighting the importance of attending to wider social issues (education quality, employment structures, institutional rigidities) that impact on youth's lives. Poor working conditions along with high unemployment have, for example, been identified as chief catalysts for the Arab Spring (ILO 2011).

Concerns about the youth 'bulge' across the Global South have projected youth to the forefront of international policy debates, with Muslim male youth in particular a key cause of concern. In this context, it seems important to question the representation of youth, and of Muslim youth, in such homogenised and undifferentiated ways within both policy texts and large-scale statistical research. What it means to be a youth, of any particular age, will differ extensively across different economic, sociocultural and political spaces. This means that as such, if we are to gain insights into youth identity constructions, we must attend to their contexts and how this shapes their national, religious, gender and ethnic belongings. Finally, despite all the above concerns, it is recognised that there is a significant absence of in-depth qualitative research into youth perspectives on many of these issues (Hardgrove et al. 2014; Sommers 2011). Furthermore, within the gerontocratic power relations of many societies, youth have also been largely invisible to and ignored by policy makers.

2.3 Troubling Identities?

The concept of identity is central to our research. Theoretically, it can be approached through different lenses, which are coloured by the shifting understandings of the epistemes of modernity, late and post-modernity. In this section, we elaborate and exemplify our theoretical understandings of identity with respect to gender, as one of the most significant structures of inequality, exploring the concept through the writings of postcolonial and poststructural theorists. We also draw out the implications for other structures of identity relevant to our interests in Muslim youth across different national contexts.

Since the structures of modernity arguably continue to resonate through the social fabrics of our contemporary worlds, in both the Global North and the Global South, we begin our discussion of the concept of identity by questioning the ways that it has been construed within modern Western philosophy. This privileged human agency and the application of reason in pursuit of social progress, an emphasis which represented a significant break with the historic dominance of religious belief. Elaborating on modern understandings of the subject, Taylor (1995) notes how its 'free and rational' self was disembodied and 'ideally disengaged' from the natural and social worlds. This works firstly, in consolidating the Cartesian separation of mind and body, in which the mind was considered more elevated as a human characteristic; secondly, it centres the subject in terms of individual 'selfhood'; and finally, it constructs this 'self' in an atomistic relationship with society. In other words, society was considered instrumentally, to be worked upon and reformed as befitted the purposes of individuals (Taylor 1995). This has relevance for the concept of the nation-state, discussed further below, as well as for the institutions of modern, liberal democracies which are premised on the defence of the freedoms of the rational autonomous self of modernity.

It was the ethos of modernity that, paradoxically, also legitimised the 'civilising mission' of European colonialism. While invoking a discourse of equality, 'every man is born equal', those who had the power to use this discourse also assumed the moral authority of their values, which included a rejection of tradition and religion, and also the superiority of their rationality and knowledge systems. Through these related sets of assumptions, the colonial subject was classified as inferior, even subhuman, in ways that allowed colonisation to be justified as a moral project.

Theorisations of the relationship of the individual and society that emerged during the course of the twentieth century importantly illuminated the significance of social structures and institutions in shaping the possibilities for agency. They also pointed to the contingencies of Western norms that were usually posited as universals, independent of contextual specificities. Different twentieth-century social theorists across a range of disciplinary perspectives recognised the relationship between the individual and society as dialectical. Rather than the modern ideal of unfettered human agency, accomplished through the autonomous action of a sovereign, knowing and rational subject, human agency was always necessarily entangled and enmeshed within historically contingent but ineluctable social structures, in ways that were both constraining and enabling. Bourdieu's theory of practice, for example, conceptualised a dynamic relation between habitus, different forms of capital and field, none of which could be considered independently of the other (Bourdieu 1990). While these dynamics are always therefore relational, strategic and positional, it is perhaps indicative of the imperative attached to agency within Western thought that Bourdieu has frequently stood accused of determinism.

In contrast to this recognition of social structures, social theorists of late modernity, focusing on the social conditions within the Global North, suggest that the disembedding of the individual from structures such as family or community, coupled with the declining authority of traditional institutions, now implies a greater level of individual agency (Giddens 1991; Beck 1992). In Beck's 'risk society', monitoring and control of the consequences of de-industrialisation and globalisation now lie beyond the reach of traditional structures and institutions, including nation-state governments. Additionally, collectivities such as trade unions that were powerful in fighting for social equality have little purchase within late modern institutions that are primarily oriented towards the individual. All of this implies that concerns relating to collective identities including social class, gender or ethnicity cease to have traction; individuals are instead constructed 'in an open-ended discursive interplay to which the classical roles of industrial society cannot do justice' (Mouffe 2005:38).

An implication of this for Beck (1992) is that individuals in late modern times have to construct 'choice biographies'. In other words, rather than biographies playing out in relatively predictable and stable ways, framed by the lifestyles of industrial societies, the 'fading' of the industrial age means that our lives are increasingly disembedded socially and historically, so that we have to confront the uncertainties of contemporary 'risk society' as individuals. This demands a greater level of self-fashioning than before:

> The proportion of the biography which is open and must be constructed is increasing. Individualization of life situations and processes thus means that biographies become self-reflexive. [..]. Decisions on education, profession, job, place of residence, spouse, number of children and so forth, with all the secondary decisions implied, no longer can be, they *must* be made. (Beck 1992:135, our emphasis)

Giddens (1991) similarly conceptualises identity in late modernity as involving a reflexive project of the self, where 'life politics' rather than nation-state politics is critical for individual self-actualisation. This 'new individualism' is viewed positively by Giddens as opening possibilities for alternative forms of democracy outside the formal, institutionalised spheres of national politics.

However, other social theorists are fiercely critical of the implications for democracy associated with the reduction of politics to 'life politics'. Rather than these opening possibilities for 'democracy from below', Mouffe (2005:40), for example, critiques how reflexive modernity places the individual at the centre of politics and forecloses the recognition of collective identities. She argues that contemporary political debate is negated by the very ethos of liberalism, in particular through its privileging of rational consensus, in ways that misrecognise the power relations and exclusions through which consensus is achieved. As Crossouard and Dunne (2015) discuss in relation to youth's active citizenship in Senegal, privileging consensus may seem benign, but it can also foster the reproduction of relations of domination. A further risk of the non-recognition of the adversarial relations of 'liberal' politics is that conflicts readily become constructed in moral terms, as 'good' versus 'evil', as has happened in the 'War on Terror' (see also Mamdani 2004 below). This makes it important to recover an agonistic understanding of politics, as being intrinsic to our sociality, a point that we take up again below in our discussion of identity.

The supposed irrelevance within late modern times of structures such as social class and gender has also provoked strong critique (Adkins 2003; Skeggs 2004). Resisting the supposed fluidity of late modern understandings of identity, Skeggs (2004) illuminates how the construction of 'choice biographies' requires the mobilisation of resources that are differentially available to us, as is a feel for what resources should be mobilised for different purposes in different contexts. Crucially, it individualises the responsibility for social risks, such as illness, unemployment and poverty, transforming these from being a state or social responsibility into a problem of 'self-care' (Lemke 2001:201). In relation to youth biographies, France and Roberts (2015) also call attention to the continuing significance of social class in supporting some youth but not others in the construction of their biographies. Further questions have been posed about the work this new individualism does in contexts of postcoloniality, where different and potentially more embedded understandings of community and collective responsibility may prevail (Spivak 2005).

In this section on identity, we have sometimes referred to the 'self' or the 'human agent'. These are both terms that encapsulate the centred, sovereign understanding of identity within modern, liberal philosophies. We have also referred to the 'subject'. This term de-centres that 'modern self' and privileges instead poststructural theories of discourse. These challenge liberal constructions of 'the knowing subject' who use their reason to arrive at 'truth' in ways that were seemingly free of power (Foucault 1970). Instead, we (and our knowledges) are constituted through discourse, in which power relations are ineluctably implicated (Foucault 1977). This undoes a modern understanding of the self, as centred, self-aware and stable. Instead, one is interpellated or hailed through discourse into particular subject positions—as a youth, a boy, a girl, a mother, a Muslim, a Christian. We do not 'control' the terms through which we are interpellated. These are social in origin and precede our coming into being through them. In this way, we are both subject *to* discourse and become subjects within discourse. This naming also brings into play particular evaluative frameworks. For example, if you are named or interpellated as a 'youth', this invokes particular norms and, depending on the context, potentially brings into play many of the ambiguities described in the preceding section.

So we 'exist' through a dependency on the address of the 'other', through the reiteration of discursive conventions and norms in which power relations are always inevitably implicated (Althusser 1972; Butler 1997). This suturing, or articulation of a subject into chains of discourse, is always socially contingent and provisional, rather than stable and fixed. It involves processes of identification, which are constituted through difference and relations to the 'other':

> it is only through the relation to the other, the relation to what it is not, to precisely what it lacks, to what has been called its *constitutive outside*

that the 'positive' meaning of any term - and thus its identity - can be constructed. (Hall 1996:4–5)

Taking up this constitutive understanding of discourse as intrinsic to our subjectivation, Hall (1996) suggests we need to put 'identity' under erasure, as a concept that requires radical rethinking. Post-structuralist thinking therefore recognises identities to be multiple and fluid, embodied rather than disembodied, constructed through systems of difference that are inherently bound up with power relations (Foucault 1980; Hall 1996; Mouffe 1992, 2005). In this decentred view of the subject, the articulation of identities is always in process, hybrid rather than singular, fractured, conflictual and inherently political.

This understanding of the subject as produced through and in discourse implies that identity categories such as 'gender' can no longer be assumed to 'reflect' any pre-existing reality or 'essence'. Rather than assuming gender to be an attribute of one's 'personal identity', we should rather consider how particular regulatory practices constitute different gender formations or gender regimes, which govern culturally intelligible notions of identity performances. Taking up the ways in which discourses 'systematically form the objects of which they speak' (Foucault 1977:49), a category such as 'gender' can therefore be considered 'performative':

> gender is always doing, although not a doing by a subject who might be said to pre-exist the deed. [..] There is no gender identity behind the expressions of gender; that identity is performatively constituted by the very 'expressions' that are said to be its results. (Butler 1990:34)

Given that this 'doing' is constituted within discursive norms of practice and intelligibility, the hierarchies through which identities come to be read as legitimate in any particular context need always to be interrogated. This is particularly so given that their construction disappears from view so that they come to be read as a naturalised 'facticity', rather than '*effects* of institutions, practices, discourses with multiple points of origin' (Butler 1990, xxxi, emphasis in the original).

Crucially, Butler's critique of the concept of gender also locates it against a wider set of concepts and norms, illuminating how sex, sexuality, gender and desire are conjoined within a particular matrix of intelligibility, in this case involving compulsory heterosexuality. Dunne (2008) provides in-depth studies of particular constellations of sex, gender and sexuality across multiple educational and social contexts in Sub-Saharan Africa. These authors call our attention to the significance of context in producing matrices of intelligibility and to the multiple ways in which gender and sexuality intersect with other social categories. Thus, socially and culturally constructed categories of identity, such as race, ethnicity, gender, religion, nationality, sexuality and class, do not act independently of one another. Rather, they interact on multiple, often simultaneous levels, contributing to systematic social inequality (Hill Collins 1991). While gender is of course central to our analysis, in all our case studies we take account of its intersections with other identity categories. These include ethnicity and nationality, that may also be naturalised as biological 'facticity'.

The emphasis by Butler on desire also highlights the significance of the affective in the articulation of identity. Rather than the privileging of rationality and the concomitant disparaging of the affective that pervades modern thought, from a poststructural perspective, the affective is understood as being integral to the articulation and suturing of identities. Taking up how the reiteration of norms produces the materialisation of our worlds, as posited by Butler (1993), Ahmed (2004) argues that these processes are affectively charged and that it is through the circulation and reiteration of affects that the social is delineated and normalised, producing the very effects of 'boundary, fixity and surface' through which our worlds materialise (Ahmed 2004:12).

Ahmed's (2004) theorisation of the affective does not therefore view emotions as individual or psychological 'dispositions'. Rather than residing in subjects or objects, or as something we 'have', emotions are 'effects of circulation' (8), where different emotions 'stick to' and delineate both subjects and objects, individuals and collectives. Instead of arising as a response to different groups or collectives, the circulation of affects within a particular discursive formation has constitutive effects, so that collectives, such as nations, ethnic, or religious groups are delineated through the circulation of feelings. These may be of strong, 'thick' belonging, or conversely of alienation. In any context, particular affects will be accorded value rather than others, so that feelings of pride, fear and disgust circulate in relation to particular objects, such as a nation, a particular race or an ethnic group. The circulation of affect associated with these collectives lead to them being naturalised as social categories and allow them to work in particular although contingent ways as social markers and boundaries, privileging some groups, while marginalising others. We take this up below more specifically in relation to the affiliations and sense of belonging that sustains the concept of the nation and its imagined community.

While relevant to all identity constructions, in our study the affective is particularly in play in the positioning of the postcolonial subject, given that discourses of colonial power remain as traces, recruited in the production of identities, and as referents in the construction of self and other. For Bhabha (2004), the space of the 'other' through which identity is constituted should be considered as 'a graphic historical and cultural specificity' for the postcolonial subject, for whom the 'problem' of identity can be seen as a 'persistent questioning of the frame, the space of representation, where the image [...] is confronted with its difference' (66). He draws on Franz Fanon to consider how the embodied postcolonial subject has to 'meet the white man's eyes' (60). Fanon finds this gaze to be filled with 'treacherous stereotypes', which include symbolic totems such as 'tom toms, cannibalism, intellectual deficiency, fetishism, racial defects', representations which all reproduce difference and exclusion. Using graphic symbolism, the space of the production of his identity is described as 'spatter[ing] my whole body with black blood' (Fanon 1986). This brings out the epistemic violence in the objectifications of the gaze of the colonial 'other' on oppressed peoples. These objectifications become inscribed within identity narratives that constitute the colonised subject. In concluding this section, we note how Bhabha (2004) also alerts us to the significance of cultural and historical contexts for the production and articulation of identities.

Identities in Context

The central interest of this book is the production of Muslim identities in different national contexts, each affected by the traces of postcoloniality, and how this is further inflected by gender. In the following section, we take up the theoretical framing outlined above, which understands context as of primordial significance for the production and performance of identities. Throughout the section, we point to the constitutive work of discourse, how its naturalisation of concepts such as the nation provides grammars of identity and belonging, in which the articulation of difference is pivotal. After considering the nation and the nation-state, we explore the different ways that religion is enmeshed within state formations, including those that claim to be secular, before turning to a consideration of how the intersecting discourses of nation and religion are pervasively gendered.

Before examining our three axes of analysis—nation, religion and gender—we reiterate the importance of the affective to our understandings of identity. Intrinsic to these understandings are identification with a collective of some kind—this could be a religious sect, a football team, a trade union, an ethnic group, a local, national or a global community. Drawing upon a discursive understanding of the construction of identity, the boundaries of these communities are always constituted through power relations and difference, and are affectively charged. They are constituted through the iterative circulation of symbolic representations in which are embedded particular histories and imaginaries. In other words, these narratives contribute to the ongoing production and the reproduction of a shared imaginary in relation to which social actors may align or distance themselves. In describing these as 'discursive', we are drawing on Foucault's understanding of discourse, as always imbricated in the material and social world, as constitutive of our ways of being and doing, and as providing grids of intelligibility through which particular objects, practices and subjectivities may be understood.

As Fanon's situation also illustrates, these narratives also work to ascribe identities, i.e. his identity construction has to work through symbolic representations and 'treacherous stereotypes' associated with his skin colour. Similarly, the circulation of narratives associating Islam with 'fundamentalisms' and with terrorism works to ascribe particular identities, in ways that precede and exceed any particular individual, marking boundaries of belonging or alienation that are intensified through the effects of circulation. These effects are always contingent in time and space—the wearing of the hijab in a Paris suburb will have different symbolic values in different Paris suburbs, which will again be very different from Dakar or Hyderabad. However, while always local, the reach of information technologies in contemporary societies also allows an interpenetration of the local with the global and the potential intensification of affects of affiliation or alienation in ways that accumulate to produce dangerously homogenised understandings of particular groups—including the problematic association of Muslims with 'Islamic fundamentalisms' that we critiqued in the opening section.

We now turn to more specific explorations of our theoretical framework with respect to our three main analytical concepts—dealing in turn with nation, religion and gender.

2.4 Citizen Identities, National Belongings and State Formation

As we have argued above, our social and historical contexts fundamentally inform who we are and shape the imaginaries that infuse our citizen identities. Taking forward a poststructural analysis, we engage now with the imaginaries that sustained the emergence of the modern (nation) state as a system of government and how this might overlap or differ from the imagined communities of the nation. We then consider the additional complexities of the fractures that were created between the state and the nation in contexts of postcoloniality, both with respect to the emergence of new nations from their colonial condition and in relation to different neo-colonial imperatives that lie within contemporary discourses of global governance.

The Flourishing of Liberal Democracies and the Imagined Communities of the Nation-State

The concept of the nation-state emerged in Western societies within modern times and in association with modern forms of liberal democracy. As a form of governance, the nation-state combined a concern for the security of particular territorial boundaries and the governing of the people within those boundaries. This allowed the flourishing of civil society, commerce and industry. Historically, this liberal framing took as its first premise the 'natural liberty' of individuals to better themselves and to pursue their own interests. The flourishing of the modern nation-state was also therefore intrinsic to the development of capitalism in the Western world. Indeed, rather than reflecting any flourishing of equality, recognition as a citizen of early modern democracies was premised on property ownership and social class positioning (Isin 1997), as well as racial, religious and ethnic hierarchies that often resulted in protracted violence between different groups (Mamdani 2004).

In describing the nation as an 'imagined community', Anderson (1991) calls attention to the work of construction involved in the forging of any nation and how this was integral to the emergence of the modern state. This work of 'imagination' involves the circulation of narratives and the policing of boundaries of belonging through symbolic representations of different groups as described above. However this work was all the more necessary for the forging of the modern state given the mass migration which took place alongside the agricultural reforms and processes of industrialisation of the modern era. As Bhabha (2004) comments, '[t]he nation fills the void left in the uprooting of communities and kin, and turns that loss into the language of metaphor'. Through metaphor, the meaning of 'home and belonging' is reconstructed, so that it can span the cultural differences of 'the imagined community of the nation-people' (200).

Bhabha (2004) is calling attention here to the performativities of the production of the nation. This involved 'nationalist pedagogies', involving the reiteration of norms and the interpellation of the national subject in both past and present:

> The people are the historical 'objects' of a nationalist pedagogy [..] the people are also the 'subjects' of a process of signification [..] as that sign of the *present* through which national life is redeemed and signified as a repeating and reproductive process. The scraps, patches, and rags of daily life must be repeatedly turned into the signs of a national culture, while the very act of the narrative performance interpellates a growing circle of national subjects. (Bhabha 2004:208–209)

For our study, it is important that this double work of production of cultural narratives and interpellation of the national subjects in past and present should be considered always in process, rather than accomplished and secure. Beck and Levy (2013) point out that while the constructed nature of the 'nation' is generally recognised, the naturalisation of the concept of the nation means that its constant (re-)figuration, i.e. the ongoing acts of 'writing the nation' that Bhabha (2004) describes above, is too readily overlooked. The production and re-circulation of these cultural narratives of nation are of particular interest in our case studies which have relatively short national histories borne out of particular extra-national, colonial and postcolonial configurations of power that encompass multiple sub-national social collectivities. These provide the discursive resources with which youth construct intelligible narratives of their identities.

Distinguishing Between State and National Belongings
We also need to emphasise how the coincidence of the imagined community of the nation and the boundaries of the nation-state is constantly in question, both historically, when state boundaries were often drawn up in very arbitrary ways, and in contemporary times of mass migration. We are making an important distinction here between 'nation' and 'state', where nation refers to a community of people who aspire to be politically self-determining, and state refers to the set of political institutions that a particular community may aspire to achieve for themselves (Miller 1995). The concept of the state points us therefore to the institutions and systems through which control and administration of a given territory is secured, including if necessary through the use of force. Historically, it has also been a key source of citizenship and rights. However, the boundaries of nation and nation-state seldom coincide (Guibernau 1996; Yuval-Davis 1997). Thus, a nation may be striving for exit from a state, for greater autonomy within a state or for the unification of different states. With the emergence of other post-national forms of citizenship, we return below to a consideration of the ways different forms of cosmopolitan belongings, including global religions, also intersect with national identities (Beck and Levy 2013).

Imagining the Nation in Postcolonial Contexts: Historical Fractures and Differentiations

We must also consider how many countries with pretentions to liberal democracy were implicated in colonial expansion, which impacted upon each of the contexts in focus in this book. From the early eighteenth century, states within Europe became recognised through a common legal framework as having sovereignty over their boundaries and the peoples living within those boundaries, so that the notion of the 'nation' and its boundaries became normalised. However, this legal framework was not seen to be relevant to large parts of the non-European world. Instead, conquest and competition flourished unfettered by the norms of commerce and European civil society. This resulted in large-scale land appropriation, the extirpation of indigenous peoples and the colonisation of Africa and Asia (Dean 2007). However, given the supposed superiority of modern Western forms of civilisation, as opposed to the 'barbarisms' of the colonies, such activity was justified morally under the rubric of the 'civilising mission' of the West. As Mignolo puts it, 'modernity and coloniality are two sides of the same coin' (2007:43). However, rather than being included as 'citizens', colonised peoples found themselves ruled over as 'subjects' (Mamdani 1996).

We further highlight the symbolic and material violence accomplished through the classificatory work of Western knowledge in colonised lands. As Said describes, from its position of hegemony, the West both managed and indeed produced 'the Orient' politically, sociologically, militarily, ideologically, scientifically and imaginatively (Said 1978:8). Rather than reflecting a pre-existing reality, Orientalism *created* 'the Orient' by 'making statements about it, authorizing views of it, describing it, by teaching it, settling it, ruling over it' (Said 1978:3). Drawing again on Foucault's understanding of discourse and power/knowledge, the work of Orientalism is in other words recognised as having constitutive force. In relation to our discussion of the imagined communities of colonised lands, the work of Orientalism importantly contributed to a reification of the differences between communities, ethnic groups and religious belief systems.

The social and material effects of Orientalism's classificatory processes were deepened and exacerbated, however, by the ways in which colonial powers devolved local rule to favoured ethnic groups, using a combination of direct and indirect rule. This led to the consolidation and installation of some ethnic groups or castes as privileged local elites, both during and after the eras of colonisation. As Nandy (1983:3) argues, processes of colonialisation brought the colonised 'to accept new social norms and cognitive categories' in ways that had irrevocable constitutive effects on the possibilities for subject formation and the constitution of the social. For Kabeer (2002), the classification of indigenous groups, coupled with indirect rule, means that 'colonised populations thus achieved their national independence organised as religious, ethnic and tribal communities rather than as individual citizens' (2002:14). Mamdani (1996) similarly suggests that after independence, politics in the ex-colonies might have been indigenised, but attempts at redistribution of power quickly reverted to regional, ethnic or familial ties, leading to modes of (national) politics that were dominated by clientelism and patrimonialism, based in divisions and differentiations that had been sharpened as an effect of colonial rule. Such divisions are shown to remain significant in the case studies that follow. For example, as shown in Chap. 6, recognition of religious differences in Nigeria which informed the rule of North and South during the eras of colonial rule continues to reverberate through youth's discourses of identity, with regional and religious hierarchies being inextricably entwined. In Lebanon, religious differences were central to the structures of local rule under the millet system of the Ottoman Empire. They later became formally embedded in the Lebanese constitution (Joseph 1999) and now remain at the heart of ongoing religious and political strife that fractures the Lebanese state and extends more widely across the region. In Chap. 7, we show how this historical structuring of the nation-state of Lebanon continues to play out, so that religion remains a central axis of differentiation in the narratives of our Lebanese youth participants.

The 'imagined community' of new nations which emerged from colonial domination has been highlighted as additionally complex, given the defining role of the West in the imagination of modernity. Chatterjee (1993) poses the significant question of what might be left for the postcolonial nation to imagine, given the defining images of modernity which had already been constituted by the West. His analysis of Indian nationalists' efforts to modernise suggests their recognition of the superiority of Europe in domains such as the economy, science and technology, and mechanisms of government. However, differentiation from Europe *was* possible through the separation of the spiritual from material domains, such that the spiritual became the domain which bore the essential and distinctive 'hallmarks' of the new postcolonial nation's cultural identity. Thus, while seeking to emulate the West in certain domains, such as the development of democratic forms of government, science and technology, Chatterjee (1993:6) argues that differentiation through the spiritual and cultural domains became a 'defining feature' of postcolonial nationalisms in Asia and Africa. Such distinctions were found to reverberate through our case studies. For example, we will see how the 'West' and its 'modernity' was sometimes emulated by Senegalese youth participants, for example in their endorsement of Senegal's espousal of secular republicanism. In contrast, local cultural norms were invoked to construct female youth's claims to equality as 'other'. (see Chap. 5). We discuss the gendered implications of the ways differentiation was articulated in the section below.

The Postcolonial Nation in a Globalised World: New Spatialities for Politics?
In the post–World War II (WWII) era, the complexities of forging new nation-states has been further complicated by the growing influence of the web of multilateral organisations that now span the Global North and Global South. Questions have been raised about the extent that these perpetuate forms of neo-colonialism, within which the Global South remains the poor relation in need of remedial intervention/ attention. If multilateral agencies such as the UN were founded in the post–World War II period to secure world peace and respect for human rights, later World Bank policies such as structural adjustment clearly impacted disproportionately on the post-colonies. Even if ostensibly benign, the promotion of universal human rights by international agencies has also been questioned for the ways they perpetuate neo-colonial relations. As Benhabib (2011:13) argues, rather than a progressive

development, their inherent individualism means that human rights discourses may also act as a 'Trojan horse', shielding the spread of neo-liberal values. Cornwall and Nyamu-Musembi (2005) also question the 'turn' to rights-based approaches by many development actors. They alert us to the ways contemporary 'rights talk' sits well with the prioritisation of partnership, participation and dialogue that now informs aid delivery, and question the instrumentalities of the use of 'rights-based' discourses in such contexts in ways that leave neo-colonial power relations undisturbed.

The international human rights regime has nevertheless been seen as provoking some 'unbundling' of the association of citizenship with the nation-state. This potentially involves more cosmopolitan forms of citizenship, and the 'emergence of new types of political subjects and new spatialities for politics' (Sassen 2006:279). However Calhoun (2008) draws attention to the multiple meanings of the term 'cosmopolitanism' and disrupts common-sense assumptions that the concept is somehow inherently benign. In its Greek origins, the 'cosmopolitan' was a citizen of the world, as opposed to a citizen of the *polis*. In contemporary everyday language, it often implies someone who is worldly, well-travelled and urbane, who is accommodating of diversity and difference. However, these forms of cosmopolitanism misrecognise their reliance on social and material privileges, and are underpinned by forms of class consciousness that assume their superiority in relation to the 'provincial' (Appiah 2006; Calhoun 2008). Other understandings of 'cosmopolitanism' are more normative. Some look to yet more developed forms of supranational governance in support of a global human rights regime (e.g. Held 1995), in ways that seem oblivious to its Western biases. Others highlight the continuing significance of local values and practices, alongside universal human obligations (Appiah 2006). The tensions between these poles lead him to describe cosmopolitanism as 'the name not of the solution but of the challenge'. We return again to different understandings of cosmopolitanism below, when addressing religion.

At this point, we note that if the significance of the modern state for citizenship might have been disrupted by the development of supranational law and supranational institutions, different authors (for example

Cheah 2006; Nash 2009; Sassen 2006) stress the continuing role of the modern state for the enforcement of human rights, but in ways that are becoming increasingly unequal. As Nash (2009) illuminates, supposedly 'cosmopolitan' understandings of citizenship have produced a proliferation of groups enjoying different citizenship status, ranging from 'super-citizens' to 'un-citizens'. The 'super-citizen' enjoys full citizenship rights, has secure employment, international mobility and so can just 'fly home' should they encounter an infringement of their human rights. On the other hand, 'marginal citizens' may have formal citizenship rights, but they are effectively debarred from claiming them because of their relative poverty, institutionalised racism or because they have been forced out by conflict. The situation of those fleeing war in Syria is a contemporary illustration of the latter. Nash (2009) suggests that rather than ushering in a new era of universal rights, the interstices between international and national legal systems may be 'concretizing' new forms of inequality. Thus, just as the concept of identity depends on its 'constitutive other', the concept of the citizen is also produced in relation to its 'other', the non-citizen. Nash (2009) describes these as 'Un-citizens', who include undocumented migrants, refugees, and those detained as part of the 'War on Terror' in 'non-places' that are outside of national jurisdictions, such as Guantanamo Bay or the camps at Bagram.

In conclusion, this section has drawn on a range of social theorists to critique the concepts of nation and of the nation-state, framed by ideologies of modernity. We have highlighted the Western origins of the nation-state alongside the paradoxical subjugation of much of the Global South during the colonial era; the further complexities that Orientalism created for the emergence of new nations in postcolonial times; and the ways this led newer nations to seek differentiation through the uniqueness of their cultures. In a globalised world, we have problematised how the promotion of international human rights may work to spread neoliberal values. Despite the claims that these may offer new forms of cosmopolitan citizenship, we conclude by suggesting that citizenship rights still mostly depend on the nation-state, although claims to rights are becoming increasingly fractured and unequal in the interstices of international and national legal systems.

2.5 Religion

We begin this section by considering the discursive grammar through which religion has been constituted within modernity and in particular with respect to the formation of the nation-state. We have highlighted above how the rejection of traditional forms of authority such as religion was integral to the emergence of modernity, which claimed instead to privilege man's (*sic*) use of reason. As Taylor (2011) comments, taking the examples of the USA and France, modern liberal democracies were therefore ostensibly constructed on the basis of a 'principled distance' between religion and the state. However, although much has been made about the supposedly 'secular' nature of modern democracies, this section will demonstrate firstly the highly variable ways that different nation-states recruit religion into their national imaginaries; secondly, the problematic claims on the part of some nation-states to be 'secular' and thirdly, the equally problematic construction of Islam as 'incapable' of secular thought. As part of the questioning of binary constructions of Islam and Christianity, we draw on authors (Mahmood 2012; Laborde 1995) who point instead to their similarities and the dynamic syncretic fusions that occur between religions in their diffusion around the world during different historical periods. We conclude the section by returning to the concept of cosmopolitanism, and how this relates to religion, particularly with respect to Muslim cosmopolitanism.

Western Democracies and Their 'Secularisms'

We turn first to Asad (2003) who explores the emergence of the concept of religion, and the different boundaries it invokes. This includes the emergence of religion as transcendent to the natural world and the later putative separation of religion and politics. In his 'anthropology' of secularism, Asad (2003) traces the emergence of a 'new grammar' associated with Christian thought, which re-positioned religion outside of the world, immanent and transcendent to it. In contrast to how Greek gods were seen as being involved in natural and social processes, the emergent Christian cosmology was 'separative', in supposing a distinction between the 'natural' and the 'supernatural' worlds (27).

In this new way of thinking, the natural world was also reconceptualised as a realm which could be manipulated, material, subject to mechanical laws, while the 'supernatural' lay beyond this, a realm that Asad (2003) describes as 'peopled by irrational events and imagined beings' (28).

Asad (2003) suggests that this prepared the ground for a new discursive grammar, allowing the emergence of the concept of 'secular space' within early modernity. This was informed by the 'disenchantment' that characterised the modern epoch, which implied 'a stripping away of myth, magic and the sacred' (13). In addition to the construction of a binary between reason and religion, this redrew the boundaries of the 'real' versus the 'illusory', the natural versus the supernatural, in ways that supposedly allowed man 'direct access to reality', and also helped to consolidate the 'myth' of secularism as intrinsic to liberal democracies (Asad 2003:13).

Although recognising that different democracies reflect different 'modern imaginaries', Asad's analysis of the American, English and French democracies that emerged in the eighteenth and nineteenth centuries nevertheless points to the continuing interpenetration of religion and the state within each of them. Echoing his arguments, Taylor (2011) disputes the primacy attached to 'secular reason'. He finds this to be a 'myth of the Enlightenment' (52), and takes issue with theorists such as Habermas and Rawls who would argue that democratic values can be founded on the use of reason alone. As Butler (2011) also points out, attempts to traduce religious belief through a critique of its cognitive status fail to attend to the ways religion works as a 'matrix of subject formation, an embedded framework for evaluations, and a mode of belonging and embodied social practice' (72).

Indeed, despite the ostensible distance posited between religion and the modern state, many social theorists have also suggested how religious values remained embedded within the values of liberal democracies. Thus, the terms of the American Declaration of Independence held strong biblical resonances from the outset (Nash 2009; Taylor 2011). In relation to the emergence of the notion of the 'secular' in the USA, Taylor (2011) points out that the term first arose in this context in the nineteenth century, when Catholics and Jews found themselves being excluded by invocations of the particular versions of Christianity of those in authority. He also notes how American Catholics were targeted in nineteenth century as 'inassimilable to democratic mores' in ways that resemble contemporary critiques of those of Islamic faith. More widely, sociologists such as Weber (1930) suggest that the ethos of capitalism and of Protestantism were mutually constitutive. In other words, contrary to the supposed secularism of the modern state, protestant religious values should be considered integral to the construction of the modern self, fostering and legitimating its strong individualism, alongside the development of capitalist values and colonial expansion. Kalberg (1997) takes up de Tocqueville's and Weber's critiques of modern democracy to illuminate how the values of ascetic Protestantism imposed a duty on the individual to work towards their own salvation and prove themselves to god, rather than any earthly authority. While potentially counterbalancing pressures to conformity within a democracy, these values imposed a duty of self-improvement and impelled the individual to prove himself (*sic*) through hard work, competition and the search for profit. Drawing upon Weber (1930), Kalberg notes how this ethos of world-oriented individualism supposed its value system to have god-given superiority, while at the same time also giving legitimacy to wealth accumulation. In other words, religious values were integrally bound up with the emergence of Western democracy, the development of capitalism and its justification of colonial expansion.

Overall, Western democracy's claims to separate the public, political sphere from that of religion must be recognised as highly contentious. Rather, as Butler (2011) suggests, some religions are already 'inside' the public sphere. Public life affirms a particular religious tradition as 'the secular', which consolidates its dominance at the same time as providing criteria for the exclusion of other faiths. Although cloaked in the language of reason, Asad (2003) concludes that 'secularism' functions as a political doctrine. In other words, as a project it seeks the 'redemption' of the rest of the world, and in so doing claims a moral high ground, which means that it can readily underwrite state-legitimated violence. Thus, while the modern liberal state might claim its foundation to be secular and rational, he finds it instead to be 'heavily invested in myth and violence' (2003:56).

Secularism, the Modernising Postcolonial Nation and Islam
The claims to secularism on the part of Western democracies are critical in the contemporary positioning of Islam in relation to the 'modern' world. Indeed, Islam and Islamic societies have been characterised as 'premodern', or even 'anti-modern', with the concept of 'the secular' found to be notable by its absence (Mamdani 2004). Such attitudes are readily discernible in contemporary France, for example in recent controversies surrounding the banning of the *hijab* in French schools. As a religious sign, these ostensibly breach the secularist principles of the French republic, whose constitution is founded on the notion of *laïcité*. While republican framings of nationality conceptualise it as involving a common culture shared by all citizens, Laborde (2008) finds this to be inherently exclusionary, and to downplay the 'ethnic-like, particularist components of French culture' (2) in ways that are oppressive of difference. She suggests that in a climate of widespread racial discrimination, the invocation of the supposedly universal values of secularism provides a legitimisation for ethnicised social relations. Rather than supporting equality between citizens therefore, principles of *laïcité* are used to rationalise and sustain ethnic discrimination within French society. We return below to the redoubling of the burden of such oppressions on women, as the 'symbolic guards' of both religious and national values.

Mamdani (2004) is also concerned to show how political Islam and secular modernity have come together in different contexts. His analysis suggests how the emergence of political Islam, for example in India or Egypt, was not led by Islamic religious scholars (the *ulama*), but by political intellectuals whose dominant concern was for societal reform. This means their discourse was 'largely secular' (4), being concerned with worldly social and political issues, rather than issues of salvation. We will show below how this is relevant in our case studies, for example in relation to the emergence of Pakistan as a nation-state.

Mamdani (2004) therefore prefers the term 'political Islam' to 'Islamic fundamentalism'. In tracing the roots of radical forms of political Islam, which espouse the use of violence, he points in particular to political encounters between Islam and the West, which led to a reworking of traditional understandings of 'jihad'. In more detail, he argues this had two main traditions (2004:50): the first (the greater jihad) involves a struggle against the weaknesses of the self, and is therefore self-directed. The second (the lesser jihad) concerns self-preservation and self-defence, so can be directed outwardly, and can involve mobilisation for social/political causes. He notes the historical infrequency of 'lesser jihad' and identifies four exceptions, all linked to anti-Western and anti-colonial struggles. He comments on how modern Western thought has misrepresented 'jihad' as an Islamic war against unbelievers and suggests instead that important strands of political Islam continue to have a modernising, largely secular ethos that seeks out societal reform. He does recognise another strand of Islamic jihad that is 'state-centred', however, and sees this as at the heart of contemporary Islamic political terror.[1] This form of jihad can also be directed against Muslims who are viewed as heretical, as we have seen in contemporary conflicts in the Middle East.

In addition to problematising reductive understandings of the concept of jihad, Mamdani (2004) also disrupts overly simplistic equations of political Islam with Islamic fundamentalism, violence or terrorism. He illuminates instead how political Islam has worked as part of national, modernising imaginaries. Mamdani's more complex account of Islam can also be compared to Badran's (2009) feminist analysis of 'secular and religious convergences' in Islam. She urges us to 'historicise' the terms, given the shifts in their meanings and inflections over time. She also asserts that the term secularism was first used in Islamic contexts in the nineteenth century within the struggles of different states for independence from colonial powers. This secular nationalism could not assume that the nation mapped onto the state, but nor did it involve resistance to religion. Instead, within the 'imagined *secular* nation, religion was taken for granted and citizens' plural religious identities accorded recognition and space' (Badran 2009:301, our emphasis). The 'pioneering secular feminisms' that developed in different Middle Eastern contexts through the late nineteenth and twentieth centuries are described by Badran (2009) as always having 'a space for religion' (246). Indeed, they drew on Islam to argue for reforms to personal status laws, that is, customary or family laws drawing on local traditions which affect women's rights with respect to issues such as custody of children, divorce and inheritance.

However, she finds the term 'secular' became set in opposition to religion in the later decades of the twentieth century, so that it came to signify 'un-Islamic, anti-Islamic or non-Islamic', and increasingly was used as an 'epithet of condemnation' by radical Islamists (Badran 2009:305). While noting how colonial and postcolonial interventions created and sedimented religious conflicts in the Middle East, for example in Syria, Iraq and Lebanon, Krämer (2013) similarly comments on contemporary sentiments which see secularism as being part of a project of modernisation imposed from the outside by colonial and postcolonial regimes, and which puts Muslim identities in jeopardy. Badran (2009) finds these 'newly ideologised and politicised' forms of Islamic discourse appropriate religion in the service of both '*umma*' and '*watan*', the first referring to a global world community of Muslims, and the latter being 'a people connected by attachment to a land or country' (303). In addition to highlighting how religion can be and has been politicised, her analysis also shows how affective attachments to the nation and the global can co-exist and intersect, rather than being mutually exclusive (see also Beck and Levy 2013 below).

We return to the ideals of a global world community in our discussion of cosmopolitanism below, but at this point reiterate firstly the extent that Western 'secularism' is informed by religious ideals and norms, and secondly, how Islam can be and has been recruited as a modernising force, in support of the emergent nationalisms of colonised nations. However, we also note how socio-political conflicts can result in a hardening of 'religious' affiliations and their politicisation in ways that may lead to 'state-centered' forms of radical Islam, and the construction of secularism as a Western imposition. Such complexities lead Burchardt and Wolhrab-Sahr (2013:607) to propose the concept of '*multiple secularities*', to support an exploration of 'the shifting symbolic meanings that the secular acquires within historically specific relations of political power and epistemic authority'. This concept seems particularly relevant to our research, for the ways it refuses binary separations of nation and religion, and recognises instead the cultural and historical contingencies of their functional differentiation in different modern state formations. In the section below, we continue to challenge binary constructions of Islam, religion and modernity, highlighting instead the complex ways they are intertwined, before turning to a discussion of religion and cosmopolitanism.

Religion: Binaries or Complex Fusions?
Much of the previous discussion depends on the articulation of binaries, such as modern versus premodern, secularism versus religion, and the West and its others, Christianity versus Islam. Mahmood's (2012) study of Islamic women's piety in Egypt is particularly useful for challenging these binaries and highlights instead the similarities in the traditions and practices of some Islamic and Christian sects. Focusing particularly on Sunni Islam and Protestant Christianity, she points, for example, to the ways that each (individual) follower is seen as capable of cultivating and inculcating the highest virtues and has individual responsibility for doing this. In Islam, this is equivalent to greater jihad. Each individual is also accountable to a transcendental authority, without further worldly intermediaries before this authority. A further shared assumption is that the pursuit of these virtues should be part of daily life, rather than through a particular religious order or through withdrawal from society. This demands work on the self, across the supposed boundaries of the secular and the religious, and the public and the private (see also Krämer 2013). In other words, 'all of life is regarded as the stage on which these values and attitudes are enacted, making any separation between the secular and the sacred difficult to maintain' (Mahmood 2012:173–174). Such similarities were particularly salient in our research in relation to Muslim and Christian male's representations of their religious practices in Nigeria (see Chap. 6). We return to Mahmood's (2012) analysis of Islamic women's piety below, to underscore its political nature and the ways their piety works with and resists masculinist norms.

The analysis by Laborde (1995) of the emergence of the Layenne brotherhood in the north-west of Senegal is also useful for underscoring how religious belief systems often involve ongoing syncretic fusions. So, for example, incoming religions and older, more 'traditional' cultural customs have been brought together in ways that allowed the development of new forms of 'African Islam' that were distinctive from those of the Middle East. The fusions of traditional beliefs with new Islamic religious practices provided forms of belonging that also allowed a sense of local distinction. As Laborde (1995) points out, 'syncretism is above all a dynamic force, a product of the interaction between traditional practices, imported religion and modernity' (7, our translation).

Before leaving this section, we note the implications of these arguments for our research, and how important it is that we attend to the contingencies of the local and its different intersecting discourses and practices. In all our case study contexts, the policing of the boundaries with respect to what counts as legitimate (local) or purer forms of 'religious' practice in relation to others, both internal and external to the nation-state, is pivotal. We nevertheless remain attentive throughout our research to the ways contemporary Western discourses homogenise political Islam and foster its equation with radical Islam (Asad 2003; Mamdani 2004), and how these may in turn produce homogenised reciprocal visions of 'others'.

Cosmopolitan Belongings?
At this point, we return to a discussion of cosmopolitanism, linked to contemporary discussions of post-national or global forms of citizenship, and consider how different understandings of cosmopolitanism might intersect with religious beliefs and practices. A common understanding of the term 'cosmopolitan' is that it involves a project of global integration which transcends nation-state institutions (Calhoun 2008). The desire to build a global community of Muslims (*ummah*) could therefore be considered as a form of cosmopolitanism. However, other visions of cosmopolitanism cohere around post-national forms of global governance (Held 1995), whose value system is bound up with the history of secularism we have critiqued above. Although European Union law has been discussed as an example of the emergence of such 'post-national' legal and political frameworks, Edmunds (2013) notes how judgements by the European Court of Human Rights have demonstrated very little sympathy for minority Islamic communities in Europe. In considering this 'failure' of cosmopolitanism, Edmunds (2013) suggests a distinction between European and Muslim

cosmopolitanisms, where 'European' cosmopolitanism assumes 'cool' affective attachments and loyalties, which resonate with the ideals of secular republicanism, and has little sympathy for the 'thick' religious attachments that might typify 'Muslim cosmopolitanism'.

Other writers offer alternative imaginaries of cosmopolitanism that helpfully resist its Eurocentric associations. Marsden's (2008) discussion of 'Muslim cosmopolitans' draws on ethnographies of Muslim peoples in northern Pakistan. His analysis takes up the dynamic intersections of different discourses (religious, ethnic and cultural), both historical and contemporary, in the production of what it means to be Muslim. This takes account of premodern Muslim cosmopolitan thought of Islamic scholars who aspired to a world that shared Islamic ideals, as well as historical and contemporary experiences of mobility in regions that have in more recent times been incorporated into British India and the Soviet Union. Rather than positing any universal cosmopolitan 'norms', this analysis privileges a 'resolute localism' where cosmopolitanism is understood as a discursive device through which 'a specific and exclusive local identity [is] objectified and valorised' (Osella and Osella 2007 in Marsden 2008:215). In addition to showing how different discourses of cosmopolitanism require participants to navigate 'very different indexes of being Muslim' across the different local and transregional contexts of their lives (2008:216), Marsden suggests how rural-rural or transregional—as much as transnational—processes may contribute to more cosmopolitan forms of belonging, as opposed to the more common associations of cosmopolitanism with global cities or elites. As we highlighted above, it is always within the particularities of the local that these cosmopolitan identities are played out.

This attention to the local is at one level sympathetic with Appiah's (2006) insistence on the significance of local values and practices as integral to cosmopolitanism, and how this constantly implicates tensions between different value systems. However, the commitment to values within Appiah's (2006) situated cosmopolitanism leads him to single out some forms of Muslim belonging as being antithetical to his understandings of cosmopolitanism. For Appiah, values intrinsic to cosmopolitanism are tolerance, pluralism (acceptance that there are many different ways of being and living) and fallibilism (awareness that our knowledge is always imperfect and provisional) (2006:144). From this understanding of cosmopolitanism, any radical (fundamental) form of Islam or Christianity that seeks to impose its understandings on others through violence is in breach of its central ideals, which leads Appiah to describe radical Islam is a form of 'counter-cosmopolitanism'.

Beck and Levy (2013) also discuss 'global Islam' through the lens of cosmopolitanism. In contrast to Appiah (2006), their discussion of the concept focuses on the new imaginaries produced through the intersections of the national and the global which are made possible through the ubiquitous use of information technologies and new media. Unlike Appiah, theirs is a non-normative understanding of cosmopolitanism; they are concerned with the analysis of global flows, rather than holding out for any utopian 'world without borders'. They describe their understanding of cosmopolitanism as 'impure', concerned with the interpenetration of the global, the national and the local in contemporary contexts where the 'Global other is in our midst' (9). Rather than seeing cosmopolitanism as one universal process, they suggest that global transformations produce different cosmopolitan 'trajectories', which intersect with national imaginaries in different ways. This challenges how the national is typically constructed in a dichotomous relationship with cosmopolitanism and highlights instead how 'cosmopolitan orientations can complement the national' (5). This is also a conflictual understanding of cosmopolitanism. It does not see cosmopolitanism as involving processes of rational consensus that will bring universal harmony. Indeed, because the global themes which they identify are framed as 'imperatives', their imposition can be coercive.

Their different themes include the global regime of human rights, the imperatives of the world market, migration and global generational civil society movements, for example the Arab Spring. However, while each of these are relevant to our study, their identification of the 'local interpenetration of world religions' as a key dynamic in the intersection of the national and the cosmopolitan seems of particular significance. As different world religions now compete with each other within the local, this gives rise to 'new forms of coexistence, interpenetration, resistance and conflict'. Their analysis therefore foregrounds conflict and tension, with the intersection of Western modernity, Christianity and Islam being seen as involving an 'everyday clash of religious universalisms' that leads to hierarchies of superiority/inferiority and the production of a 'radical otherness' (15–16). This analysis tends to collapse differences within world religions all the same. Our case studies will also suggest the construction 'radical otherness' to be a powerful dynamic within world religions. Like Mamdani (2004), Beck and Levy (2013) find that the sharp differentiations between 'we' and 'others' that are intrinsic to these constructions can readily become aligned with moral distinctions between 'Good' and 'Evil'.

To conclude this discussion of cosmopolitanism, it will be clear that it is a slippery term and that very different understandings of it can be invoked. Firstly, as identified earlier, the concept is often associated with a form of urbanity that misrecognises the elite forms of capital through which it is sustained. Secondly, cosmopolitanism can involve an appeal to different forms of universalism, although this can be the (secular) rationalities of modern governance, or religious affiliations with deep (affective) attachments. Thirdly, whether the concept is taken forward in philosophical (Appiah 2006) or in ethnographic (Marsden 2008) terms, one is quickly summonsed to confront how any 'universalism' plays out in particular contexts, in ways that are likely to be contradictory and conflictual. Fourthly, while some writers (for example Appiah 2006; Held 1995) propose normative understandings of cosmopolitanism (even if very different from each other), others (Marsden 2008; Beck and Levy 2013) do not espouse any cosmopolitan 'project', but seek to analyse cosmopolitanism as a product of intersecting discourses, both historical and contemporary.

It is these latter understandings that are of particular interest to us—we do not seek in our analysis to propose any normative 'cosmopolitan' ideals but rather attend to the ways different discourses of cosmopolitanism intrude into the contexts of research, and in so doing, animate the production of citizen identities in a performative way. Beck and Levy (2013) highlight the contemporary circulation of global discourses in the production of different forms of cosmopolitanism. Importantly, Marsden's (2008) analysis further signals the salience of attending to historical formations that contribute to the sedimentation of identity discourses across time and space. In our case studies, we explore how aspirations to construct a global *ummah* sometimes involved articulation of hierarchies between different versions of Islam—see in particular how authoritative, absolutist notions of Islam were used to close down discussion in male Muslim focus groups in Nigeria, with other more syncretic forms of practice being dismissed as inauthentic, as well as the fracturing of Islam along sectarian lines in Lebanon (Chaps. 6 and 7, respectively). However, we also note the almost total silence in all discussions of cosmopolitanism about gender—a silence which belies an assumed, masculine norm which nevertheless depends on its constitutive other.

2.6 Intersections of Gender, Nation, Religion

At multiple points in the discussion above, we have signalled our intention to return to gender. We open this concluding section therefore by first highlighting that all of the above is gendered, and of the importance of deconstructing the social and cultural embeddedness of gender hierarchies. To give some small illustrations, our everyday ways of living and being are constantly entangled with the iteration of gender norms, for example in differences in the clothes we wear, our embodiments, our social relations including their divisions of labour and the material spaces that we occupy. In relation to the construction of identity, our poststructural theorisation understands these differentiations as discursively constituted within historically contingent grids of intelligibility, which have over time involved classificatory systems which depend upon the binary opposition of signs (Foucault 1970). As Adams St. Pierre (2000:481) elaborates, such binaries include the opposition of culture/nature, mind/body, rational/irrational (emotional), subject/object, where the first is recognised as male, with the female 'always positioned at the wrong side of [such] binaries and at the bottom of [such] hierarchies'.

In relation to liberal theories, one can add to these binaries the opposition of the public and the private, as well as the inner and outer, and the spiritual and the material—all of which are central in the gendering of modernity and the construction of the modern nation-state.

Feminist critiques have focused on the close associations of masculinity with the culture and practices of nationalism, including male domination of decision-making positions, male dominance in the division of labour and male regulation of female rights, labour and sexuality (Nagel 1998; Pateman 1988). Thus, in the opposition of the public and private, women are relegated to the private domain, outside of the public sphere, positioned by Kant (1992/1784) as 'the feebler sex', subject to the emotions, in ways that necessarily compromise their capacity to exercise their reason. The patriarchal assumptions of the disembodied, rational subject in modern liberal theory are critiqued for the curtailment of women's participation as citizens. As Mouffe (1992) points out, however, this critique is limited by its essentialised understanding of women and does not adequately undo the ways that patriarchy is embedded in liberal understandings of the self.

The patriarchal positioning of women within national imaginaries has also been identified by many different theorists. Yuval-Davis and Anthias (1989) signal the ways women occupy a distinct symbolic role in nationalism. They are biological reproducers of national and ethnic collectivities, responsible for the inculcation of proper norms of behaviour. As signifiers of ethnic/national differences, they are vital to the ideological reproduction of the collectivity and transmission of its culture. Thus, women are symbolically important as the 'mothers' of the nation, an analogy which aligns women's honour with the that of the family as well as the nation, and ensures that women's honour is placed under male scrutiny (Nagel 1998). As shown below, cultural norms associated with the nation are also bound up with the practices of the self and the policing of norms associated with religious codes (Mahmood 2012).

The position of women has been identified as being particularly significant in the formation of national imaginaries of postcolonial nations. For Chatterjee (1993), a consequence of accepting Europe's superiority in fields such as the economy, science and technology and modes of governance, was the need to differentiate one's national culture from that of the ex-coloniser. In the demarcation of the public and the private, the material from the spiritual and the cultural, it became all the more important to defend the cultural, as a space which had successfully resisted colonisation and which therefore represented the 'essence' of national culture. As Chatterjee (1993) illuminates however, the responsibility for nurturing these dimensions has fallen primarily on women, thus making them subject to new and redoubled forms of patriarchy under both colonial and postcolonial gender regimes.

Overall, women's bodies are an important boundary marker for the nation; they function as a surface on which different regimes of power/knowledge are inscribed and where difference is defined (Foucault 1977). As Mayer argues, through the body:

> the mythical unity of national 'imagined communities' is maintained and ideologically reproduced by a whole system of symbolic 'border guards' (Mayer 2000:18).

These 'border guards' serve to identify people as members or non-members of a specific collectivity through cultural codes of style of dress and behaviour, as well as through customs, religion, language and the construction of different forms of masculinities and femininities. Mayer also notes the relationship between gender and colonialism by suggesting that nationalism developed in reaction to imperialism and to imperialism's 'feminization and infantilization both of the colonies themselves and of indigenous men' (Mayer 2000:14). She suggests that as colonial powers challenged their masculinity, indigenous men emphasised both control over their own bodies as well as control over 'their' women's bodies. In this way, 'men's sense of masculinity has, increasingly, come to depend on preserving women's femininity, modesty and religiosity' (Mayer 2000:15). These arguments are shown to remain relevant to each of our case contexts, in which the policing of national and religious ideals is accomplished particularly through the policing of women, in which women themselves are agentive.

Our insistence on recognising women's agency leads us to contemporary constructions of Muslim women, which frequently puts their agency into question, with women who espouse Islam being seen as non-agential, within subordinate and patriarchal gender relations. The ethnographic study of the 'politics of piety' of Egyptian Muslim women in Cairo by Mahmood (2012) provides a valuable counterpoise to such assumptions, drawing on Butler and Foucault to critique secular-liberal understandings of the subject, its agency and of politics. Rather than necessarily requiring the re-signification of norms, Mahmood locates agency in the ways that 'norms are lived and inhabited, aspired to, reached for, and consummated' (22). She also shows how the women in her study sought to transform many aspects of their social lives through styles of dress and speech, standards of entertainment, issues related to financial and household management, care for the poor and in influencing the terms of public debate. Even within women's cultivation of norms such as '*sabr*', involving perseverance in the face of difficulty without complaint, which is considered to be an 'essential attribute of a pious character' (171–172), she finds agency to be integral to what might initially appear to be 'passivity'. Thus, '*sabr*' 'does not mark a reluctance to act [...] it is a constructive project... a site of considerable investment, struggle and achievement' (Mahmood 2012:174). Overall, her analysis speaks back to stereotypical constructions of Arab and/or Muslim women as passive and subordinated, as well as highlighting how these women drew on Islam in their struggles against social injustice.

Agency here is not understood in Western liberal terms as being voluntaristic and associated with the ideals of freedom and emancipation. Instead, agency is intrinsic within particular modes of subjectivation that prevail in specific contexts. Mahmood draws on Foucault to argue that modes of subjectivation implicate particular historical sets of ethical practices, where ethics is understood as a 'modality of power' involving 'practices, techniques, discourses through which a subject transforms herself in order to achieve a particular state of being, happiness or truth' (Mahmood 2012:28). As discussed in our methodology chapter, this leads us to privilege a discursive analysis that does not locate agency in individuals, but in the inhabiting of subject positions and norms in the ways Mahmood (2012) describes. This enables a consideration of religion in terms of its attributions of authority, modes of subjectivation and different technologies of the self. This offers a way of exploring the discursive entanglements with ideas of nation and gender which may diverge or intersect with the dominant public discourse of citizenship in each particular context. A specific example of this would be the ways religion was recruited by male and by female Muslim youth as a distinguishing feature of Senegalese nationality, although alongside expressions of pride in its secular democracy, and in ways that were highly gendered. We trace this to the collective memories of the work done by Islamic leaders in the past to support Senegal's emergence as an independent nation against the external other of France, work that was identified as being both religious and political.

Overall, our interest is in how these multiple threads are invoked and made coherent by youth, and although finding in our different case studies that the gendered intersection of nation and religion often resulted in subordinated femininities, we are also concerned in our analysis to show the active production and axes of contestation of such subject positions.

2.7 Conclusion

The purpose of this book is an exploration of how young Muslims integrate or differentiate the three themes of nation, religion and gender in their identity constructions within four distinctive Muslim-majority contexts. This chapter has contextualised these three significant axes of youth identity. It has explored different theoretical lenses for considering the concept of identity itself and of gender. In this section, we position our study within poststructural and postcolonial understandings of identity, as an ongoing discursive accomplishment, that is fluid and dynamic, even if always involving the reiteration of the symbolic representations of national and religious belonging that are shot through with traces of the past. We highlight in particular how identity is constructed through difference, and in relation to the 'other', where the constant reiteration of different boundaries of belonging, involve both inclusions and exclusions.

From this perspective, we then turned to a discussion of nation, highlighting its Western origins and signalling the multiple additional complexities of national identifications for postcolonial nation-states. In particular, we pointed to the work of Orientalism, how this contributed to the suturing of differences that were deepened and sharpened by the ways colonial administrations worked. We explored how this often fractured the imaginaries of the nation in many postcolonial contexts, so that the postcolonial nation's claim to uniqueness is produced in differentiation from multiple internal, as well as external 'others'.

We then explored the concept of religion, deconstructing its binary construction against both modernity and secularism, and modernity and Islam, and showing how Islam has been integral to struggles for independence of postcolonial nations, recruited in support of political and social reforms, rather than necessarily sitting in any antithetical relation to modernity. Anticipating our later case studies, we will show, for example, the entanglement of religion in the forging of the nation of Pakistan, in its differentiation as a nation in contra-distinction to the external others of India. Similarly in Senegal, African Islam was integral to the national imaginary, in ways that allowed differentiation from its colonial past, as well as conferring distinction in relation to other African nations. In contrast, we take up the significance of the internal other in the construction of the nation in Nigeria and Lebanon, and how traces of the internal historical (religious) divisions which were significant in their emergence as independent nation-states continue to reverberate within youth discourses. We finally turned to gender, to illuminate its persistence within national and religious affiliations, and indeed how it is through gender that the cultural distinctiveness of the postcolonial nation is often policed and sustained.

The chapter which follows will present a detailed account of our research methodology and research methods. We describe how our interest in the internal and external 'others' through which national and religious identities are accomplished was taken forward in the design of our interview schedule. In keeping with our awareness of the gendered dynamics of youth's identity productions, we also describe how we took account of gender in our interview sampling practices and in the conduct of the research more generally. After describing our research processes, we then turn to the different country cases, where we explore the multiple configurations of youth identity production within their different contexts.

Note

1. Mamdani (2004) traces the call for an armed jihad to two key thinkers, Abdul A'la Mawdudi from Pakistan and Sayyid Qutb from Egypt. Writing in the aftermath of the creation of Pakistan, Mawdudi is described as the first Islamic thinker to make armed struggle central to jihad and to call for universal jihad to establish a global Islamic community. However, Mamdani makes a key differentiation between the 'society-centered' jihad embraced by Qutb, as opposed to the 'state-centered' jihad embraced by Mawdudi. In more detail, Qutb is described as advocating an Islamic road to modernity, embracing its pursuit of knowledge and the physical sciences, although rejecting Western culture and philosophy. This was therefore a *modernising* form of Islam, which sought reforms within state jurisdictions. It includes the possibility of ongoing reinterpretation of shari'a law (the term for this institutionalised practice being *itjihad*), so that this evolves in response to changing contexts. In contrast, the 'state-centered' jihad of Mawdudi sought to constitute a universal Islamic *ummah* that was global in reach, extending beyond the boundaries of any 'nation-state'. It is also radical in seeing the 'gates of *itjihad*' as 'forever closed' (612). Mamdani argues that this state-centred form of radical Islam informs contemporary Islamic political terror.

References

Adams St Pierre, E. (2000). Poststructural feminism in education: An overview. *Qualitative Studies in Education, 13*(5), 477–515.

Adkins, L. (2003). Reflexivity. Freedom or habit of gender? *Theory, Culture & Society, 20*(6), 21–42.

African Union. (2006). *African Youth Charter*. Banjul: African Union Commission.

Ahmed, S. (2004). *The cultural politics of emotion*. Edinburgh: Edinburgh University Press.

Althusser, L. (1972). Ideology and ideological state apparatuses. In *Lenin and philosophy and other essays*. New York and London: Monthly Review Press.

Amin, S. (2013). Demography. In S. Joseph & M. L. Booth (Eds.), *Women in Islamic cultures: Disciplinary paradigms and approaches: 2003–2013* (pp. 65–86). Leiden and Boston: Brill.

Anderson, B. (1991). *Imagined communities: Reflections on the origin and spread of nationalism.* London: Verso.

Appiah, K. A. (2006). *Cosmopolitanism. Ethics in a world of strangers.* London: Penguin.

Asad, T. (2003). *Formations of the secular. Christinity, Islam, modernity.* Stanford: Stanford University Press.

Badran, M. (2009). *Feminism in Islam. Secular and religious convergences.* Oxford: Oneworld Publications.

Beck, U. (1992). *Risk society. Towards a new modernity.* London: Sage.

Beck, U., & Levy, D. (2013). Cosmopolitanized nations: Re-imagining collectivity in world risk society. *Theory, Culture & Society, 30*(2), 3–31.

Beehner, L. (2007). *The effects of 'youth bulge' on civil conflicts.* New York: Council on Foreign Relations.

Benhabib, S. (2011). *Dignity in adversity. Human rights in troubled times.* Malden, MA: Polity Press.

Bhabha, H. K. (2004). *The location of culture.* London and New York: Routledge.

Bourdieu, P. (1990). *The logic of practice.* Cambridge: Polity Press.

Burchardt, M., & Wohlrab-Sahr, M. (2013). Multiple secularities: Religion and modernity in the global age—Introduction. *International Sociology, 28*(6), 605–611.

Butler, J. (1990). *Gender trouble. Feminism and the subversion of identity.* London and New York: Routledge.

Butler, J. (1993). *Bodies that matter. On the discursive limits of "sex".* London and New York: Routledge.

Butler, J. (1997). *Excitable speech. A politics of the performative.* London and New York: Routledge.

Butler, J. (2011). Is Judaism Zionism? In J. Butler, J. Habermas, C. Taylor, & C. West (Eds.), *The power of religion in the public sphere* (pp. 70–92). New York: Columbia University Press.

Butler, J., Habermas, J., Taylor, C., & West, C. (2011). The power of religion in the public sphere. New York: Columbia University Press.

Calhoun, C. (2008). Cosmopolitanism in the modern social imaginary. *Daedalus, 137*(3), 105–114.

Chatterjee, P. (1993). *The nation and its fragments. Colonial and postcolonial histories.* Chichester: Princeton University Press.

Cheah, P. (2006). Cosmopolitanism. *Theory, Culture & Society, 23*(2–3), 486–496.

Cole, J. (2011). A cultural dialectics of generational change. The view from contemporary Africa. *Review of Research in Education, 35,* 60–88.

Cornwall, A., & Nyamu-Musembi, N. (2005). Why rights, why now? Reflections on the rise of rights in International Development Discourse. *IDS Bulletin, 38*(1), 9–18.

Crossouard, B., & Dunne, M. (2015). Politics and youth citizenship in Senegal: The policing of dissent and diversity. *International Review of Education, 61*(1), 43–60.

Dean, M. (2007). *Governing societies. Political perspectives on domestic and international rule.* Maidenhead: Open University Press.

Dunne, M. (ed.) (2008). *Gender, sexuality and development: education and society in Sub-Saharan Africa.* Rotterdam, Sense Publishers

Edmunds, J. (2013). Human rights, Islam and the failure of cosmopolitanism. *Ethnicities, 13*(6), 671–688.

Evans, R., & Lo Forte, C. (2012). A global review. UNHCR's engagement with displaced youth. Geneva: UNHCR Policy Development and Evaluation Service (PDES).

Fanon, F. (1986). *Black skin, white masks.* London: Pluto.

Foucault, M. (1970). *The order of things. An archaeology of the human sciences.* New York: Vintage/Random House.

Foucault, M. (1977). *Discipline and punishment: The birth of the prison* (A. Sheridan, Trans.). London: Allen Lane.

Foucault, M. (1980). Truth and power. In C. Gordon & G. Burchell (Eds.), *Power/knowledge. Selected interviews and other writings* (pp. 109–133). Harlow: Pearson Education.

France, A., & Roberts, S. (2015). The problem of social generations: A critique of the new emerging orthodoxy in youth studies. *Journal of Youth Studies, 18*(2), 215–230.

Giddens, A. (1991). *Modernity and self-identity.* Cambridge: Polity Press.

Guibernau, M. (1996). *Nationalisms: The nation-state and nationalism in the twentieth century.* Cambridge: Wiley.

Hall, S. (1996). Introduction: Who needs 'Identity'? In S. Hall & P. du Gay (Eds.), *Questions of cultural identity* (pp. 1–17). London: Sage.

Hardgrove, A., Pells, K., Boyden, J., & Dornan, P. (2014). *Youth vulnerabilities in life course transitions. Occasional paper.* New York: UNDP Human Development Report Office.

Held, D. (1995). *Democracy and the global order: From the modern state to cosmopolitan governance.* Cambridge: Polity Press.

Hill Collins, P. (1991). *Black feminist thought. Knowledge, consciousness and the politics of empowerment*. New York and London: Routledge.

International Labour Organisation. (2011). Youth unemployment in the Arab world is a major cause for rebellion. Retrieved from http://www.ilo.org/global/about-the-ilo/newsroom/features/WCMS_154078/lang–en/index.htm

International Labour Organisation (ILO). (2013). *Global employment trends for youth 2013. A generation at risk*. ILO: Geneva.

International Labour Organisation (ILO). (2014). *Global employment trends. The risk of a jobless recovery*. ILO: Geneva.

International Labour Organisation (ILO). (2015). *Global employment trends for youth 2015: Scaling up investments in decent jobs for youth*. Geneva: ILO.

Isin, E. F. (1997). Who is the new citizen? Towards a genealogy. *Citizenship Studies, 1*(1), 115–132.

Joseph, S. (1999). Descent of the nation: Kinship and citizenship in Lebanon. *Citizenship Studies, 3*(3), 295–318.

Kabeer, N. (2002). Citizenship and the boundaries of the acknowledged community: Identity, affiliation and exclusion. *IDS working paper 171*. Falmer: Institute of Development Studies.

Kalberg, S. (1997). Tocqueville and weber on the sociological origins of citizenship: The political culture of American democracy. *Citizenship Studies, 1*(2), 199–222.

Kant, E. (1992/1784). An answer to the question: What is enlightenment? In P. Waugh (Ed.), *Postmodernism. A reader* (pp. 89–95). London: Edward Arnold.

Krämer, G. (2013). Modern but not secular: Religion, identity and the *ordre public* in the Arab Middle East. *International Sociology, 28*(6), 629–644.

Laborde, C. (1995). *La confrerie layenne et les Lebou du Senegal: Islam et culture traditionnelle en Afrique*. Bordeaux: Centre d'étude d'Afrique noire, Institut d'études politiques de Bordeaux.

Laborde, C. (2008). *Critical republicanism: The Hijab controversy and political philosophy*. Oxford: Oxford University Press.

Lemke, T. (2001). The birth of bio-politics: Michel foucault's lecture at the collège de France on neo-liberal governmentality. *Economy and Society, 30*(2), 190–207.

Mahmood, S. (2012). *Politics of piety: The Islamic revival and the feminist subject*. Princeton, NJ and Oxford: Princeton University Press.

Mamdani, M. (1996). *Citizen and subject. Contemporary Africa and the legacy of late colonialism*, Princeton, NJ: Princeton University Press.

Mamdani, M. (2004). *Good Muslim, bad Muslim. America, the Cold War, and the roots of terror.* New York: Panthean Books.

Marsden, M. (2008). Muslim cosmopolitans? Transnational life in Northern Pakistan. *Journal of Asian Studies, 67*(1), 213–247.

Mayer, T. (2000). Gender ironies of nationalism: Setting the stage. In T. Mayer (Ed.), *Gender ironies of nationalism: Sexing the nation* (pp. 1–24). London: Routledge.

Mignolo, W. D. (2007). Coloniality and modernity/rationality. *Cultural Studies, 21*(2–3), 155–165.

Miller, D. (1995). *On nationality.* Oxford: Clarendon.

Mouffe, C. (1992). Feminism, citizenship and radical democratic politics. In J. Scott & J. Butler (Eds.), *Feminists theorize the political* (pp. 367–384). New York: Routledge.

Mouffe, C. (2005). *On the political.* London and New York: Routledge.

Nagel, J. (1998). Masculinity and nationalism: Gender and sexuality in the making of nations. *Ethnic and Racial Studies, 21*(2), 242–269.

Nandy, A. (1983). *The intimate enemy. Loss and recovery of self under colonialism.* Delhi: Oxford University Press.

Nash, K. (2009). Between citizenship and human rights. *Sociology, 43*(6), 1067–1083.

Osello, F., & Osello, C. (2007). 'I am Gulf': The production of cosmopolitanism in Kozhhikode, Kerala, India. In E. Simpson & K. Kresse (Eds.), *Struggling with history; Islam and cosmopolitanism in the Western Indian Ocean.* London: Hirst.

Pateman, C. (1988). *The sexual contract.* Cambridge: Polity Press.

Pew Forum on Religion and Public Life. (2011). *The future of the global muslim population: Projections for 2010–2030.* Washington, DC: Pew Research Center.

Said, E. (1978). *Orientalism.* New York: Panthean Books.

Sassen, S. (2006). *Territory, authority, rights: From medieval to global assemblages.* Princeton, NJ: Princeton University Press.

Skeggs, B. (2004). Exchange, value and affect: Bourdieu and the 'self'. In L. Adkins & B. Skeggs (Eds.), *Feminism after Bourdieu* (pp. 75–97). Oxford: Blackwell.

Sommers, M. (2006). *Youth and conflict. A brief review of relevant literature.* Washington, DC: USAID.

Sommers, M. (2011). Governance, security and culture: Assessing Africa's youth bulge. *International Journal of Conflict and Violence, 5*(2), 292–303.

Spivak, G. C. (2005). Use and abuse of human rights. *Boundary, 32*(1), 131–189.

Taylor, C. (1995). *Philosophical arguments*. Cambridge, MA: Harvard University Press.

Taylor, C. (2011). Why we need a radical redefinition of secularism. In E. Mendieta & J. Vanantwerpen (Eds.), *The power of religion in the public sphere* (pp. 34–59). New York: Columbia University Press.

UNESCO. (2013a). *Be skilled, be employed, be the change generation. Education for all global monitoring report youth version*. Paris: UNESCO.

UNESCO. (2013b). *Statistics on youth*. Paris: UNESCO.

United Nations. (1995). *World programme of action for youth to the year 2000 and beyond. Resolution 50/81*. New York: United Nations.

Urdal, H. (2012). *A clash of generations? Youth bulges and political violence. Expert paper No. 2012/1*. New York: United Nations Department of Economic and Social Affairs Population Division.

Weber, M. (1930). *The protestant ethic and the spirit of capitalism* (T. Parsons, Trans.). London: Butler and Tanner.

World Bank. (2006). *World development report 2007: Development and the next generation*. Washington, DC: World Bank.

Yuval-Davis, N. (1997). *Gender and nationhood*. London: Sage.

Yuval-Davis, N., & Anthias, F. (1989). *Woman–nation–gender*. Basingstoke: Macmillan.

3

The Research

Abstract This chapter sets out our approach to the research. It outlines our collective engagement in the research development processes from its inception through to the analysis and writing. We begin by providing a rationale for the study that locates it within wider contemporary concerns and global debates. In a policy context that describes multiple 'hopes' and 'fears' associated with youth, Muslim youth and the Global South, our empirical focus was on accessing youth voices. Our intention was to resist and 'trouble' the homogenised western accounts of Muslim youth through in-depth explorations of the various narratives they used to name and claim their own sense of belonging through their engagement with nation, religion, ethnicity and gender. Our case study approach in four different national contexts was designed to capture the plurality of youth voices. Spanning three regions of the globe—South Asia, Middle East and West Africa—the country cases, Pakistan, Senegal, Nigeria and Lebanon, are all predominantly Muslim states in the Global South. They each have distinctive colonial histories that have shaped their emergence as nation states, the narratives of belonging of their citizens and youth's articulations of identity. In each location, we engaged in a series of focus group discussions, in most cases with the support of local youth researchers. This approach was informed by our concern to privilege youth voices and to listen to the multiple different ways in which youth themselves construct and perform their identities. The details of the research in each context and reflections on its limitations are explored further in subsequent chapters.

3.1 Research Rationale

In the previous chapters of this book, we outlined how important youth are in contemporary policy circles. We related this to the high percentages of youth in the populations of many nation-states, particularly in the Global South. Coupled with their socio-demographic importance, youth are also a concern because of their non-integration into the labour market. Alongside the limited successes of international efforts to ensure universal access to quality education identified in the latest Global Monitoring Report (UNESCO 2015), youth employment has remained obdurate around the world, even in the face of a wider global economic recovery and development. All of this feeds into fears of youth disaffection and alienation from society, potentially fostering a rejection of conventional avenues of protest that might be associated with constitutional democracy and leading instead to youth radicalisation, particularly within 'fundamentalist' forms of religious expression. Given that Islam is a predominant religion in the Global South, youth radicalism (especially that of male youth) has become associated with Islamic fundamentalism and with terrorist activities. Crucially, in this bundle of associations, understandings of 'Islam' are invariably homogenised; any nuanced engagement with the diversity of different interpretative frameworks and forms of practice that might have developed across the many different contexts of Islamic worship in the Global South is singularly absent. Typically, little account is taken of the different inflections of Muslim belonging that might have emerged within the new nation-state formations, forged during the last century, as they cast off earlier eras of colonial domination.

We critique these overly homogenised assumptions and their Western neo-colonial biases in Chap. 2 (Geographies of Identity) but note that despite the concerns that 'youth' as a social category has provoked in high-level policy circles, little research has been done which attends in an in-depth way to the voices of youth from different predominantly Islamic states in the Global South. Our approach to our research has instead been informed by our concern to listen to the multiple different ways in which youth themselves construct and perform their identities through their engagement with nation, religion, ethnicity and gender. With a view to resisting and disrupting homogenised representations of Muslim youth identity, 'troubling' them, we have explicitly sought to explore the pluralities of youth identity formations in three different regions—South Asia, Middle East and West Africa—and in four different national contexts—Lebanon, Pakistan and two contrasting West African countries, Nigeria and Senegal. We have privileged youth voices not only through their inclusion as focus group discussants, but also through our inclusion of 'youth researchers' in case study contexts. Nevertheless, we acknowledge the limitations of a research approach based primarily on focus group data, which cannot achieve the depth provided in more ethnographical studies as exemplified in the work of Mahmood (2012).

3.2 Research Contexts

This concern to explore youth voices also builds on the extensive previous research we have conducted in these different regions, which has similarly privileged youth perspectives. This includes previous research in which the research team were all involved, focusing on citizenship and the perspectives of marginalised groups, particularly girls, in the Occupied Palestinian Territories, Pakistan and Senegal (Dunne et al. 2014). In South Asia, further in-depth research includes the study by Dr. Naureen Durrani of the interaction of Pakistani national identity with religion, gender and ethnicity, including the implications of these interactions for social cohesion, tolerance for diversity and gender relations (Durrani 2007, 2008, 2013; Durrani and Dunne 2010). In the Middle East, a further extended study by Dr. Kathleen Fincham focused on how exilic Palestinian youth in Lebanon constructed their identities in the context of statelessness, again focusing on the intersections of nationality, gender and religion (Fincham 2010, 2012a, b, 2013a, b). In Sub-Saharan Africa, social and educational inequalities, as well as gender and sexuality, have been in strong focus within many different research studies (see, for example Crossouard and Dunne 2015; Dunne 2008; Dunne and Leach 2005; Dunne et al. 2014; Leach and Dunne 2007).

All of these studies have focused on youth identity constructions and performance. As outlined in Chap. 2 (Geographies of Identity), they all embrace an understanding of identity construction as discursively produced through articulations of difference and relations to the 'other'. Thus, in defining one's identity as 'Pakistani', differentiations are made against other national categories, which are saturated with hierarchical evaluations about their distinguishing features. By understanding different youth's perspectives on the significant 'others' against which they define themselves, we gain deeper appreciation of how youth are positioned within systems of difference and how they agentively position other youths through articulations of difference. These systems of difference reflect wider structures of inequality that are constantly implicated in the production of our social realities, and are intrinsic to any efforts on the part of educators or international agencies to attend to inequality, including gender inequalities. With respect to the inclusion of youth as researchers, while this may have been advocated by different agencies, it is typically informed by a rather simplistic desire to access 'authentic' youth voices, as if these could re-present youth realities in a transparent way. As we discuss in Dunne et al. (2015), this privileges western conceptions of the subject and takes up a simplistic representational understanding of 'voice'. Identity also tends to be assumed to reflect an individual 'essence', rather than recognising the constitutive force of discourse in the performance of our identities. These representational understandings typically neglect the dynamics of the interviews themselves, instead of attending to them as spaces in which youth bring into being and perform their different identities in an ongoing way. The dynamics of the youth researchers' engagements are discussed further below, in the section describing the conduct of the research, as well as in the four different case study chapters.

This research project has sought to explore youth identity formations in four distinctly different contexts in order to attend to the different inflections of Islamic belonging that might prevail in different nation-state formations, in different world regions, with quite different geo-political histories of imperial and colonial rule. The four national contexts of our research are Pakistan, Senegal, Nigeria and Lebanon. In Table 3.1, we present a selected range of indicators to provide insights into their socio-demographic profiles and their positioning within different global ranking systems. We draw on these sources with caution as, although useful in sketching an initial profile, we are aware of fallibilities of such data, their multiple elisions and silences, which are in no small way related to their productive force and political import.

With these cautions, our sources suggest that Nigeria and Lebanon are marginally Muslim-majority countries. Muslims are estimated at 50 and 54% of their populations, respectively. In contrast, Pakistan and Senegal are predominantly Muslim, with Muslims making up 96 and 94% of their populations, respectively. Socio-demographically, each country has a high percentage of youth, ranging from 17.2% in Lebanon to 21.5% in Pakistan. The 2015 gender gap ranking by the World Economic Forum suggests that considerable gender inequalities prevail in all four contexts. Out of 145 countries, the countries such as Pakistan, Lebanon, Nigeria and Senegal were ranked 144th, 138th, 125th and 72nd, respectively (World Economic Forum 2015). With the exception of Lebanon that has reached parity, all the case study countries have considerable gender inequalities in favour of males in relation to education, youth literacy and youth employment.

While our case countries resemble each other in several ways, they are particularly distinct with respect to their different nation-state formations. Each experienced different forms of colonial rule and exploitation over decades, in particular by Britain (in the case of Pakistan and Nigeria) and by France (in the case of Lebanon and Senegal). As part of their emergence as independent nation-states during the last century, all four countries have sought to put in place parliamentary democracies. However, these each involve quite different constitutional formations, in which the role of religion is differently demarcated in ways that reflect the traces of their colonial and postcolonial histories. Details of

Table 3.1 Case study country statistical comparisons

	Pakistan	Senegal	Nigeria	Lebanon
Total population (2016)[a] (000)	188,144	14,967	183,523	5,054
Area[b] (km^2)	796,095	196,722	923,768	10,400
Annual population growth rate (2016)[a] (%)	1.6	2.8	2.8	1.1
Population below poverty line (US$1.25 a day) (2002–2012)[a] (%)	21	29.6	68	No data available
Youth population (15–24 years)[b] (%)	21.5	20.5	19.3	17.20
Muslim population[b] (%)	96	94	50	54
Gender Ranking[c] (/145)	144	72	125	138
Fragile States ranking (2015)[d] (/178)	13	60	14	41
Youth literacy rate 15–24 years (2005–2013)[a] Total (F/M)	73 (64/80)	56 (51/61)	66 (58/76)	99 (99/98)
School life expectancy (2013)[a] Total (F/M)	7.8 (7.0/8.5)	7.9 (7.8/8.1)[e]	7.6 (6.9/8.3)[e]	13.8 (13.6/13.9)
Youth unemployment rate[b] (%) Total (F/M)	7.7 (10.5/7)[f]	12.7 (19/8.3)[f]	No data available	22.1 (21.5/22.5)[f]

[a]UNESCO (2016). *Global Education Monitoring Report.* Paris: UNESCO. Retrieved 10 May 2016 from http://en.unesco.org/gem-report/node/6

[b]Central Intelligence Agency (CIA) (2014) World Factbook. Retrieved 10 May 2016, from https://www.cia.gov/library/publications/the-world-factbook/geos/sg.html

[c]World Economic Forum (2015). *Global Gender Gap Report.* Geneva: World Economic Forum. Retrieved 10 May 2016, from http://reports.weforum.org/global-gender-gap-report-2015/ Rankings given are out of 145 countries. Rank 1 has the lowest gender gap

[d]The Fund For Peace (2015). Fragile States Index 2015. Retrieved 12 May 2016, from http://fsi.fundforpeace.org/ Rankings given are out of 178 countries. Rank 1 is most fragile

[e]UNESCO (2015). *Global Monitoring Report 2000–2015 Achievements and Challenges.* Paris: UNESCO. The most recent available data for Senegal refers to 2011 and for Nigeria to 1999

[f]Data for Pakistan 2008, Senegal 2011, Lebanon 2007

the respective histories of our case study countries are discussed in-depth in the relevant chapters. At this point, we outline some key constitutional differences which set their respective state formations apart from the other, focusing in particular on the place of religion in their respective democratic constitutions.

Turning first to Senegal, this case presents what would seem to be a clear separation of government and religion. Thus, when becoming independent, its leaders followed a largely French model of a secular republic, in which any appeal to religion (as well as other particularities such as gender, ethnicity and language) was formally debarred. However, the other three case study contexts all gave some degree of recognition to religion within their national constitutions. Nigeria, emerging from British colonial rule, set up a federal republic, in which formal recognition was given to three different regions in an attempt to recognise their religious differences. Although not formally part of the constitution, some sources hint at an unofficial rotation of the Nigerian presidency, to ensure this alternates between those of Muslim and Christian faiths. In its parliamentary democracy, Lebanon has given strong acknowledgement to the significance of different religious communities, being a rare example of a 'confessionalist' constitution. This is a system of government that gives formal recognition to different religious communities. In the case of Lebanon, this gives recognition to 18 different religious sects, of which four are Muslim. It has also acknowledged religious differences by the formal institution of power-sharing across key government positions, so that the Lebanese President must be a Maronite Christian, the Prime Minister a Sunni Muslim and the Speaker of the Parliament a Shi'a Muslim. As an Islamic Republic, the constitution of Pakistan embraces Islam as a founding principle of the nation-state, as it emerged from the partition of India at the end of British colonial rule. While in its inception in 1947, Pakistan sought to institute a constitutional democracy. It has since seen several military coup d'états which have installed military presidents.

With the possible exception of Senegal, all of our case study countries have experienced significant levels of conflict since becoming independent. The Fund For Peace (2015) Index of Fragile States ranks Pakistan as 13th, Nigeria as 14th, Lebanon as 41st and Senegal as 60th out of 178 countries. Their different contexts are discussed in full in the relevant case study chapters, as the histories and geographies of each have profound bearing on the ways that youth construct their identities and articulate their belongings with respect to 'others' external and internal to their national location.

3.3 Research Approach and Research Methods

This section outlines the ways that the research was developed and conducted, from the development of the instruments to the analysis and reporting of different case studies. Given that we sought to privilege youth voice in an in-depth way, a qualitative approach to the research was used. Our main source of data was focus group discussions with different youth, supported by observations in the research context, including observations of the interview processes as well as the wider setting. In addition, the socio-demographic characteristics of the participants were explored through an individually completed bio-data sheet (see Appendix A for the generic format). The fieldwork phase of the research was conducted mainly during the later months of 2014 although more specific details of this are given in the respective chapters. Building on researcher familiarity with each national context, the focus group discussions and observations were arranged and conducted mostly during a 2-week fieldwork visit. In the case of Nigeria, focus group discussions were conducted in two phases—a piloting phase in 2011–2012 and the main data collection phase completed in early 2014. The first phase of the Nigerian case study was important for shaping the research instruments that included a bio-data sheet and focus group interview schedule. These were adapted and tweaked to fit the specifics of the national case and the particular group of youth respondents.

The identification of the main research sites in each country context was largely done with the support of the local contacts of the UK-based lead researchers. As pointed out above, each of these researchers had previously worked in their case study country and their case country research relations were valuable—indeed indispensable—in the identification of the research locations and approaches to potential respondents.

Our strategy for the composition of the focus groups was to bring together youth with common characteristics which we considered to be important in shaping their identity formations. This strategy was to facilitate greater freedoms for the expression of any potentially sensitive issues and to maximise the affective intensities of the interactions. In each context, the interview sample was constructed as far as possible by convening sex-segregated and religiously segregated focus groups with male and female youth of Muslim and Christian faith. As educational institutions tended to be the main point of access to youth, where possible, we also sought to include youth who were out of education and convened separate focus group discussion with these youth respondents. These 'out-of-education' youth were a mix of those employed in the formal or informal sector, underemployed or unemployed. The rationale for this distinction was that in contexts where school expectancy is low (see Table 3.1), access to youth through education would tend to include those of higher socio-economic status. Indeed, as the 'out-of-education' groups only represent 15% of the total sample, the research has privileged the accounts from more elite youth. This is less marked in Lebanon where the levels of educational uptake are significantly higher than those in the other country cases.

As important as national statistics are to provide a schematic overview of each country context, they also gloss over significant social differences within populations. With the wider emphasis of this research at the local level, in each case study we attempted to capture some of these within nation differences even though it was not possible to convene separate focus group discussions to span the multiple axes of difference in each context. The range and configuration of the focus group discussions in each country case varied and these are described in more detail in the respective chapters. The overall numbers of youth respondents involved in the study across the four different case study contexts are presented in Table 3.2.

In three contexts (Lebanon, Nigeria and Pakistan), the initial approach to respondents was made through research contacts within different educational institutions. The interviews were carried out in the institutional contexts of schools or higher education. In Senegal, youth participants in previous research were involved in identifying the focus group respondents. Across all the case studies, focus groups were planned where possible to involve between four and six participants. Numbers varied between one and six youth. In many cases, the smaller numbers indicate the difficulties of identifying potential participants in certain categories. For example, in Senegal, the relatively educated status

Table 3.2 Sample across country cases

	Pakistan	Senegal	Nigeria	Lebanon	Total
FGDs	13	18	17	10	58
Total (F/M/mix)	(7/6/0)	(9/9/0)	(9/8/0)	(4/4/2)	(29/27/2)
Youth	65	75	78	58	276
Female	28	35	44	31	138
Male	37	40	34	27	138
Muslim	60	47	45	52	204
Shia	6	0	0	52	58
Sufi	0	47	0	0	47
Sunni	52	0	45	0	97
Undisclosed	2	0	0	0	2
Christian	5	28	33	6	72
Age range	19–28	16–35	18–36	16–24	16–36
Mean age	23	24	24	19	
In education	56	64	72	58	234
Out of education	9	11	6	0	42

of Christians meant that it was difficult to identify Christian respondents outside of higher education.

As our research was focused on youth, the age of respondents was also important. Table 3.2 shows differences in the age range for each country. Where respondents were accessed through personal contacts, the age requirements were more difficult to stipulate than for those in educational institutions. As a result, we used respondents' self-identification with the category of youth which despite a significant span all fell within accepted definitions of the African Union (2006).

In order to gain a fuller appreciation of the background of the focus group participants, a bio-data sheet was developed, which probed aspects such as ethnicity, religion and sect, their main languages, their nationality, region of origin and the region in which they currently resided. It also probed their family background, asking for similar information about their mother and their father. The bio-data sheet, included in a generic form as Appendix A, was translated into French, Arabic, Urdu and other relevant local languages for the different case study contexts. All participants completed this before the focus group discussion, sometimes with some help from the youth researchers if a participant was not literate or spoke other local languages. These data were later transferred to Excel to develop a statistical description of the interview sample in each context. After completing the bio-data sheet, each participant was asked to write a short statement on the back to say how they would introduce themselves to another youth of a different nationality whom they were meeting for the first time. In many cases, this statement was revisited at the end of the focus group, asking each participant to add anything that had emerged as significant from the discussion they had just contributed to.

A generic interview schedule was also developed to support the discussions with the participants across all of the case studies and is included as Appendix B. This focused on participants' views of nationality, religion, ethnicity and gender in turn, while also intersecting each of these categories. In the course of the discussions, after being asked to talk about what made a good or ideal national of their country, respondents were asked what made a good or ideal man and then woman from their country. Similarly, when probing ethnic affiliations, the intersection of ethnicity with religion and with gender was explored through questions such as *'Is being a Muslim (or Christian) different for people who are from different ethnic groups?'* and *'How is being a woman different in different ethnic groups?'* These questions explicitly intersected the key social structures that we intended to explore. At the same time, we were attendant to the ways youth spontaneously intersected them, as illustrated, for example, when they identified religious leaders in response to questions about the national figures that were important to them.

Overall, the intention was not to follow the interview schedule in a rigid way, but to provoke discussion about the intersection of the multiple aspects of youth identities and indeed to create opportunities for them to perform their identities within the interview through their ongoing demarcations of difference within and across the group. The schedule also included some questions about generational differences and questions on information technology. It concluded with a question on which aspect of their identity the participants saw as being the most important and a further question on whether there were significant tensions between any particular aspects of their identities. The interview length was estimated as being 1 h. They varied in length between around 40 min and one and a half hours.

As indicated above, the focus group discussions were supported by local researchers in each context, either involving them alongside the lead UK-based researcher or sometimes in conducting the interviews independently. This was particularly the case in Senegal, where Barbara could not interact with youth who spoke Wolof rather than French, and also in Nigeria, where the latter series of interviews was conducted at a time when security issues made it impossible for Máiréad to travel to that area. The youth researchers could be assumed not to be positioned as 'other' by the respondents in terms of generational differences. This is typically one of the key rationales for including youth as researchers. This works in a similar way for local researchers who could also be assumed not to be positioned as 'other' on national or in some cases ethnic grounds. In the face of multiple potential axes of positional difference, in most contexts it was possible to match the researchers with the respondent groups in terms of religion and gender. In the majority of our cases, we were able to facilitate interviews with female Muslim youth by female Muslim youth researchers and similarly for males and other religious groups. Informed by the experience of mixed group focus group discussion in the first piloting phase in Nigeria, the aim of this matching was to allow respondents more freedom to engage together with sensitive issues.

As each of the case study contexts was quite different, the exact configurations of the focus group participants varied and these are discussed in more detail in the relevant chapters. The fieldwork in most cases involved youth researchers. They were invaluable for their local support, including the ways that they could bring local knowledge to the discussions, which allowed them to probe responses in interesting ways and to expand and reflect on what had been said after the interviews. Their interjections during the focus group discussions were also significant. For example, at some points the discussions provoked strong reactions from the youth researchers, so that they intervened to query or sometimes even to correct assertions made by participants. As we reported in our previous study of youth citizenship, which was also supported by youth researchers (Dunne et al. 2015), the youth researchers might have blurred the boundaries of respondent and researcher, but these interjections were particularly interesting for their indication of strong lines of difference that clearly mattered to them.

Our observations in each of our case study contexts of course also sought to take account of our own identities, reflexively examining how we were positioned (and positioning) in our interactions with youth researchers and the respondents. We discuss this in more detail in the different case study chapters, but note here that while the UK-based researchers all had previous experience of their case study context, our relationships to the context varied considerably.

Ethical approval for the research was secured from the University of Sussex Social Sciences review panel. In the conduct of the research, the research purposes and research processes were reviewed with all of the participants at the beginning of the focus group. This was also provided on an information sheet which was developed for the project, translated into the relevant language for each context and given to each participant. This included asking participants' permission to record, transcribe and translate into English the focus group discussions for analysis and reporting in this book, as well as further academic presentations and publications. All participants were guaranteed confidentiality and anonymity, and were asked to respect the confidentiality and anonymity of the others in their focus group. The opening discussion also explained that if they wished to leave, they could do so at any point, and if they stayed, this was understood to signal their willingness to participate. This way of securing participants' consent drew on our previous experiences of working in these different contexts, and our awareness that the practice of asking for written consent would not be culturally acceptable, and would be likely to arouse suspicion.

The research process was collaborative throughout and it built on previous empirical research projects and writing by the same research team. Brought together by overlapping interests and perspectives, the team worked together to structure the fieldwork and develop the instruments. Based on their experience, each research team member had a specific responsibility for one of the country cases and the gathering of data through engagement with youth in that context. After the fieldwork phases, the interview data were translated and transcribed into English and the preliminary analysis was conducted by the respective research team member. Through a series of research team meetings, the analyses were discussed and refined. Commonalities and differences within and across cases were explored through iterations with the theoretical framing, the contextual specificities and the data. The structures for the text were also developed such that each of the case studies is presented in a similar way. Each case study first positions the case within its socio-historical and socio-demographic context, before describing the specifics of the research sample and processes. Each case study then turns to the analysis of youth's identity affiliations and performances with respect to nation, religion and gender and concludes by summarising the key issues identified within that case. The continual iterative engagements of the research team with the different country cases allowed a cross-case synthesis, which is presented in the concluding chapter of this book. At this point, we turn to our presentation of the different country case studies in the following four chapters.

References

African Union. (2006). *African Youth Charter*. Banjul: African Union Commission.
Central Intelligence Agency (CIA). (2014). *World factbook—Senegal*. Retrieved March 22, 2015, from https://www.cia.gov/library/publications/the-world-factbook/geos/sg.html.
Crossouard, B., & Dunne, M. (2015). Politics and youth citizenship in Senegal: The policing of dissent and diversity. *International Review of Education, 61*(1), 43–60.
Dunne, M. (Ed.). (2008). *Gender, sexuality and development: Education and society in sub-Saharan Africa*. Rotterdam: Sense Publishers.
Dunne, M., Leach, F., Chilisa, B., Maundeni, T., Tabulawa, R., Kutor, N., et al. (2005). *Schools as gendered institutions: The impact on retention and achievement*. London: DfID.
Dunne, M., Durrani, N., Crossouard, B., & Fincham, K. (2014). *Youth as active citizens report. Youth working towards their rights to education and sexual and reproductive health*. Brighton: University of Sussex; The Hague: Oxfam Novib.

Dunne, M., Durrani, N., Crossouard, B., & Fincham, K. (2015). Youth researching youth: Methodological reflections from a multi-country study of youth claiming rights to education and sexual reproductive health. In S. Bastien & H. B. Holmarsdottir (Eds.), *Youth at the margins: Experiences from engaging youth in research worldwide* (pp. 299–316). Rotterdam: Sense Publishers.

Durrani, N. (2007). Identity wars in the curriculum: Gender and the military in Pakistani national identity. In F. Leach & M. Dunne (Eds.), *Education, conflict and reconciliation: International perspectives* (pp. 253–268). Bern: Peter Lang.

Durrani, N. (2008). Schooling the 'other': Representation of gender and national identities in Pakistani curriculum texts. *Compare: A Journal of Comparative and International Education, 38*(5), 595–610.

Durrani, N. (2013). Pakistan: Curriculum and the construction of national identity. In M. Ahmad (Ed.), *Education in West Central Asia. Education around the world* (pp. 221–239). London: Bloomsbury Academic.

Durrani, N., & Dunne, M. (2010). Curriculum and national identity: Exploring the links between religion and nation in Pakistan. *Journal of Curriculum Studies, 42*(2), 215–240.

Fincham, K. (2010). The construction of the Palestinian girl: Voices from South Lebanon. *Girlhood Studies, 3*(1), 34–54.

Fincham, K. (2012a). Nationalist narratives, boundaries and social inclusion/exclusion in Palestinian camps in South Lebanon. *Compare, 42*(2), 303–324.

Fincham, K. (2012b). Learning the nation in exile: Constructing youth identities, belonging and 'citizenship' in Palestinian refugee camps in South Lebanon. *Comparative Education* (special issue: Youth Citizenship and the Politics of Belonging), *48*(1), 119–133.

Fincham, K. (2013a). Constructions, contradictions and reconfigurations of 'Manhood' among youth in Palestinian camps in Lebanon. *International Journal of Educational Development, 37,* 48–56.

Fincham, K. (2013b). Shifting youth identities and notions of 'Citizenship' in the Palestinian diaspora: The case of Lebanon. In D. Kiwan (Ed.), *Naturalization policies, education and citizenship: Multicultural and multi-nation societies in international perspective*. London: Palgrave Macmillan.

The Fund For Peace. (2015). *Fragile states index 2015*. Retrieved May 12, 2016, from http://fsi.fundforpeace.org/.

Leach, F., & Dunne, M. (Eds.). (2007). *Education, conflict and reconciliation. International perspectives*. Oxford: Peter Lang.

Mahmood, S. (2012). *Politics of piety: The Islamic revival and the feminist subject*. Princeton, NJ and Oxford: Princeton University Press.

UNESCO. (2015). *Global monitoring report 2015: Achievements and challenges*. Paris: UNESCO.

UNESCO. (2016). *Global education monitoring report*. Paris. Retrieved May 10, 2016, from http://en.unesco.org/gem-report/node/6.

World Economic Forum. (2015). *Global gender gap report*. Geneva: World Economic Forum. Retrieved May 10, 2016, from http://reports.weforum.org/global-gender-gap-report-2015/.

4

Pakistan: Converging Imaginaries in an Islamic State

Abstract This chapter explores how Pakistani youth make sense of themselves in relation to the social world and the ways their identifications intersect with nation, religion, gender and ethnicity. Youth navigate their identities in a socio-political context of a Muslim majority state, which traces its genesis to a religious identity. A total of 65 youth, 28 women and 37 men, participated in 13 single-sex focus group discussions. The youth express an explicit sense of national identity imagined through (Sunni) Islam, which overlays a homogenous unity on internal diversity. Nevertheless, aspirations to compliance with 'proper' Islam co-exist alongside commitments to secular democracy and equal citizenship rights. The discursive construction of multiple antagonistic non-Muslim 'others' tends to solidify Islam as a boundary between 'us' and 'them'. This fractures the nation through the construction of internal 'others'—non-Muslim Pakistanis and 'improper' Muslims who deviate from hegemonic ways of enacting Muslim identities. The confluence of religious, national and ethnic identifications within a conflict-affected context produces strong gendered subjectivities. This fosters the accumulation of highly militarised masculinities in defence of the nation, Islam and women, and positions women as symbolic border-guards between 'us' and 'them' and carriers of national/religious traditions. While youth discourses indicate local and global influences on the dynamics of national and religious identifications, gender positions and relations appear to be largely stable, essentialised and naturalised.

We begin our four country case studies with the narratives of youth from the Islamic Republic of Pakistan. To situate the youth accounts, this chapter first presents the Pakistan context by offering a discussion of the creation of the state and the nation-building challenges that this young nation has faced in its short history as an independent country. It then outlines the research approach, methods and sample, elaborating on the discussion offered in Chap. 3. The findings begin with the ways the youth imagine the nation and the signifiers they draw upon to construct similarity. This is followed by a discussion of how religion is deployed simultaneously to draw similarity and difference and the inevitable construction of the internal 'others' it entails. Next, the gendered construction of the 'ideal' Pakistani citizen is presented. Finally, the analysis focuses on the centrality of the antagonistic external 'other' to the construction of Pakistani identity and the gendered effects it produces.

4.1   Introduction and Context

Geography
Located in the north-west of South Asia, and at the junction between the Middle East and Central Asia, Pakistan occupies a position of great geostrategic significance. It borders four countries—India in the east, Afghanistan and Iran in the west and China in the north-east—and the Arabian Sea in the south. It comprises four administrative divisions called provinces, namely Balochistan, Khyber Pakhtunkhwa (KP),[1] Punjab and Sindh. Additionally, it has a capital territory (Islamabad) and two autonomous territories—Azad Jammu and Kashmir and Gilgit-Baltistan (GB)—and a group of Federally Administered Tribal Areas (FATA).[2]

History

With 96% of its estimated 189 million citizens being Muslim (Government of Pakistan [GoP] 1998), Pakistan is the second largest Muslim-majority country in the world and the only nuclear-armed Muslim state. It came into existence in 1947 with the end of British colonial rule, resulting in the partition of British India into the sovereign states of Hindu-majority India and Muslim-majority Pakistan. The Pakistan Movement was nationalist rather than religious in orientation and led by secular modernist leaders of the All India Muslim League, with a strong participation of Muslim youth in tertiary and higher education (HE). Nevertheless, religion was the marker on the basis of which Muslims from diverse ethnic, linguistic, regional and class backgrounds within the then united India discursively constructed themselves as members of a political community and won their claim to a sovereign state.

To understand what led to the emergence of Muslim nationalism in India, one needs to step back in history. The expansion of Islam in India truly began with the conquest of Sindh by Muhammad bin Qasim, an Umayyad general, in 711 AD. Cohen (2005) claims that by 1290 nearly all of India was under the loose control of Muslim rulers. After a further two and a half centuries in which conflicts between Indo-Islamic, Hindu and Sikh groups took place, the Mughals established their (Muslim) empire in the early sixteenth century. By the time the British arrived in India, Muslims constituted roughly one-quarter of the Indian population. Cohen (2005:20) attributes the flourishing of Islam in India to 'inter-marriage [particularly between the elites], conversion [particularly because of the Sufi movement], the attractiveness of Islamic egalitarianism, and social and political advantages in a context of Muslim rulers'.

The mutiny of 1857 brought an end to Muslim rule in India and resulted in a crisis of identity for Indian Muslims (Ahmed 1997). While both Hindus and Muslims took part in the uprising, the British divide and rule policy following the mutiny was seen by many as pro-Hindu and anti-Muslim. After crushing the mutiny, the British fundamentally refashioned the political, social and economic structures of India in ways that gave Muslims 'little social space and no political power' (Cohen 2005:23). Devji (2011) attributes the emergence of the Muslim 'community' in India directly to colonialism. The destruction of royal and aristocratic forms of power among Muslims gave way to religious authority, which for the first time stood outside the patronage of the former. The separation from political authority transformed the Muslim community into a 'religious entity' in the political sense (Devji 2011:111). The secular politics of colonialism made the Muslim community a site of contestation and competition between the different groups of divines and laymen over the meaning and vision of the community. The discursive wars over the community's identity were particularly intense in the Urdu-speaking community in northern India between the Sunni clerics, who sought to 'recast Islam in their own image' and the 'reformists' led by Syed Ahmed Khan (1817–1898) whose project was to modernise Muslims (Devji 2011:111). With the introduction of limited franchise to India along religious lines in 1906 by the Raj, this community, which until now had shaped the construction of the Muslim nation but was a minority within local population dynamics, had to give space to the Muslims from other regions whose numbers were substantial at the local level. In 1940, Jinnah merged the idea of Pakistan with the state of Pakistan by arguing that the Hindus and Muslims constituted two nations, each deserving of their own state. The creation of Pakistan was the result of the 'conscious manipulation of selected symbols of Muslim identity by Muslim elite groups in economic and political competition with each other and with elite groups among the Hindus' (Brass 1971:41). In these contestations, Jinnah's version became victorious as the Muslim masses identified with his model, thereby 'recognizing each others as members of a community with particular interests' (Hussain 2000:134).

The partition of India along religious lines resulted in one of the biggest mass migrations in history, with some 14.5 million people crossing borders on both sides, amidst violence, looting and rioting in which an estimated one million people died and 75,000 women were raped (Butalia 2000). These traumatic events made Islam central to official and popular discourses of national identity and an antagonistic non-Muslim 'other' vital to the collective memory. As we explain later, a range of factors—political instability, secessionist movements, internal and external conflicts—further reinforced the centrality of Islam and external 'others' to Pakistan's identity.

Religion

The mass migration strengthened the dominance of Muslims in Pakistan. Nonetheless, Pakistan has a small religious minority (4%), comprising Christians (the largest group), Hindus (mostly settled in the border districts of Sindh), Parsis (Zoroastrians) and the Ahmadi community (who consider themselves Muslims but were declared non-Muslims by the state in 1974) (GoP 1998).

The majority of Muslims follow the Sunni sect, and the adherents of Shi'a Islam constitute a substantial minority.[3] The issue of the succession of Prophet Muhammad (PBUH[4]) divided Muslims into two sects. Sunni Muslims chose Abu Bakr as his successor, while Shi'a Muslims believe that Ali, the Prophet's son-in-law, was designated as the successor after the Prophet (PBUH). Most Sunnis observe the Hanafi *fiqh* or body of laws and follow one of the two basic schools of interpretation—the Barelvi (influenced by mystical Sufi tradition) and the Deobandi, which calls for the establishment of an Islamic state governed by its interpretation of Islamic law in Pakistan. A third group, Ahle Hadith, heavily influenced by the Wahhabi movement in Saudi Arabia, is the most orthodox. Likewise, Pakistan's Shi'a community is internally differentiated and includes the Ismaili and the Ithna Ashariyya. The latter are the most populous and have a substantial presence in Karachi, Lahore and southern Punjab. The diverse and contested nature of Islamic thought and practice in Pakistan raises challenges for its management, which the state has turned into an opportunity by appropriating the right to define who counts as Muslim (Iqtidar 2012).

Ethnicity and Nation Building

Pakistan's religious 'homogeneity' stands in sharp contrast to its ethnic and linguistic diversity. Language being the main marker of ethnicity, Pakistan contains five major ethnic groups: Punjabis[5] (55%), Pakhtuns[6] (15%), Sindhis (14%), Mohajirs[7] (8%) and Balochs (4%) and several minority ethno-linguistic groups (5%) (GoP 1998). Each ethnic group is primarily concentrated in its home province, that is Sindhis in Sindh, the Baloch in Balochistan, Punjabis in Punjab and Pakhtuns in KP, with most Mohajirs residing in urban Sindh. Pakhtuns and Punjabis are, however, found throughout Pakistan. The participation of different ethnic groups in Pakistan's governance is inequitable and so is socio-economic development across and within the provinces. With more than half of Pakistan's population concentrated in Punjab, this province dominates the socio-economic and political landscape of Pakistan. In terms of the Human Development Index (HDI), Punjab (0.6699) is Pakistan's most developed province, followed by Sindh (0.6262), KP (0.6065) and Balochistan (0.5557) (Arif 2013). For geostrategic reasons, Punjab was a garrison province under the Raj since the late nineteenth century, with the Government of India pouring 'billions of rupees into the Punjab for the building of strategic railways, roads and cantonment towns' (Yong 2005:20). With Punjabis categorised as one of the 'martial' races, Punjab became popularly known as the 'sword arm of the Raj' (Yong 2005:17). This was accompanied by huge investment made in the agricultural sector through the development of large-scale irrigation networks. Loyalty of the Punjab recruits to the Raj was ensured through the landed rural elites who also included Muslim religious leaders associated with Sufi shrines called *sajjada nashins* or *pirs* (Gilmartin 1979). It was these *pirs* who provided religious leadership in much of western Punjab. The British strengthened the hold of these intermediaries over their peasants by isolating rural communities from the growing economic influence of the cities. The dominance of the civil–military oligarchy established under the Raj explains the dominance of this group in independent Pakistan (Yong 2005).

The dominance of the Punjabi ethnic group, both in political structures and in the military, fuels resentment and grievances among the smaller ethnic groups. With the exception of Punjab, each of Pakistan's provinces has seen secessionist movements. The disintegration of Pakistan and the creation of Bangladesh in 1971 was one such movement. In this case, the Bengalis in East Pakistan, who were numerically the largest ethnic group, were under-represented in both political structures and the military. Furthermore, the military government of Ayub Khan pursued a political project of making the 'Bengalis into "good" and "pure" Muslims', which further alienated the Bengalis (Saikia 2014:298). In 1970, in Pakistan's first ever general election, the Bengali nationalist party, the Awami League under Sheikh Mujibur Rahman, emerged as the single largest party, winning 160 out of 300 seats, followed by Pakistan Peoples Party led by Zulfikar Ali Bhutto in West Pakistan winning 81 seats. Nevertheless, Rahman was not allowed to form a government by General Yahya Khan, which led to civil unrest in East Pakistan. The use of force against Bengalis by the Pakistan Army resulted in a separatist movement, which ultimately succeeded in the creation of Bangladesh with the support of the Indian military.

The smaller ethnic groups in Pakistan have different relationships with the official nation-building project. We begin the discussion with Sindh, which became part of the Raj in 1843. This region remained a peripheral part of the Mughal Empire and received little attention from the Raj in terms of development and 'modernisation' (Cohen 2005). At independence, its social structures and leadership, along with a repressive feudal order, remained intact. Sindh had a secular regional party dominated by landlords before partition, but Sindhis nonetheless sided with the Muslim League, as they feared being dominated economically and politically by Hindus under Congress. Sindhis became a minority in Karachi and other bigger cities in Sindh because the bulk of the Urdu-speaking refugees migrating from northern India settled in Karachi and urban Sindh at partition. Moreover, Sindh has also been receiving an influx of Punjabis, Pakhtuns and the Baloch. The threat from these 'outsiders' has served to sharpen Sindhi ethnicity (Hussain 2000). Till 1970, Sindhis were under-represented in all state institutions, but the government of Zulfikar Ali Bhutto, an ethnic Sindhi, sought to address Sindhi grievances (Rashid and Shaheed 1993). The Mohajirs were in the forefront of the Pakistan Movement and the construction of a 'Muslim' nation, as discussed earlier, and were part of Pakistan's ruling elite along with Punjabis until politically marginalised in the 1970s by the rise of strong ethno-linguistic forces under Zulfikar Ali Bhutto (Rashid and Shaheed 1993). In 1980, the Mohajir Qaumi Mahaz (MQM) party emerged as the dominant representative of the Mohajirs, which demanded official recognition as the fifth ethnic group. The economic and political decline of this relatively privileged community transformed their Islamic Pakistani nationalist identity into an ethnic (Mohajir) identity.

Moving the focus now to Balochistan, the Baloch tribes are settled in the rough terrain that covers so much of Pakistan, Afghanistan and Iran. The Baloch have an autonomous history which remained largely unchanged under the British as the latter utilised this region as a buffer state to contain the influence of a potential Soviet intervention. Balochistan is rich in natural gas and coal but is Pakistan's poorest province. It is the largest province in land mass but is home to only 5% of Pakistan's population. Furthermore, it is a multi-ethnic province, with the Baloch population enjoying only a small majority. Since Pakistan's independence, the state has had armed conflicts with the Baloch on four occasions (1948, 1958, 1962 and 1973) (Cohen 2005). Since January 2005, a fierce military confrontation between Baloch nationalists and the military has been going on over Baloch demands for political and economic autonomy (Grare 2006). The Eighteenth Amendment to the Constitution of Pakistan in 2010 devolved greater power and a better and more equitable financial package to provinces which in the long run could potentially alleviate Baloch resentment (Adeney 2012).

We end this discussion with an extended focus on Pakhtuns and KP, as the majority of the research participants in this case study are Pakhtuns and KP is the main research site. The Pakhtuns, although internally differentiated along clan and tribal lines, are settled predominantly in Afghanistan and Pakistan and share a number of characteristics including the Pashto language, a code of conduct, Pakhtunwali, and a desire for self-rule. Central to Pakhtunwali are three concepts: *nang* or honour involves 'the protection of sexual propriety'; *badal* or revenge is linked with honour and upholds the dictum of 'an eye for an eye and a tooth for a tooth'; and *melmastia* or hospitality emphasises 'maintaining loyalty to friends and allies, and providing protection to whoever seeks it, including an enemy' (Saikal 2010:5–6). In 2007, an estimated 72.5 million Pakhtun population lived in Afghanistan and Pakistan (Saikal 2010); of these, 12.5 million Pakhtuns constituted 42% of Afghanistan's population, where they are the largest ethnic group, while some 30 million formed 16% of Pakistan's population, where they are the second largest ethnic group. Within Pakistan,

Pakhtuns are concentrated in KP (the largest ethnic group), Karachi in Sindh, Punjab, FATA (the overwhelming majority) and Balochistan (the second largest group).[8] Malik (2016:102) asserts that of all the Muslim groups, the Pakhtuns were 'the most Orientalised people' during the colonial era, 'whose tribal system, stories of Aryan-versus-Semitic origins and "instinctive" penchant for violence were enthusiastically recorded' and circulated. This Orientalised construction of the Pakhtuns 'happened through a binary discourse of denigration and romanticisation' under the Raj and has been deployed extensively by European and North American writers since 9/11 to mark Pakhtun identity with 'primitiveness, violence, chicanery, puritanism and unbridled masculinity' (Malik 2016:102).

Pakhtuns were categorised as one of the 'martial' races, 'extolled as exemplary soldiers', and were recruited in large numbers in the British military (Rand and Wegner 2012:234). Nevertheless, Pakhtuns have been subjugated and subjected to external interventions and they have done the same to other groups.[9] While Pakhtuns have seldom acted as a collective, the anti-colonial movement under the leadership of Khan Abdul Ghaffar Khan developed a strong sense of ethnic consciousness within the KP Pakhtuns (then the NWFP). After independence, this consciousness assumed the form of sub-nationalism in opposition to the Pakistani state, which was perceived as an instrument of Punjabi domination (Rashid and Shaheed 1993). Because Pakhtuns along with Punjabis dominate the Pakistani military, today Pakhtuns are fully integrated into the state structure and market economy. Nevertheless, since 9/11 the Pakhtun populations in FATA and KP have been the main victims of the violence emanating from the 'War on Terror', with 1.56 million people internally displaced (Internal Displacement Monitoring Centre 2015).

Democracy, the Military and India

Although Pakistan was conceived as a secular democracy, it is yet to develop a stable democratic system. Nevertheless, formal democratic processes have been consolidated in the last 8 years.[10] In March 2013, for the first time in Pakistan's history, power was transferred democratically from one elected government to another after it had completed its full term. Nevertheless, on four occasions the military has directly assumed power. More recently, there has been a shift in the power structure of the Pakistani state, and the military no longer enjoys exclusive power, although it still remains the most powerful institution. In addition, the judiciary has emerged as a strong institution and the media is increasingly playing an important role in strengthening transparency by intense coverage of policies (Cohen 2011).

The dominance of the military is strengthened by permanent antagonism with India. The enduring rivalry between the two countries, particularly over Kashmir, is evidenced by four wars (1948, 1965, 1971 and 1999) and a series of interstate crises. While India continues to blame Pakistan for supporting militancy in Kashmir and sponsoring terrorism on its land, Pakistan too accuses India of supporting the Baloch insurgency and sponsoring terrorism in Karachi, KP and FATA.

Islam, Pakistani Identity and Conflict

We now turn to the centrality of Islam to Pakistani identity, to highlight the power asymmetries it constructs and the conflicts this creates. The political relationship of Islam to the Pakistani state has remained contentious. Since independence, Islam has been invoked in the discourse of the nation in order to hold the diverse ethnic groups and the unevenly developed regions together. Since the secession of East Pakistan in 1971, Islam has been ferociously mobilised to contain ethnicity and forge national unity. However, it was the military regime of General Zia-ul-Haq (1977–1988), which sought to Islamise the state and society. While his Islamising project had a huge impact on social life, religious and sectarian strife, militarisation and gender relations, it nonetheless failed to challenge the secular foundations of the state or the secular interests of the state elite (Akhtar et al. 2006). Islamisation also coincided with the Soviet invasion of Afghanistan in 1979, resulting in the forging of a nexus between the military and the religious right. The *jihad* spawned an Islam that still casts a shadow over Pakistan in the form of militant Islamic groups.

The regulation of Muslim citizenry by the state and the manipulation of religious difference by domestic and international elements have caused much bloodshed and instability in the country. Violence has particularly escalated since Pakistan became a frontline state in the global 'War on Terror'. At the time of fieldwork, Pakistan ranked 10th on the global ranking of fragile states. In broad terms, three aspects of the relationship between religion and conflict are significant. In recent years, violence, especially between the dominant Sunni and the minority Shi'a sects, has left them and worshippers at Sufi shrines increasingly targeted by militant Sunni groups (Yusuf 2012). A second aspect of religious conflict relates to interfaith violence targeted against Pakistan's non-Muslim citizens (Amnesty International 2015). Religious minorities are marginalised politically, socially and economically and are discriminated against through the misuse of the infamous blasphemy law (Yusuf 2012). A third, and the most critical dimension of religious conflict that engulfs Pakistan today, relates to the complexity arising from battles, both discursive and armed, over different versions of national identity and its intersections with Islamic identity, which solidified as a result of support by the state for local and foreign *jihadi* elements, with the material support of the West and Saudi Arabia (Cohen 2011). As a frontline state in the global 'War on Terror', suicide bombings, armed attacks and killings by various Islamist armed groups continue to claim hundreds of lives with further violence inflicted by security agencies in counterterrorism operations (Amnesty International 2015).

Alongside religious conflict, interethnic struggles between the Mohajirs and the Pakhtuns over state resources and political tensions between the urban-based Muttahida Qaumi Movement and rural-based Pakistan Peoples Party have fuelled an ongoing violent conflict in Pakistan's largest city, Karachi. To summarise, religiously motivated terrorism in Pakistan, with KP as its epicentre, ethnic insurgency and sectarian violence in Balochistan and ethnic/political and sectarian violence in Karachi are the major obstacles to a peaceful Pakistan.

Gender

The management of religious thought and practice as a key mechanism in the production of the ideal Pakistani citizen has particular consequences for the construction of gender, in particular, the 'proper' Muslim woman (Durrani 2008). The tribal and feudal culture in Pakistan combines with the entanglement of Islam with the

Pakistani identity in ways which restrict the legitimate performances of Pakistani women in the public and private spheres. Any deviation from these normal ways of being makes women extremely vulnerable to attacks. Despite some positive legislation,[11] and the increase in the number of reserved women seats in government at the local, provincial and national levels, the Pakistan Women's Human Rights Organization (2015) has reported an increase in violence against women, including domestic violence, forced marriage, early marriage, rape, mutilation, honour killing, vigilante justice and acid attacks. It is not therefore surprising that Pakistan ranks second from the bottom (144/145 countries) on the Gender Gap Index, measured by the World Economic Forum (2016) (see Table 3.1). The 'ideal' male citizens, on the other hand, are positioned as protectors of the ideological frontiers of the nation and the enforcers of the nation's moral code on women. This of course normalises violence and encourages masculinist identities for men.

Youth

With a median age of 21 and two-thirds of its population less than 30 years of age, Pakistan's population is extremely youthful (Kugelman 2011). Of all the four case study countries, Pakistan has the highest proportion of people aged 15–24 years (see Table 3.1). Youth are thus critical to shaping the future of Pakistan. While education is seen as the key vehicle for taking advantage of its youth bulge, Pakistan's national education sector presents a dismal picture. Although since 2010, under Article 25-A of the Constitution of Pakistan, the provision of free and compulsory education to all children between the ages of 5 and 16 years is a constitutional right, a staggering 25 million children and adolescents within that age bracket are denied the right to education (Alif Ailaan 2014). This is despite the fact that Pakistan has extended several incentives for over a decade to increase enrolment and retain students including: (i) free distribution of textbooks in public sector schools; (ii) abolition of tuition fees in public sector schools; and (iii) the provision of monthly scholarships/stipends to female students in middle and high schools in rural areas of selected marginalised districts (MET and SHE 2013). The educational exclusion has both a gender and regional dimension. For example, while the overall youth literacy rate is 73%, the rate for males (80%) is higher than that for females (64%) (Table 3.1). In addition, provincial inequities exist in gender parity in youth literacy rates. For example, the gender gap in youth literacy is the smallest in Punjab (0.80), followed by Sindh (0.77), with gaps much bigger in KP (0.60) and Balochistan (0.51) (Government of Pakistan 2014). While the state share in the education market is declining consistently relative to the private sector, the state holds its influence through control over the contents of education. Until 2010, a centralised national curriculum was applied across Pakistan in state schools and private schools, with the exception of elite schools, which follow the Cambridge examination system. After 2010, curriculum development has been devolved to the provinces. However, all four provinces have adopted the national curriculum that was developed prior to devolution, and the National Curriculum Council has been developed to ensure coordination and uniformity in education across the country.

Youth face daunting economic challenges. While Pakistan's gross domestic product (GDP) growth rate in 2015 was 4.2%, it is estimated that a GDP growth of at least 9% would be needed to employ its 80–90 million people under the age of 20 (Kugelman 2011). Currently, the youth unemployment rate stands at 7.7%, with figures for female (10.5%) higher than male youth (7%) (Table 3.1). Additionally, while female youth participation shows an increase, it is primarily among the illiterate rural young women in the unskilled sector. According to the International Labour Organization (ILO 2012), less than one in five Pakistani women participates in the labour market. Female youth not only have higher unemployment rates, but also earn less compared to male youth across all occupations (Aslam and Kingdon 2012). Pakistan comes second to last in economic empowerment of women according to the Global Gender Gap Report 2015 (World Economic Forum 2015).

Table 4.1 The Pakistan sample

Religion	Gender		Total
	Female	Male	
Muslim	24	36	60
Christian	4	1	5
Total	28	37	65

With these contextual constraints, the prospects of a youth dividend can quickly transform into a 'time bomb' (Kugelman 2011). Youth radicalisation is particularly seen as a risk. As the preceding discussion makes it abundantly clear, Pakistani youth are exposed to both the 'push' and the 'pull' factors of radicalisation (Yusuf 2011). The push factors include: (i) the construction of essentialised identities through schooling that promotes polarisation, intolerance, conflict and divisions (Durrani and Dunne 2010); (ii) relative deprivation and inequality in realising basic rights including access to (quality) education; and (iii) the absence of a culture of meritocracy. The pull factors of youth radicalisation include a demand for and easy access to Islamist militants and a ready cause to fight for (Yusuf 2011).

4.2 The Research

The findings presented in the next section draw on the narratives of 65 youth, comprising 28 women and 37 men (see Table 4.1), gathered through 13 single-sex focus group discussions (FGDs), 7 with female and 6 with male participants. Twelve FGDs were conducted in Peshawar, the capital city of KP, and one in Karachi, the capital city of Sindh. The Peshawar FGDs were conducted between 24 November and 6 December 2014, and the one in Karachi was conducted in March 2015. Eleven of the twelve FGDs in Peshawar were held in a university campus. The 12th FGD with Christian females was conducted in a Catholic school serving disadvantaged Christian students in Peshawar. The 13th FGD in Karachi was conducted with Shi'a Ismaili women in a women's hostel attached to a university. All FGDs in Peshawar were conducted in Urdu and translated into English. The FGD in Karachi was conducted in English. All FGDs were audio-recorded and fully transcribed.

With respect to *age*, the youngest participant was 19 and the oldest 28 years old. However, the majority of the participants were between 21 and 25 years, with a mean age of 23 years (both median and mode = 22 years). The ethno-religious characteristics of the participants reflect those of the research locations. In terms of *religion*, 92% were Muslims and 8% were Christians. All Muslims from KP identified themselves as Sunni, while two preferred not to disclose their sect. With respect to *ethnicity*, an overwhelming majority were Pakhtuns (74%). All Punjabi-speaking participants identified with KP as their home province and with the Christian faith. Thus, like the population from which the sample was selected, ethnicity overlapped with religion. With 99.4 and 99.6% of their inhabitants being Muslim, KP and FATA are the most religiously homogeneous regions, followed by Balochistan (98.7%), Punjab (97.2%) and Sindh (91.3%) (GoP 1998). Likewise, around three-quarters of the population in KP (74%) and 99.1% in FATA are Pakhtuns. Moreover, Pakhtuns are predominantly Sunni. Given the predominance of Pakhtuns within the research group as a whole, the findings and conclusions of this case study should be treated with appropriate caution, as ethnic groups in Pakistan may differ in their relationship to the official national identity.

Peshawar, being the provincial capital, attracts people from all parts of the province. Likewise, the youth belonged to a wide range of districts in KP, including the central, southern and northern regions of KP and FATA. An interesting feature of the sample was the absence of interaction across ethnic, religious and cultural boundaries. For example, unlike the Senegalese sample, there was no instance of cross-religious and just two cases of cross-ethnic households. With two exceptions, all participants had spent all their lives in KP, with some only visiting some cities in Punjab and Sindh for a short time. This lack of encounter with other ways of being, as we will illustrate in the next section, produced strong insularity. The FGD in Karachi was particularly arranged to bring some diversity by capturing the voice of Shi'a Ismailis, a minority Muslim sect. These were all women from GB.

When the FGDs were conducted, the majority of the participants were studying for an undergraduate or postgraduate qualification. With only 5% of Pakistanis having access to HE (British Council 2009), the youth participants were a relatively select group. Only nine participants were in employment. Of these, four were school teachers and university graduates, all of whom were female Christians; and five were in low- or semi-skilled jobs, such as cleaning, catering and laboratory technology. The latter were all men, four Muslims and one Christian. They were less educated, though all had at least a secondary school leaving certificate.

Researcher's identity was particularly important in collecting the narratives of youth. All FGDs in Peshawar were facilitated by Naureen, a Pakhtun herself, who has work experience as an academic in Peshawar. This gave her unique access to the research participants in a region that is classified as very high risk in terms of terrorism threat levels. Access to the participants was arranged by her former colleagues. Naureen was introduced to the participants as 'an alumna' and 'a former faculty member' of the university in which the participants were accessed through gatekeepers, i.e. heads of departments. This mutual connection was further enhanced by her ethnic and cultural proximity. Access to the Catholic school was facilitated by Naureen's Christian colleague, which helped in gaining the participants' trust which she further enhanced through her gender and making references to her own Catholic schooling in KP. The FGD with the Shi'a Ismailis was conducted by a Shi'a Ismaili female, who, at the time of data collection, was a postdoctoral researcher at a UK university and was known personally to the participants. This enabled the creation of a trusting atmosphere for accessing the voice of this Muslim minority sect.

It would be useful to explain the use of identity categories in the quotes given in the next sections. FGDs in this chapter are not identified by place. This is because all but one FGD took place in Peshawar. The only FGD held in Karachi was held with Ismaili youth. Therefore, any reference to an Ismaili indicates that the discussion took place in Karachi. All FGDs have been numbered (for example FGD1 … FGD13) and so are all participants (for example P1 … P65). Each quote indicates gender and ethnicity in full. Religion is indicated for Christian and Ismaili youth only. Where religion is not indicated, the participant is Sunni.

4.3 Constructing the Nation

The narratives of Pakistani youth begin with the ways they imagine the nation and the sources they draw upon in expressing a sense of pride in the Pakistani nation.

Initial Self-definition

Pakistani identity was very prominent in the initial self-definitions that the youth expressed in their bio-data sheets and the FGDs. Overall, 65% of participants incorporated their Pakistani nationality in their self-description (male = 59%; female = 73%). Several participants highlighted the significance of context, the nature of the encounter and the audience or the interlocutor as key factors that would shape their self-description. In Chap. 2, we argued that we are multiply-constituted across different discourses and that our mobilisation of identity markers is contextual and strategic. The youth reflected on the difficult nature of the question of self-definition in an international context, arguing that this would very much depend on the encounter and the histories embedded within it and that within different contexts they might choose to give prominence to one identity over another: 'the *introduction will be tailored to the context*' (FGD13-P60-Ismaili female). This highlights that identities 'are not a priori givens', and that their construction mobilises 'both personal biography and group history' and are thus 'socially produced' (Brah 2007:12).

National Identity, Citizenship and Democracy

The Pakistani identity appeared to be a kind of meta-identity through which the youth are '*recognised*' and '*identified*' by others and which gives them '*honour*' and '*existence*' (FGD8-P36-Pakhtun male). Many animated discussions of national pride emerged when the youth were encouraged to articulate their understandings of Pakistani identity. Although a range of reasons were offered for their pride in being Pakistani, the 'naturalness' and 'obviousness' of such feelings were also acknowledged. Although the impact of education and the media was clearly discernible on their self-identification, they felt that their national and religious identities were somehow 'natural' rather than discursively constructed. It was a '*natural feeling*' to be proud of their '*homeland*' and to '*have a natural attachment to it*' (FGD12-P56-Christian female):

> P23: We get such patriotic feelings naturally. We live here, get our education here and are born and bred here. (FGD5-Pakhtun female)

National identity embodies historical continuity, connecting a group of people to a particular territory (Miller 1995). The youth felt '*naturally*' connected to their '*motherland*', where their '*forefathers and great-grand parents*' had lived and which would also be home to their '*coming generation*' (FGD13-P60-Ismaili female). References were made to the sacrifices their ancestors had made in freeing the nation from the shackles of imperial rule:

> P35: I am proud of our ancestors who fought against the British colonisation and oppression, be they leaders of the Muslim League or the Khudai Khidmatgar.[12] Their resistance and struggle got us our independence and sovereignty. (FGD8-Pakhtun male)

This sense of belongingness was further heightened by invoking the discourse of citizenship and the concomitant language of rights and obligations. Across the FGDs, youth expressed gratitude for living in a '*sovereign*' and '*free*' country where they enjoy a set of rights and are required to fulfil certain obligations. Only '*the stateless*' like '*the Palestinians fully appreciate the value of belonging to a state*' and '*the freedom to move*' and '*self-expression*' (FGD8-P33-Pakhtun male). The legal aspect of nationality was particularly salient in the narratives of non-Muslim youth and those from the minority Muslim sect:

> P57: We have freedom. Pakistan provides us education and other rights. (FGD12-Christian female)

The distinctiveness of Pakistanis provoked heated discussions. While several youth resorted to Islam in marking Pakistanis out, which we discuss in the next section, racial characteristics, such as skin colour and physical features, were also mentioned, but these were critiqued for being shared with other South Asians like 'Indians'. By contrast, the Urdu language and accent, and the Pakistani dress code, *shalwar qameez*, were more readily accepted as identifiers of Pakistanis. Fellow citizens were also identified in less tangible ways such as '*you identify your own people when you see them*' (FGD12-P56-Christian female). The metaphor of family was often invoked to stress '*the hospitable, loving and caring nature*' of Pakistanis and their '*concern for others, particularly in a foreign country, they will definitely give us their time and will show feelings of love and support*' (FGD13-P61-Ismaili female).

While several symbols and markers of Pakistani identity were articulated to justify their sense of pride, the most frequently cited signifier loaded with the greatest affect was 'Islam'. Next in frequency were Pakistan Army and the nuclear arsenal, both of which also produced considerable affect. All three were linked through a discourse of 'difference' and the construction of the external global 'other' and embedded in the discourse of 'terrorism' and the 'War on Terror'. We turn to analyse these further in Sects. 4.4 and 4.6.

Following the above three markers, the youth strongly linked '*freedom*' to Pakistani identity. Nations dream of being free, and the symbol of this freedom is the sovereign state (Anderson 1991). The timing of data collection is crucial here as the sit-in organised by Imran Khan's Pakistan Tehreek-e-Insaf, popularly called *Azadi* (Freedom) March, which lasted from 14 August to 17 December 2014, was still going on. A huge number of youth participated in the sit-in, which was held against the Nawaz Sharif government over claims of systematic rigging in the 2013 election. Across religious affiliations and gender boundaries, the youth expressed pride in having the freedom to '*express your views*', '*make your own decisions*' and be '*independent*' (FGD13-P63-Ismaili female).

> P28: It's a free state. There is no compulsion. I am a free man. I can go anywhere. There are no restrictions on me. (FGD6-Pakhtun male)

Another positive marker was Pakistan's diversity, such as '*a variety of terrains like mountains, plains and deserts*' and '*different seasons*' (FGD4-P16-Pakhtun male). While managing this diversity, which includes '*religions*', '*cultures*', '*languages*' and '*lifestyles*', and requires '*tolerance*' and '*respecting each other's identities*', it is nonetheless remarkable that '*Pakistanis are living together with peace, with calmness and with all these attitudes of love and support for each other*' (FGD13-P64-Ismaili female). Particularly, in times of crisis, be it a natural disaster—floods, earthquake or a security tragedy—internal displacement due to insurgency and counterterrorism operations, all internal divisions are put behind and all Pakistanis '*stand as one nation to help those who are affected*' (FGD8-P33-Pakhtun male). This highlights that under normal circumstances, our experience of national belongingness is unremarkable. It is only in times of struggle that the nation ceases to be contestable and taken for granted.

The youth's patriotic expressions were not uncritical though and they appeared to be reflexive in assessing Pakistan's development and security challenges. The lack of stable democratic structures was voiced by several youth. Political instability was termed as the '*root cause of all other challenges*' (FGD13-P65-Ismaili female) alongside 'weak democracy' because of 'military takeovers' (FGD6-P29-Pakhtun male). The military, which is a key identifier of Pakistani identity (see Sect. 4.6), was strongly critiqued for contributing to political instability and accused by some for Islamisation of the state that led to gender/religious inequalities:

> P48: Whenever there is a democratic government the army stages a coup. The army doesn't let democracy be strengthened in this country. (FGD10-Pakhtun male)
>
> P65: Zia-ul-Haq imposed religion and five time prayers and the dress code and he defined everything … that was the turning point of our history, turning point for women's inequality, and … religious violence. (FGD13-Ismaili female)

However, political leadership was also criticised for rampant corruption, nepotism and '*a lack of rule of law where the rich and the poor are equal*' (FGD1-P5-Pakhtun male). Nevertheless, the majority of the national icons that the youth discussed in their accounts were from politics.[13] The most popular national icon, admired particularly by Pakhtun youth in HE, was Imran Khan (24%). He was hailed for being '*honest*' and '*sincere*' and for '*creating awareness about rights and duties*' (FGD5-P24-Pakhtun female). Following him, in order of popularity, the national icons included Muhammad Ali Jinnah (22%), Pakistan's founding father; Allama Muhammad Iqbal (18%), the poet, philosopher and Muslim League leader, who for the first time put forward the idea of a separate homeland for Indian Muslims; and Abdul Sattar Edhi (13%), the philanthropist, social activist and founder of the Edhi Foundation, one of the largest non-profit social welfare organisations in the world. All of the aforementioned popular national icons are men and Sunni Muslims.[14]

To conclude, the youth construct their 'similarity' using a range of signifiers: land, dress code, language, physical characteristics and feelings of community. Democracy and the associated freedoms and rights also produce strong affect. This indicates the youth do not see the development of secular, constitutional government and society as incompatible with an Islamic republic. While all of the above are important in producing a shared identity, it is religion and 'difference', reinforced by historical conflicts with India and contemporary conflict in the context of the 'War on Terror', through which the Pakistani nation is discursively produced. The construction of difference through an external 'other' appears to produce similarity at the national and local levels. We continue to develop the centrality of Islam and external others to the construction of Pakistani identity in Sects. 4.4 and 4.6.

4.4 Religion, Unity and Divisions

Turning now to the articulation of religious identity, only 16% of participants, all Muslims, used this marker in their self-description (male = 3%; female = 31%). The use of religion in their self-identification was much higher for females than for males, while the former also made a greater use of identity markers overall. Given the centrality of Islam to Pakistani identity and the subsequent marginalisation of non-Islamic religions in Pakistan, it is understandable that the five non-Muslim youth did not identify themselves through articulation of their Christianity. Several Muslim youth highlighted that on an international stage, their nationality '*naturally*' becomes their '*primary identity*' through which other people would identify them. Nevertheless, the

Muslim youth imagined the nation predominantly through religion as discussed below.

Islam, National Pride and Unity

Islam was the marker that drew boundaries between 'us' and 'them' as the youth imagined a world demarcated by religion through an imaginary of the 'Muslim World':

> P42: The Islamic Republic of Pakistan is the 2nd largest country of the Muslim world. (FGD9-Pakhtun female)
>
> P44: Pakistan has the largest number of religious scholars; it produces the largest number of people who know the Qur'an by heart, and has the largest number of madaris [religious schools]. (FGD10-Pakhtun male)

The youth took pride in their being '*born in a Muslim family*' and for being '*raised in an Islamic society*' and '*in an Islamic environment*' (FDG4-P18-Pakhtun male). It was '*a great solace to know that as a Muslim*' they will '*ultimately go to heaven*' (FGD8-P38-Hazarewal male). As the quote below indicates, the creation of the Pakistani state on the basis of religion was seen as a unique characteristic, shared only with Israel, and this aroused a sense of great pride:

> P1: There are only two states in the world formed on the basis of ideology, Israel and Pakistan. So Pakistan means pak (pure), a land where pure people live. (FGD1-Pakhtun male)
>
> P41: Pakistan came into being on the basis of La Ilaha IllAllah[15] [There is no God but Allah]. (FGD7-Pakhtun female)

Islam was contrasted with other religions and was termed '*a perfect religion from all aspects*' which gives '*guidance in each and every aspect of life*', offers '*complete instructions regarding all rituals and rights, be it the rights of the child, matters of property or the rights of men and women*' and helps them inform their '*actions and thoughts*' (FGD8-P34-Pakhtun male).

Religion, like national identity, is a cohesive force that mobilises individuals through rites and ceremonies (Durkheim 1912). From this perspective, religious congregations, like national gatherings, may serve to bolster national unity, ease ethnic tensions and recruit citizens for various political objectives. On the other hand, religion and religious rites can also serve as a marker of difference, for example against a nation-state. Shared symbolism is integral to nationhood, and for the Pakistani youth, Islam is the locus of the collective symbolism as it supplies them the myths, symbols and memories which serve to form the basis of Pakistani nation. Their understandings of what it means to be a Muslim highlighted a range of notions including rituals, beliefs and actions. While all Muslim youth were Muslim through genealogy, it was beliefs and embodied ritual practices which were salient in the narratives of both Sunni and Ismaili Muslims. The youth's 'similarity' as Pakistani emanated from '*believing in one God, Allah*', being the '*followers of Prophet Muhammad (PBUH), the last messenger of Allah*', and '*believing in the Qur'an*', which instructs them '*how to spend life according to Islamic point of view*' (FGD13-P65 Ismaili female). Muslim-ness was associated with 'pure' and 'right' beliefs. In addition to '*understanding the meaning of Qur'an*', the obligatory Muslim prayer, *namaz,* offered five times a day, was a key ritual invoked to symbolise both Pakistaniness and Muslim-ness. Nevertheless, some youth, particularly the Ismaili females, also pointed out that Muslim-ness '*is not about offering prayers*' or '*wearing Islamic dress*' but is performed '*in actions, in deeds and in behaviour*' (FGD13-P65-Ismaili female).

'Good Muslims' and Global Terrorism
Another dominant theme in youth's understanding of Islam was 'peace'. As discussed in Chap. 3, the discourse of the 'War on Terror' and the media representations of global terrorism position Muslim (male) youth as 'Good Muslims' or 'Bad Muslims' (Mamdani 2004). These binaries serve to contain and control the representations of 'Islam and Muslims', which in turn advances Eurocentrism and Orientalism, perpetuating and legitimising the construction of Islam and Muslims as terrorists.

Both Muslim men and women took up the 'Good/Passive Muslim' subject position in articulating their understandings of Islam.

> P62: They [terrorists] are not our people; they are not Muslims; they are not true Muslims; Islam teaches unity, Islam teaches love, peace, prosperity, and affection. (FGD13-Ismail female)
>
> P7: Islam means peace. A Muslim is a person who spreads peace. (FGD2-Pakhtun female)

The youth, both Muslim and non-Muslim, were extremely critical of the media, both international and national, for constructing a terrorist subjectivity for them. The media was believed to '*exaggerate such incidents as terrorism and militancy*' (FGD3-P13-Pakhtun female). While the Pakistani media was criticised for '*creating sensationalism to entertain people for their own financial gains without even bothering about its impact on the country*' (FGD12-P56-Christian female), the international media was particularly seen as '*implicated in creating a negative image for Pakistan*' (FGD12-P57-Christian female).

> P37: … we are not terrorists, we are peaceful people who love education. Why is the world determined to name us as terrorists? Even when they [the US and its allies] interfere in our internal affairs and play with our integrity, we remain positive [non-violent]. (FGD7-Pakhtun male)

Given this international gaze on young Pakistanis/Muslims, the youth felt pressurised to resist these terrorist and violent identities and in doing so positioned themselves as 'Good Muslims' as indicated by the above extract.

Islam, Democracy and Rights

In Chap. 2 we contrasted the 'thick' affective Muslim cosmopolitanism rooted in religious attachments to the global *ummah* with the 'thin' notions of European cosmopolitanism which privilege the rational and a separation of religion and the state (Edmunds 2013). The youth's narratives invoked 'thick' affective cosmopolitanism, particularly expressed within the context of the global 'other', which we discuss in Sect. 4.6.

Nevertheless, they also expressed solidarity across religious boundaries and co-opted Islam alongside democracy and the development of welfare state: '*It was Islam, which for the first time, gave the concept of democracy and a welfare state*' (P40-Pakhtun female). Many Muslim youth expressed the belief that running Pakistan on '*truly Islamic principles*' could help realise the purpose for which Pakistan was created, that is '*a place where people, both Muslims and minority groups enjoy independence, rights and fulfil all their needs*' (FGD13-P62-Ismaili female):

> P36: The Islamic requirement is not just to take care of the needs of other Muslims but all human beings. (FGD8-Pakhtun male)
>
> P2: We support peace and prosperity for the whole world. We raise our voice for the right thing. (FGD1-Hazarewal male)
>
> P15: If there is some injustice happening somewhere, as Muslims and as human beings we condemn it. I am proud as we always raise our voice … against cruelty. (FGD4-Pakhtun male)

Thus, indicating once again that the youth saw Islam compatible with democracy, rights, freedom and the welfare of all citizens and non-citizens irrespective of religion.

The Conflation of Religion and Ethnicity
When encouraged to think how Pakistani Muslims are different from other Muslims, the initial and most common response was '*There is no difference between Muslims … as Islam is a complete way of life irrespective of where you live*' (FGD8-P33-Pakhtun male). The youth had difficulty in distinguishing between Islam and Muslims as for them there existed an 'obvious', 'natural' and 'universal' way of performing Muslim identity. It was after much debate and interrogation that essentialised notions of being a Muslim gave way to acknowledging the cultural and regional impact on the practices and performances of Muslims. This distinction further established the dominance of Pakistanis, as the youth considered their practice of Islam purer and more legitimate. Although it was conceded that '*while din* (religion) *is the same, cultural differences lead to difference in practices*', the image of a 'true' Muslim remained

dominant: '*A true Muslim will behave in a similar fashion everywhere irrespective of geographical differences*' (FGD8-P36-Pakhtun male).

These notions of a 'true' Muslim strongly overlapped with ethnicity. Although some participants indicated that they '*are first a proud Muslim, then a Pakistani and then a Pakhtun*',Pakhtun ethnicity overlaps strongly with religion and at times signifies it (FGD8-P33-Pakhtun male). A close examination of their accounts indicated that Pakhtun identity was often being used to signify Islam and 'true' believers. When the youth were encouraged to think how Muslims across different provinces in Pakistan could be distinguished, spontaneous expressions of pride in Pakhtun-ness emerged, which were heavily overlaid with a conservative form of Muslim-ness. Ethnic identity construction, like national identity, requires the drawing of boundaries vis-à-vis 'others' (Barth 1969) and involves cultural similarity and the construction of difference (Calhoun 1997). The Pakhtun youth constructed their Pakhtun identity predominantly against the Punjabis, drawing a thicker boundary of Islam to border police what counts as 'true' Muslims. This might be because Punjab is geographically closer to KP than the other provinces and the two ethnic groups have economic interactions too. Additionally, both Punjabis and Pakhtuns are disproportionately represented in the military:

> P37: In KP, Islam is strictly followed in all aspects of life. There is a strong overlap between Islam and Pakhtunwali [the Pakhtun code of conduct]. When Qais Abdur Rasheed was invited to embrace Islam and when he was given all the details about Islam and Islamic way of life, he said that there wasn't much difference between Islam and Pakhtunwali and that both strongly overlapped ... So he accepted the message of Islam. (FGD8-Pakhtun male)
>
> P8: Pakhtuns follow Islam strictly… Punjabis don't. They visit graves and shrines. They do not observe fast. (FGD2-Pakhtun female)

Pakhtuns claim that their relationship to Islam is as old as Islam itself. They assert that their professed ancestor, Qais bin Rasheed, became a Muslim and a disciple of the Prophet Muhammad (PBUH) at a time when Arabs were still fighting against Islam (Barth 1969; Ahmed

1976; Glatzer 2002). Pakhtuns see Islam as a practical expression of the Pakhtun code of conduct called Pakhtunwali. These myths of authenticity were invoked in establishing the Pakhtun superiority over Punjabis:

> P45: Whenever an un-Islamic law is passed Pakhtuns demonstrate against it. If a law is passed that is in contradiction to Islam or something happens that violates Islamic laws, Pakhtuns are on the streets to protest. (FGD10-Pakhtun male)

Thus, for the Pakhtun youth, all three identities—nationality, religion and ethnicity—were mutually reinforcing and were further bolstered through the construction of the external 'other', also identified through religion, as discussed in Sect. 4.6.

Religion and the Internal 'Other'
The conflation of Islam with Pakistani identity bolsters a sense of unity for the Muslim youth, since '*all Muslims are brothers [sic]*'; therefore, Islam offers them '*a natural connection with other Pakistanis*' (FGD8-P34-Pakhtun male). This unified national identity is forged using inclusionary and exclusionary processes to construct 'insiders' and 'outsiders'—those who belong within and those who are outside the selfhood of the state. Since national identity is about questions of belonging to the collectivity and entitlement to make claims on it, it inevitably unites and divides at the same time. This has implications for citizenship, access to political power and resources and personal processes of identification and authenticity (Durrani and Dunne 2010). Given that religion marks the boundary between 'us' and 'them', it also serves as a boundary mechanism for marking internal 'others'. The national solidarity expressed through Islam by the Muslim youth placed the non-Muslims at the margins of the Pakistani nation:

> P11: They [non-Muslim Pakistanis] are very good. They mind their own business. They do not interfere in our affairs. (FGD2-Pakhtun female)

This suggests a disjuncture between citizenship and national identity, where the former merely represents a legal relationship between the state and the citizens, whereas the latter reflects authenticity and a sense of belonging. Thus, despite entitlement to full formal citizenship, the 'majority' may exclude the 'outsiders' within from belonging to the nation. The non-Muslim Pakistanis were not imagined as fellow members of the Pakistani nation. Although less tangible, this form of exclusion may still have negative social and material implications for the excluded individuals/groups as expressed below by the Christian female in relation to perceived inequity in the job market.

Social interaction across the religious boundaries and everyday encounters with other ways of practising a faith appeared crucial to producing a sense of community that is inclusive of internal diversity. However, it was also evident that for the vast majority of the participating youth, such opportunities were few and far between.

> P25: We have had interactions with non-Muslims; they are loyal to Pakistan and we would have been the same if we were non-Muslims. (FGD5-Pakhtun female)

When the youth were encouraged to imagine life on the other side of the religious fence in Pakistan—in other words, how life would be different if the Christian youth were Muslim in Pakistan and vice versa—the Christian females' responses indicated their feeling of marginality in the Pakistani nation, as well as a perceived inequality in access to jobs and other resources:

> P58: We would be confident like them [Muslim citizens] in society and would have no problem getting jobs. We would have more freedom. We would be less reliant on important people to work on our issues. We would be confident enough to make demands on the state directly. (FGD12-Christian female)

Thus, despite the constitutional guarantee of equal rights,[16] the exclusion from national identity may negatively impact the 'redistribution' (access to material resources), 'recognition' (cultural recognition) and 'representation' (parity in political participation) of the non-Muslim citizens (Fraser 2009). It was evident that religion/Islam was fracturing the Pakistani nation: '*The main problem is religion ... Christianity in Pakistan does not get its due place and regard. Not always but sometimes you feel it*' (FGD12-P58-Christian female).

The majority of the Muslim youth found it extremely hard to imagine themselves as non-Muslims. Some understood it as conversion:

> I am a bit reluctant to answer this question. According to Islam, if you convert to another religion, it is tantamount to putting yourself in fire. (FGD1-P5-Pakhtun male)

After much explaining that the aim of the question was to explore how they thought non-Muslims experience life in Pakistan, some claimed their life would be '*no different*' or that they would still be '*OK*' as '*the policies and the constitution of this country provide equal rights to minorities*' (FGD12-P60-Ismaili female):

> P49: Rights of minorities are protected in Pakistan to a large extent. There are quotas for them in education, jobs and other places. (FGD10-Pakhtun male)

Those who could differentiate between formal inclusion in the state and affective inclusion in the nation were less optimistic, acknowledging that '*within local communities, non-Muslim Pakistanis are second class citizens*' (FGD7-P30-Pakhtun female) and that as a non-Muslim in Pakistan, they may be '*miserable*', '*marginalized*' or marked as '*infidels*' (FGD13-P61-Ismaili female).

Religion/Islam is the boundary separating 'us' and 'them'. The partition and repartition of the self, which involved religious conflict and a non-Muslim 'other', appear significant. Contemporary conflict involving global non-Muslim 'others', as discussed in Sect. 4.6, further reinforces the construction of the Muslim nation. National imagination through Islam sits well with the ethnic/Pakhtun identity of the youth, bolstering their unity through the subsuming of Pakhtun-ness into Pakistani identity. Nevertheless, the affective investment in images of the 'true' believer/Muslim enables the youth to police the boundaries of 'true' religion which fractures this religious/national unity. Furthermore, imagining the nation through erecting thick boundaries of Islam marks the non-Muslim Pakistanis as the outsiders within, excluding them from the Pakistani community, which has economic, social, cultural and political implications for them.

4.5 Constructing the 'Ideal' Pakistani Citizen: Gendering the Nation

The confluence of national and religious identifications discussed in the earlier section has particular implications for the construction of gender identities that we now explore. We first analyse the construction of gender in everyday life and then focus on the key sites in the public performance of Pakistani identity (Sect. 4.6). The construction of national identity is about constructing an ideal image of the nation, which remains incomplete without a corresponding construction of the 'ideal' woman and man. The youth constructed the 'ideal' Pakistani woman and man through dress codes, work and space, all of which were gendered and intersected with religion and ethnicity.

Dress code or clothing is the most obvious symbol used to signal association with a 'nation' or 'gender' (Durrani 2008). Nevertheless, this nationalisation of bodies is highly gendered, particularly in postcolonial states, where women represent national traditions and serve to fulfil nationalism's conservative drive towards traditional continuity, while men represent national modernity and serve to satisfy nationalism's desire to be seen as progressive (McClintok 1997). While the youth noted the Pakistani national dress, qameez and shalwar, as a marker by which Pakistanis are distinguished, it was also acknowledged that the Pakistani dress code was a reliable identifier of Pakistani women compared to men. Although all female youth, including Christian females, adhered to the Pakistani dress code, many young men were in Western attire. The overlapping of Islamic with Pakistani identity further gendered the dress code:

P63: A Muslim woman should cover her head. (FGD13-Ismaili Muslim)

4 Pakistan: Converging Imaginaries in an Islamic State

All the Muslim women in Peshawar had covered their heads. In addition, they had covered themselves with either a chador or a burka.[17] Furthermore, with two exceptions, all Muslim women in Peshawar were veiled (had covered their face), in the educational spaces and during the FGDs. This 'appropriate' and homogenised physical appearance of Pakistani women simultaneously draws boundaries between Pakistani men and women and between Muslim and non-Muslim women (Durrani 2008). While the gendered dress code strengthens the association of Pakistani identity with Islam, it also acts as a 'gaze' through which Muslim women are regulated and policed (Foucault 1977). This regulatory 'gaze' upon women extends to the policing maintained by the male stare, noted by both male and female respondents/participants. This surveillance of women's bodies, seen as being particularly stronger in KP, not only constructs a power asymmetry between men and women but also acts as a panopticon, enabling women to become their own 'overseer', 'exercising this surveillance over, and against, [themselves]' (Foucault 1980:155).

> P64: If a piece of cloth could enhance our dignity in the eyes of community to such a level, there is no reason for us to go out without covering our head. (FGD13-Ismaili female)

This also shows Muslim women's desire to position themselves appropriately within available discourses. In addition to religion, other identity markers were also at play in the construction of the gendered dress code. For example, a Muslim woman in Peshawar who had not covered her face attributed veiling to (Pakhtun) culture rather than to Islam:

> P31: In Pakistan we have mixed up culture and religion. Religion tells you not to cover your face but culture tells you otherwise. (FGD7-Hazarewal female)

Likewise, both Pakhtun men and women took great pride in Pakhtun women being *'more religious, even more so than Pakhtun men'*, with strict observance of *'purdah in KP and Balochistan'* seen as evidence of the *'purity'* of *'our women'* (FGD11-P54-Pakhtun male). Likewise, the intersection between place and gender is evident from the ways the Ismaili females negotiated the gendered dress code between their hometown in GB and Karachi:

> P64: We kind of ... change our lifestyle according to the situation because we have to survive. For example, when I was in GB, I never let my dupatta fall off my head. But when I came here [Karachi], I saw in [the university], I was the only woman covering my head. So the second day I covered my head, then for a week I did so, then I thought no one is noticing whether she is covering her head with dupatta or not and then I stopped. (FGD13-Ismaili female)

Anderson (1991) considers national identity as similar to kinship and religion, which is helpful in explaining why women have come to assume the role of the bearers of cultural values and traditions. 'If the nation is an extended family writ large, then women's role is to carry out the tasks of nurturance and reproduction' (Moghadam 1994:4). Across the FGDs, the 'ideal' Pakistani woman was portrayed as the biological and cultural reproducer of the nation and the 'ideal' Pakistani man as provider and protector of the national image and women's 'purity' and 'modesty' and the 'moral code'. Needless to say, this gendering is explicitly heteronormative. A woman's first and foremost duty to the nation is giving birth to the next generation, bringing them up as good Pakistanis and *'taking care of their moral, physical, emotional and other needs'* (FGD1-P3-Pakhtun male):

> P39: Her first priority should be her home. Some educated women prioritise work over family and domestic responsibilities ... By ignoring the home, they ignore the whole generation so she is not fulfilling her prime responsibility. (FGD9-Peshawari female)

> P3: She should help her husband and back him up and stand by him. Because if she helps her husband he will work more which is to the benefit of all but if she is in paid employment she cannot offer her husband this support. (FGD1-Pakhtun male)

By contrast, the 'ideal' Pakistani man is '*a man of action*' (FGD2-P10-Pakhtun female) and '*has a sense of responsibility for himself, for his family, for his country*' (FGD13-P63-Ismaili female). He prioritises '*national over self-interests*', '*works for the development of Pakistan*' and '*earns a good name for Pakistan*' (FGD6-P28-Pakhtun male).

P36: He is responsible for protecting his house. (FGD8-Pakhtun male)

While both Islam and Pakhtun ethnicity intersect in the construction of a gendered division of labour, the accounts of the Christian females indicated that '*irrespective of religion, many men do not allow women to have a job*' and that '*there is no freedom for women*' because '*it is just the culture here*' (FGD12-P56). Likewise, the Christian male confirmed that '*household chores are done by women. Even if she is employed, she still does household chores*' (FGD11-P55).

Across the FGDs, a strong emphasis on the education of women was evident, because '*if mothers are educated they will help bring up better children*' (FGD1-P6-Pakhtun male). It was also clear that women's access to education was very unevenly distributed, with women from remote rural areas particularly disadvantaged in accessing this socially desirable and powerful subject position. Nonetheless, '*irrespective of the level of education she receives, a woman's ultimate goal is to get married*', with very little societal sanction '*to enter the work place*' (FGD8-P36-Pakhtun male). Despite gaining a professional qualification, many women would end up '*staying home*' leaving the '*work place to men*', as they study '*to just get very good proposals, just for marriage. After marriage, they are just sitting at home*' (FGD13-P65-Ismaili females).

This gendered division of labour promotes gendered power relations as well as 'the division of space into domestic, which is associated with women, and the public which is considered a male domain' (Durrani 2008:608). The accounts of Muslim youth indicated the institutionalisation of gendered spatial division, which is created through the exclusion of women from the public sphere. This reinforces male dominance and endorses gender segregation. Moreover, it defines male subjectivity in relation to control over space and female subjectivity in terms of being controlled and kept under surveillance (Leslie 1993). This unequal spatial divide is sanctioned and naturalised through local Islamic discourses:

> P8: In Islamic society, male is dominant … He is responsible to work outside and women are expected to stay home in our Pakhtun culture. (FGD2-Pakhtun female)
>
> P33: In Islam the rightful place of a woman is within the four walls of her house. (FGD8-Pakhtun male)

In addition, ethnicity converged with religion to draw strict spatial boundaries that promoted gender segregation and restricted female mobility: '*we place certain restrictions on women because of our ethnic culture. In Pakhtun society if your women go out to shops, bazars etc. it is seen very badly*' (FGD8-P37-Pakhtun male). Educational spaces appeared to be the only public arenas which women could inhabit legitimately.

> P51: It all comes to education. Those who are not educated will stay home. (FGD11-Pakhtun male)

Nevertheless, even the mobility of educated women is strictly regulated. They are 'free' to access particular spaces, at particular times and under particular conditions, such as '*with the permission of her husband or her family*' (FGD11-P53-Pakhtun male). All female FGDs were conducted at a time when academic classes were in session, as the females were required to go back home as soon as their classes were finished. Both the discourses of religion and ethnicity were drawn to define the rightful role, space and place of Pakistani women:

> P51: We have freedom but don't give it to women. … We give them freedom allowed by Islam and Pakhtun society. (FGD11-Pakhtun male)

However, these ethnoreligious discourses did not externally impose on the thought of the youth (Foucault 1986); rather, they enabled the youth to work on themselves, to produce themselves in particular ways:

> P40: Even when we have permission, we will not go on our own without a male. We think, what people will think of us? ... Even when we have to go to visit an archaeological museum [for academic work], if our brother can't accompany us, we will ask our class-fellows to go with us but will not go on our own. We do not like it [going out alone]. (FGD9-Pakhtun female)

This illustrates how religion is a 'mode of belonging and embodied social practice' (Butler 2011:72), rather than a matter of rational choice. Thus, the dominant discourses worked through the implicit consent of the youth who desired to constitute themselves correctly within the discourses available, even if it meant taking up subject positions which may be seen as irrational. The consensual regulation of the youth was apparent, as it seemed they had fully identified the subject positions they were offered within the dominant discourses with their own interests.

If discourses are an 'instrument of power', they can also be 'a hindrance, a stumbling-block, a point of resistance and a starting point for an opposing strategy' (Foucault 1978:101). The very few youth who resisted the dominant gendered subject positions were mainly men and they drew on Islamic discourses to produce an alternative discourse:

> P35: People use Islamic discourse to set the limits of women and define their role ... But we do not hear what the Prophet (PBUH) has said about the status of women ... I do not think there is difference [between men and women]. What men want they can do; what women want they should do. (FGD8-Pakhtun male)

Islam is thus appropriated both to construct gender power asymmetries and to destabilise and subvert them.

4.6 Gendering the Nation Through the External 'Other'

Having discussed the gendered construction of Pakistani identity in the banal realm of everyday life (Billig 1995), we now focus on the gendering of the Pakistani identity through the construction of the external 'other' and the discourse of the 'War on Terror', both of which construct the public performance of Pakistani identity in a gendered way.

As Sect. 4.2 has made abundantly clear, conflict has remained rife in the history and politics of Pakistan. This has special significance for the construction of the 'other' without which national identity cannot be imagined. The youth cited several antagonistic non-Muslim external 'others'—India, Israel, the USA—to distinguish their Pakistani Muslim self. India was seen as antagonistic, drawing on the collective memory of war, conflict, partition and trauma and its ongoing efforts to 'harm' Pakistan's integrity through covert intelligence operations. The USA was critiqued not only for the violence perpetrated on Pakistanis/Pakhtuns in the context of the 'War on Terror' but also the policies it has allegedly pursued to annihilate the Muslim nation. Again, it is in the context of 'thick' religious solidarity (Muslim cosmopolitanism) that Israel is abhorred for the atrocities it commits against fellow Muslims–Palestinians.

Nations are built upon stories of collective existence in which the past is constantly defined and redefined. The different wars with India were conjured by the youth to construct a national(istic) past:

> P34: The 1965 war with India is a great historic event, when a much bigger and stronger country attacked us and we fully defended ourselves. (FGD8-Pakhtun male)

With specific reference to Pakistan, the collective memory or amnesia of these wars is nurtured through the national curriculum and state-sanctioned textbooks (Durrani 2008), grand national ceremonies and representations on television and the print media. Every year, the 1965 Indo-Pakistan war is commemorated on 6th of September, a public holiday in Pakistan, popularly called 'Defence Day'. Television programmes are broadcast, and the print media publishes special editions to honour the bravery and sacrifices of the Pakistan Army. The collective memory of the wars with India reinforces 'the Islam under siege' discourse, which circulates at all levels of Pakistani society:

4 Pakistan: Converging Imaginaries in an Islamic State

> P29: We think that Islam will be annihilated through a conspiracy … we have radicalised the people and have created a fear in them that India can attack us stealthily anytime and that Islam is struggling for its existence and that obscenity will gain control in our land. (FGD6-Pakhtun male)

In addition to India, Israel was positioned as an antagonist in the discourse of the 'other': *'Israel always conspires against the Islamic world and Pakistan. They have occupied Palestine'* (FGD10-P44 Pakhtun male). However, the most significant 'other' was the USA, identified so for *'interfering too much in Pakistan's affairs'* and *'trying to run Pakistan'* (FGD2-P9 Pakhtun female), but more specifically with reference to the 'War on Terror'. Among the very few female icons that the youth identified with was Aafia Siddiqui,[18] *'the daughter of Pakistan'*, *'whose handing over to the USA'* was articulated with great national shame (FGD10-P43-Pakhtun male):

> P8: She suffers for Islam. She is imprisoned. She is not fulfilling their [the US] demands and is being tortured. Obviously, they are against Islam so they are after Afia. (FGD2-Pakhtun female)

Thus, both discourses—the 'other' and the 'War on Terror'—conflate Islam and Pakistan, which serves to construct both as feminine and in need of protection. This tends to offer specific gendered subject positions to Pakistani men—defenders of the territorial borders and the ideological boundaries of the nation, including the policing of internal 'others', that is those who deviate from the dominant ways of being a Pakistani. In addition, it portrays the Pakistan Army as the main signifier of Pakistani identity.

Across gender and ethnic and religious divides, the Pakistan Army offered the youth both a sense of pride and promise of protection from the many national/religious enemies:

> P37: Pakistan has a very strong and independent military … Powerful countries, such as the US, China and India recognise the might of Pakistan Army. (FGD8-Pakhtun male)

> P38: I am proud of the fact when chief of the Indian Military says that Pakistan Military is one of the strongest militaries in the world. To hear such praise from your enemy makes me feel proud. (FGD8-Hazarewal male)

Likewise, Pakistan's nuclear arsenal offered a strong sense of protection from the numerous non-Muslim 'others' and a great sense of pride: '*India would have attacked us had we not exploded our nuclear device. It has given us a sense of security*' (FGD10-P46-Chitrali male). Dr. Abdul Qadeer Khan, the founding scientist of Pakistan's Nuclear Programme, was praised for '*giving the Muslim world its first atomic bomb*' (FGD7-P41-Pakhtun female). Likewise, Zulfikar Ali Bhutto, under whose premiership the programme started, and Nawaz Sharif, during whose regime Pakistan conducted nuclear tests, were both praised:

> P62: Although, it [detonation of nuclear bomb] alarmed other countries, but for Pakistan it was a historic event as now Pakistan is identified as a stronger country defense-wise. (FGD13-Ismaili female)

While the discourse of the 'War on Terror' enables the American audiences to affectively invest in the images of national identity (Solomon 2014), it is also drawn upon by Pakistani youth to make such affective investment in the Muslim nation, which of course is gendered. This is because 'once a discourse is established, it begins to have a life of its own and can be used selectively by all manner of groups, including those which it excludes' (Brah 2007:137).

> P3: Why can't we reveal who is behind the terrorism and for what purpose? Well the purpose is very clear. I feel it is to defame and stigmatize Islam and wipe Islam out of this country. The other day Munawar Sahib argued that Jihad in Islam is fee Sabilillah [Only for Allah and not for personal gains].[19] Many political parties have strongly reacted to this statement … [and have] accused Munawar of inciting people to participate in terrorism. But what he was saying is not un-Islamic. Jihad is legitimate in Islam. The Prophet (PBUH) said, "Jihad will continue till the very end". (FGD1-Pakhtun male)

4 Pakistan: Converging Imaginaries in an Islamic State 115

The discourse of the 'War on Terror' thus reinforces Orientalism and Eurocentrism, and at the same time, it bolsters Islamism or political Islam, as illustrated above. Mamdani's (2004) distinction between 'lesser' jihad (concerning self-preservation and self-defence in the face of hostility including mobilisation for social/political causes) and 'greater' jihad (an inner struggle against the weakness of the self, discussed in Chap. 2) is pertinent here. The discourse of the 'War on Terror' appears to present 'Islam under siege' and promotes 'thick' cosmopolitanism, which is articulated predominantly by male youth. Pakhtun identity, with its close connection to Islam, as discussed earlier, and KP being the frontline region in the Soviet–Afghan war and now in the 'War on Terror', were also implicated in the construction of 'us' versus global 'them':

> P33: Have you thought why all the enemies are after Pakistan and the Pakhtuns of KP? Why is the KP engulfed in crisis? It's because KP is the Oxford of Islam. For worldly knowledge, Oxford is the greatest seat of learning. For Islamic knowledge, you go to KP. (FGD8-Pakhtun male)

> P45: It is our observation … that whenever Islam is involved, for example during the Soviet invasion of Afghanistan, Pakhtuns contributed the most. (FGD10-Pakhtun male)

Thus, knowledge of the Muslim (Pakistani) youth is produced through competing discourses—'Bad Muslims' or terrorists and Islamism and global jihad—and each is linked to a contestation over power. Whichever discourse will emerge as dominant will decide the 'truth' of the Muslim/Pakistani youth.

More importantly, the confluence of the discourses of the 'other' and the 'War on Terror' constructs a mullah–military alliance that further constructs gendered subjectivities for Pakistani men and women and reinforces women's marginality in the public performance of Pakistani identity. While the significance of the 'biggest jihad as self-reformation and fighting your *nafs* (self)' was acknowledged (FGD8-P34 Pakhtun male), internal policing, often achieved violently, of those who deviate from the 'normal' and 'obvious' ways of being a 'proper' Pakistani/

Muslim was also reported: '[*Militant wings of political parties*] *make their narrative and association with Jihad and push them to prevent people by force from indulging in un-Islamic activities*' (FGD6-P29-Pakhtun male).

To summarise the preceding two sections, gender and Pakistani identities are reciprocally and discursively constructed and both involve hierarchical relations. Because of the dominant national imagination through Islam, gender and what is considered to be acceptable womanhood are appropriated through religious discourses, norms and practices. In addition to religion, ethnicity, rural/urban location and the construction of the 'other' intersect with gender. These confluences produce gendered effects and gender asymmetries and make women the symbolic border guards of the Pakistani nation, with their primary role being biological and cultural reproducers. By contrast, men are identified as leaders and defenders of the nation's territorial and ideological borders and protectors of women's 'purity' and 'moral code'. These convergences produce discourses which favour the mullah–military alliance and which render the democracy and citizenship discourse fragile. The latter has particular implications for the construction of internal 'others'—non-Muslims in particular but also non-dominant Muslim sects—who are pushed to the margins of the nation at the affective level. This in turn impacts negatively on the claims these marginalised groups can make on the nation.

4.7 Conclusions

The discourses of Pakistani youth indicate an explicit sense of national identity imagined through (Sunni) Islam, which overlays a homogeneous unity on the internal social, religious, ethnic and cultural heterogeneity, for the majority of (Sunni) Muslim youth. The discursive construction of multiple antagonistic non-Muslim 'others' and the contemporary violence lived daily, particularly in KP, tend to solidify Islam as a boundary between 'us' and 'them'. In addition, Pakhtun ethnicity further reinforces national imagination through Islam. All three discourses—the nation, the 'other' and *Pakhtunwali*—converge to tighten the representations of the nation around Islam. This serves to conflate

Pakistan with Islam, which has specific implications for (gender) power relations within and beyond Pakistan.

Religion is central to the national identifications of the Sunni and Ismaili youth, both of whom understood Islam as a set of (universal) beliefs and rituals, implying the greater jihad discussed in Chap. 2. In addition, the youth readily took up the subject position of the 'Good Muslim' that is constructed by the discourse of the 'War on Terror', insisting on Islam as a religion of peace and occasionally articulating cosmopolitanism across religious boundaries. However, the Sunni/Pakhtun youth's understanding of Islam suggests 'hegemonic', 'proper' and 'true' ways of performing Muslim identities, which intersects with Pakhtun ethnicity and gender. These hegemonic notions of the performance of 'proper' Muslim encourage the policing of the boundaries with respect to what counts as legitimate or purer forms of Islamic practice. In addition, it undermines the national solidarity produced through Islam by the inscription of 'improper' Muslims on those who deviate from the hegemonic ways of enacting Muslim identities.

Despite the salience of Islam in the national imaginary, the youth deploy discourses of secular democracy and citizenship in the construction of the nation. Rather than religious leaders, the national icons the youth identified with the most are political leaders admired for awakening the Muslim nation and working to establish a welfare state for Pakistanis where all citizens, irrespective of other identity markers, will have access to equal rights and have the ability to hold the government accountable. Likewise, while across gender and religious belonging, the military is the signifier that produces strong identifications, particularly through the deployment of discourses of the 'other' and the 'War on Terror', within the invocation of citizenship discourses, it is positioned as the 'other' and strongly critiqued for political instability and the Islamisation of the polity. Thus, the youth's identities are constructed across multiple discourses, which are at times contradictory.

In contrast to the Muslim youth, the Christian youth construct the nation through the discourses of 'home', 'territory' and citizenship. Islam simultaneously unites and divides the Pakistani nation. Both narratives clearly indicate the separation of citizenship from national identity, where the non-Muslim Pakistanis are included as citizens but excluded from the nation and local community. This less tangible exclusion nonetheless supports inequity in 'redistribution', 'recognition' and 'representation' for the non-Muslim citizens (Fraser 2009).

The convergence of Islam with Pakistani identity is further reinforced through antagonistic multiple non-Muslim 'others', especially India, Israel and the USA and the discourse of the 'War on Terror'. This discursively portrays Islam and Pakistan under siege, which strengthens the power of the military and the religious elites in the circulation of images of the nation. In particular, the discourse of the 'War on Terror' enables the Pakhtun male to make affective investments in the national identity and the global *ummah* and tends to reinforce political Islam and potential militarisation of male identities.

The above has particular implications for gender identities and relations. In the context of contemporary conflict experienced daily by the youth, the above intersections construct the Pakistani nation in a highly gendered way, where the male youth/the military/the religious elite are positioned as leaders and defenders of the nation and protector of women's morality and women are positioned as good mothers and carriers of national/religious traditions and symbolic border guards between 'us' and 'them'. Complex gendered identifications are thus produced by the superimposition of (Sunni) Islam on Pakistani identity, the collective memory of wars involving non-Muslim global 'others', the discourses of the 'War on Terror' and 'Islam under siege', ethnic identifications and locality—urban versus rural—and local culture. While Christian females are less subjected to disciplinary regimes such as gendered dress code and gendered space, the gendered division of work is apparent across the religious divide.

The vast majority of Pakhtun youth strongly identify with the gendered subject positions offered by the discourses of the nation, religion and ethnicity, suggesting a case of effective constitution of subjectivity as the youth identify these subject positions with their interests (Weedon 1997). The success of these discourses works, not through external imposition, but by enabling the youth to work on themselves through self-regulation and policing and through desire and affect.

Resistance to these dominant discourses is predominantly offered by men using Islam as an alternative discourse, for example pointing to the equality of men and women in the Qur'an. This indicates the significance of men in changing the national and gendered norms in Pakistan. Furthermore, the deployment of Islam as a resistance discourse is evident in changing national norms, which in turn may support the transformation of gendered norms. To gain dominance, these alternative discourses would require to be in circulation and win Pakistanis over to increase their social power (Weedon 1997). Education appears to be an important institution in enhancing the social power of resistance discourses and to challenge the gender norms as it is seen important by all youth in the construction of the 'good' citizen. Given that the vast majority of the youth performed highly gendered subjectivities, despite being educated, the radical transformation of the educational discourse itself appears crucial.

This chapter has explored the ways in which the Pakistani state was carved out of British India through the discursive construction of the Muslim nation, prompted by social and political imperatives in colonial India. We have analysed the ways youth have navigated their identities through the intersection of nation, religion and gender within the sociopolitical context of a Muslim-majority state which traces its genesis to a religious identity and which has a current and past history of conflicts involving antagonistic external 'others'. In the next chapter, we shift our exploration to Senegal, which is a Muslim-majority state but a secular republic and, unlike Pakistan, has enjoyed a relatively peaceful existence since independence.

Notes

1. Called the North-West Frontier Province (NWFP) until 2010 when it was renamed as part of the 18th Amendment to the Constitution.
2. For a map of Pakistan, see https://www.cia.gov/library/publications/the-world-factbook/geos/pk.html.
3. There are no official figures on Muslim sects, and different estimates provide varying data. According to Cohen (2005), Sunnis form 85% and Shi'as 12% of the Muslim population.

4. Abbreviation of 'PBUH', a phrase that Muslims say each time the name of the Prophet is mentioned as a mark of respect.
5. 44% speak Punjabi and 11% speak Siraiki, a Punjabi variant. Punjabi and Siraiki are mutually understandable. For over two decades, the Siraiki-speaking Punjabis have been trying to be accepted as a distinct ethnic group in Punjab.
6. The difference between Pakhtun and Pashtun/Pushtun is linguistic, a 'kh' instead of a 'sh' sound. The 'kh' sound is used by Pakhtuns of Peshawar Valley and northern parts of the KP, while the softer sound 'sh' is used by Pakhtuns in the south of Pakistan and in Afghanistan.
7. These people speak Urdu natively, the national language in Pakistan.
8. These regions are ordered according to the absolute numbers of Pakhtun population from the largest in KP (26 million) to the smallest in FATA and Balochistan (5.5 million each) (https://en.wikipedia.org/wiki/Pashtun_diaspora).
9. For example, the area ruled by the Lodi dynasty (1451–1526) extended over much of Pakistan and northern India, while that of the Suri dynasty (1540–1557) included eastern Afghanistan, Pakistan, and northern India extending up to Bengal. At its peak, the area ruled by the Durrani dynasty (1747–1862) included all of Afghanistan, most of Pakistan and part of northern India.
10. The notion of a 'secular' democratic state created on the basis of religion as a marker of nationhood may contradict 'Western' understandings of the secular, but only because of the invisibility of the religions that are already 'inside' the nation-state.
11. For example, in December 2011, the parliament passed the Prevention of Anti-Women Practices (Criminal Law Amendment) Act and the Acid Control and Acid Crime Prevention Act, offering greater protection for women against gender-based violence.
12. Also called *Surkh Posh* or Red Shirts movement. It was a non-violent movement against the British Raj by Pakhtuns of the North-West Frontier Province of British India, led by the Pakhtun nationalist, Khan Abdul Ghaffar Khan.
13. Religious leaders were mentioned only when the participants were asked who their favourite Muslim icon was. The majority identified with the Prophet (PBUH). Following that, the Sunnis, both males and females, identified with the second Caliph, Umar bin al-Khattab, and the Ismaili females with the Agha Khan. A small number of Sunni

youth identified with 'moderate' religious scholars—Tariq Jameel and Javed Ghamidi.
14. While Jinnah was born into an Ismaili Shi'a household, he moved towards the Sunni sect quite early in life (Ahmed 1997).
15. La ilaha illa'llah is the first and foremost important article of Islamic faith. It means 'there is none who is rightfully worshipped, apart from Allah' (Abdul-Rahman 2003:20). This was the most popular political slogan used by Muslims in the Pakistan Movement.
16. However, non-Muslims are constitutionally barred from becoming head of the state.
17. Chador is a full-body cloak, worn by women in both urban and rural KP. Women may cover their face with it as well. Pakhtun women from rural locations traditionally wore a kind of burka called shuttlecock, which is an outer garment that covers the entire body and has a grille over the face that the woman looks through. However, the burka that the research participants wore was similar to the abaya worn in the Arab world. It is a loose and long coatlike garment and was worn with a niqab to cover the head and face.
18. Dr. Aafia Siddiqui is a Pakistani national, who studied in the USA. She was arrested in Afghanistan in 2008, with documents and notes for making bombs. She was tried and convicted of assault and attempted murder of a US Army Captain in Afghanistan by a New York court in 2010 and sentenced to 86 years in prison. Siddiqui denied the charges.
19. Former Ameer of Jamaat-e-Islami, (JI) Syed Munawar Hasan, speaking at the annual JI conference in Lahore on 22 November 2014, claimed that Muslims have been commanded to wage jihad and qital only in the name of Allah, and fighting for any personal cause, prejudice, property and wealth was un-Islamic. He argued that both Jihad and Qital fee sabilillah are the solutions to the country's security problems rather than electoral and democratic politics.

References

Abdul-Rahman, M. S. (2003). Islam: questions and answers. London: MSA Publications Limited.

Adeney, K. (2012). A step towards inclusive federalism in Pakistan? The politics of the 18th Amendment. *Publius: The Journal of Federalism, 42*(4), 539–565.

Ahmed, A. S. (1976). *Millennium and charisma among Pathans: A critical essay in social anthropology*. London: Routledge.

Ahmed, A. S. (1997). *Jinnah, Pakistan and Islamic identity: The search for Saladin*. London: Routledge.

Akhtar, A. S., Amirali, A., & Raza, M. A. (2006). Reading between the lines: The mullah–military alliance in Pakistan. *Contemporary South Asia, 15*(4), 383–397.

Alif Ailaan. (2014). *25 million broken promises: The crisis of Pakistan's out-of-school children*. Islamabad: Alif Ailaan.

Amnesty International. (2015). *Amnesty International Report 2014/15: Pakistan*. Retrieved September 2, 2015, from https://www.amnesty.org/en/countries/asia-and-the-pacific/pakistan/report-pakistan/.

Anderson, B. (1991). *Imagined communities: Reflections on the origin and spread of nationalism*. London: Verso.

Arif, G. M. (2013). *Pakistan poverty profile*. Retrieved from http://www.bisp.gov.pk/PIDEReports/poverty.pdf.

Aslam, M., & Kingdon, G. (2012). Can education be a path to gender equality in the labour market? An update on Pakistan. *Comparative Education, 48*(2), 211–229.

Barth, F. (1969). Pathan identity and its maintenance. In F. Barth (Ed.), *Ethnic groups and boundaries: The social organization of cultural difference* (pp. 117–134). Long Grove, IL: Waveland Press.

Billig, M. (1995). *Banal nationalism*. London: Sage.

Brah, F. (2007). Non-binarized identities of similarity and difference. In M. Wetherell, M. Laflèche, & R. Berkeley (Eds.), *Identity, ethnic diversity and community cohesion* (pp. 136–146). London: Sage.

Brass, P. R. (1971). Elite groups, symbol manipulation, and ethnic identity among the Muslims of South Asia. In D. Taylor & M. Yapp (Eds.), *Political identity in South Asia* (pp. 35–77). London: Curzon Press.

British Council. (2009). *Pakistan: The next generation*. Retrieved March 25, 2012, from http://www.britishcouncil.org/pakistan-next-generation-report-download.htm.

Butalia, U. (2000). *The other side of silence: Voices from the partition of India*. Durham: Duke University Press.

Butler, J. (2011). Is Judaism Zionism? In J. Butler, J. Habermas, C. Taylor, & C. West (Eds.), *The power of religion in the public sphere* (pp. 70–92). New York: Columbia University Press.

Calhoun, C. (1997). *Nationalism*. Buckingham: Open University Press.

Cohen, S. P. (2005). *The idea of Pakistan*. Lahore: Vanguard.
Cohen, S. P. (2011). *The future of Pakistan*. Washington, DC: The Brookings Institution.
Devji, F. (2011). The idea of a Muslim community: British India 1857–1906. In M. Maussen, V. Bader, & A. Moors (Eds.), *Colonial and post-colonial governance of Islam: Ruptures and continuities* (pp. 111–132). Amsterdam: Amsterdam University Press.
Durkheim, E. (1912). *The elementary forms of religious life* (K. E. Fields, Trans.). New York: Free Press.
Durrani, N. (2008). Schooling the 'other': Representation of gender and national identities in Pakistani curriculum texts. *Compare: A Journal of Comparative and International Education, 38*(5), 595–610.
Durrani, N., & Dunne, M. (2010). Curriculum and national identity: Exploring the links between religion and nation in Pakistan. *Journal of Curriculum Studies, 42*(2), 215–240.
Edmunds, J. (2013). Human rights, Islam and the failure of cosmopolitanism. *Ethnicities, 13*(6), 671–688.
Foucault, M. (1977). *Discipline and punishment: The birth of the prison* (A. Sheridan, Trans.). London: Allen Lane.
Foucault, M. (1978). *The history of sexuality: An introduction*. Hammondsworth: Penguin.
Foucault, M. (1980). Truth and power. In C. Gordon & G. Burchell (Eds.), *Power/knowledge. Selected interviews and other writings* (pp. 109–133). Harlow: Pearson Education.
Foucault, M. (1986). The archaeology of knowledge. London: Tavistock Publications.
Fraser, N. (2009). *Scales of justice: Reimagining political space in a globalizing world*. New York: Columbia University Press.
Gilmartin, D. (1979). Religious leadership and the Pakistan movement in the Punjab. *Modern Asian Studies, 13*(3), 485–517.
Glatzer, B. (2002). The Pashtun tribal system. In G. Pfeffer & D. K. Behera (Eds.), *Concept of tribal society. Contemporary society. Tribal studies* (Vol. 5, pp. 265–282). New Delhi: Concept Publishers.
Government of Pakistan. (1998). *Percentage population by religion, mother tongue, and disability 1998, Pakistan*. Retrieved March 05, 2007, from http://www.pap.org.pk/statistics/population.htm#tab1.4.
Government of Pakistan. (2014). *Population, labour force and employment: Pakistan economic survey 2013–14*. Islamabad: Finance Division, Government of Pakistan.

Grare, F. (2006). *Pakistan: The resurgence of Baluch nationalism*. Washington, DC: Carnegie Endowment for International Peace.

Hussain, A. (2000). Peregrinations of Pakistani nationalism. In M. Leifer (Ed.), *Asian nationalism* (pp. 126–152). London and New York: Routledge.

Internal Displacement Monitoring Centre. (2015). *Pakistan: Solutions to displacement elusive for both new and protracted IDPs*. Geneva: IDMC.

International Labour Organisation (ILO). (2012). *Global employment trends for youth*. Geneva: ILO.

Iqtidar, H. (2012). State management of religion in Pakistan and dilemmas of citizenship. *Citizenship Studies, 16*(8), 1013–1028.

Kugelman, M. (2011). Pakistan's demographics: Possibilities, perils, and prescriptions. In M. Kugelman & R. M. Hathaway (Eds.), *Reaping the dividend: Overcoming Pakistan's demographic challenges* (pp. 5–29). Washington, DC: Woodrow Wilson International Center for Scholars.

Leslie, D. A. (1993). Femininity, post-fordism, and the "new traditionalism". *Environment and Planning D: Society and Space, 11*(6), 689–708.

Malik, I. (2016). Pashtun identity formation and Taliban politics: Grand narratives and the contemporary searchlight. In S. Gregory (Ed.), *Democratic transition and security in Pakistan* (pp. 102–123). Abingdon: Routledge.

Mamdani, M. (2004). *Good Muslim, bad Muslim. America, the Cold War, and the roots of terror*. New York: Pantheon Books.

McClintock, A. (1997). "No longer in a future heaven": Gender, race and nationalism. In A. McClintock, A. Mufti, & E. Shohat (Eds.), *Dangerous liaisons: Gender, nation and post-colonial perspectives* (pp. 89–112). Minneapolis: University of Minnesota Press.

MET & SHE. (2013). *National plan of action 2013–2016: Achieving universal primary education in Pakistan*. MDG Acceleration Framework. Ministry of Education, Trainings and Standards in Higher Education.

Miller, D. (1995). *On nationality*. Oxford: Clarendon.

Moghadam, V. M. (1994). Introduction and overview. In V. M. Moghadam (Ed.), *Gender and national identity: Women and politics in Muslim societies* (pp. 1–17). London: Zed Books.

Pakistan Women's Human Rights Organisation. (2015). *Pakistani women's human rights organization*. Retrieved October 18, 2015, from http://www.pakistaniwomen.org.

Rand, G., & Wagner, K. A. (2012). Recruiting the 'martial races': Identities and military service in colonial India. *Patterns of Prejudice, 46*(3–4), 232–254.

Rashid, A., & Shaheed, F. (1993). *Pakistan: Ethno-politics and contending elites* (UNRISD Discussion Paper 45). Switzerland: United Nations Research Institute for Social Development.

Saikal, A. (2010). Afghanistan and Pakistan: The question of Pashtun nationalism? *Journal of Muslim Minority Affairs, 30*(1), 5–17.

Saikia, Y. (2014). Ayub Khan and modern Islam: Transforming citizens and the nation in Pakistan. *South Asia: Journal of South Asian Studies, 37*(2), 292–305.

Solomon, T. (2014). Affective investment in the war on terror. In M. Bentley & J. Holland (Eds.), *Obama's foreign policy: Ending the war on terror.* Series. Abingdon: Routledge.

Weedon, C. (1997). *Feminist practice and poststructuralist theory.* Oxford: Blackwell.

World Economic Forum. (2016). *Global gender gap report.* Geneva: World Economic Forum. Retrieved May 10, 2016, from http://reports.weforum.org/global-gender-gap-report-2015/.

Yong, T. T. (2005). *The Garrison state: Military, government and society in colonial Punjab, 1849–1947.* New Delhi: Sage.

Yusuf, H. (2012). *Sectarian violence: Pakistan's greatest security threat? Norwegian peacebuilding resource centre.* Retrieved February 26, 2013, from http://www.peacebuilding.no/var/ezflow_site/storage/original/application/949e7f9b2db9f947c95656e5b54e389e.pdf.

Yusuf, M. (2011). A society on the precipice? Examining the prospects of youth radicalisation in Pakistan. In M. Kugelman & R. M. Hathaway (Eds.), *Reaping the dividend: Overcoming Pakistan's demographic challenges* (pp. 76–105). Washington, DC: Woodrow Wilson International Center for Scholars.

5

Senegal: Muslim Youth Identities in a Secular Nation

Abstract This chapter presents an analysis of the ways youth in Senegal articulated their identities with respect to nation, religion and gender. Identity was understood as an ongoing discursive production involving differentiation against constitutive 'others'. Youth's identity constructions were explored through focus group discussions which gave space for their identity work. The focus groups involved 75 youth (35 females and 40 males) in Dakar and its vicinity. Forty-seven of these were Muslim and 28 were Christian. Senegal is a predominantly Muslim country which became a secular republic after gaining independence from France in the 1960s. The analysis highlights the complex ways in which nation, gender and religion intersected in youth's identity constructions. Youth's narratives show how their national and religious affiliations were sutured together, in contrast to the strong separation of nation and religion that is assumed within some understandings of the modern 'secular' nation. The entanglement of their religious and national belongings was also integral to the ways their nation was defined against its colonial past, with Sufi leaders in particular being singled out as national heroes for having unified the nation in opposition to the colonial other. Senegalese youth further proclaimed the distinctiveness of Senegalese or

'African' Islam. Its fusions with traditional customs and beliefs allowed Islam to take root in multiple syncretic forms across Senegal. This syncretism and 'Africanity' were valued, and constructed in opposition to the other of the 'diabolized' or 'jihadist' Islam that youth felt was practised in other contexts, such as the Middle East, or Afghanistan. However in relation to gender, considerable tensions were evident in how this intersected with youth's discourses of nation, religion and ethnicity. Within national, religious and sometimes ethic discourses, powerful gender hierarchies emerged, which often left women constructed in a subordinated position. Each of these discourses (nation, religion and ethnicity) could be recruited individually to justify unequal gender norms. Their power is intensified when recruited together, and conjoined with potentially negative associations with modernity as an imposition from the Global North. Although contested in female focus groups in particular, promises of equality that are supposedly at the heart of republican values prove evanescent.

5.1 Introduction and Context

Senegal is located on the Atlantic coast of Sub-Saharan Africa and is a Muslim-majority country, with around 94% of its people being Muslim, alongside a small minority of Christians. It became a nation-state after gaining independence from France in 1960. Its republican democracy was based on the French constitution and proclaims its secular character. While public protest has sometimes descended into violence, Senegal has not seen the kinds of political instability experienced by many of its African neighbours. In contrast to the case of Pakistan, discussed in the previous chapter, transfer of power has taken place without military coups. After another rotation of political leadership in the last presidential and legislative elections in 2012, the country gained international acclaim as a 'beacon of African democracy' (BBC News Africa 2012). In contemporary times, when Islam can be demonised and constructed as inimical to secular principles of government, the intersection of nation, religion, ethnicity and gender in youth's identity constructions becomes especially interesting to explore in the Senegalese context.

5 Senegal: Muslim Youth Identities in a Secular Nation

The Chapter first addresses the Senegal context in more detail. It then provides some expansions on the research methodology related to the Senegal case, building on the overall depiction of the research in Chap. 3, before turning to the analysis of youth's constructions of their identities in relation to nation, religion and gender.

5.2 The Senegalese Context

The Republic of Senegal is located in the Sahel region on the Atlantic coast of West Africa. Neighbouring states are Mauritania, Mali, Guinea-Bissau, Guinea and Gambia, the latter being an enclave in the south of the country around the River Gambia (see Fig. 5.1). With a surface area of 196,722 km², it has an estimated population of 14,967,000 and an annual population growth rate of 2.8% (UNESCO 2016). Although a

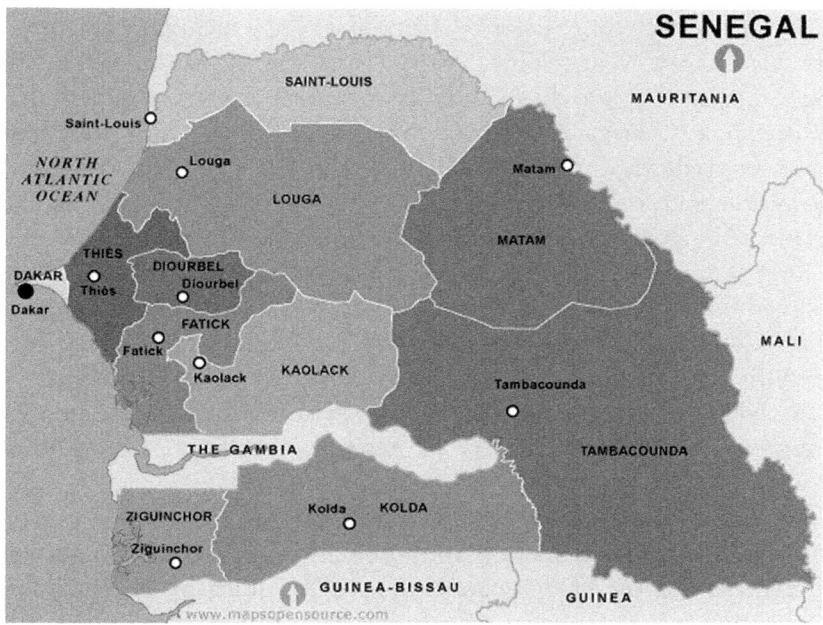

Fig. 5.1 Map of Senegal.
Source http://www.mapsopensource.com/senegal-regions-map.html

lower middle-income country, its economy remains vulnerable to poor harvests, a factor contributing to what has been seen as a low average annual economic growth of 3.3% over the last 10 years, in comparison with 6% for Sub-Saharan Africa as a whole (World Bank 2014). Senegal is ranked in 114th place out of 124 countries in the Human Development Index (World Economic Forum 2015b). UNESCO (2016) report that 29.6% of Senegal's population live below the poverty line (earning less than $1.25 a day). Like many African countries, the Senegalese population is young: 20.5% are between the ages of 15 and 24, and 63% are aged under 24. The youth unemployment rate is reported as being 12.7%, this being 19% for females and 8.3% for males (CIA 2014).

Politically, Senegal became an independent state in 1960. Although different European countries had competed for trade along Senegal's coast from the fifteenth century onwards, it was ruled by France from 1895 as part of French West Africa (Afrique Occidentale Française or AOF). This vast 'super-colony' (Conklin 1997) included contemporary Mauritania, Mali, Guinea, Ivory Coast, Benin, Burkino Faso and Niger. Dakar was latterly AOF's administrative capital, although representation of Senegal's colonial subjects was limited; only four *communes* (a territorial unit within French administration) could elect a *député* (electoral representative) to sit in the French National Assembly in Paris. Alongside the development of commerce, the notion of a 'civilizing mission' was integral to France's colonial expansion, based on the assumed 'superiority of French culture and the perfectibility of humankind' (Conklin 1997). However, Conklin also points to the fragility of the AOF's administrative structures, so that indirect rule through local intermediaries was expedient to its French administrators. These local intermediaries included leaders of Senegal's Muslim (Sufi) brotherhoods.

Under the leadership of its first president, Leopold Senghor, independent Senegal proclaimed its commitment to secular republican government, taking the French constitution as its model. In Senegal's new constitution, political parties were barred from appealing to racial, ethnic, religious, linguistic, gender or regional identities (Hartman 2010). Invocations of Senegal's 'secular' democratic principles in contemporary media suggest these be central to the national imaginary, one recent example being Gaye's (2015) critique of ex-President Wade's continued presence on Senegal's political stage. In this, he attacks the role of 'familial or amicable ties', arguing that they have 'no place in a republic, where issues between citizens must be dealt with along republican principals, based on the equality of all before the law, each worthy of equal dignity and respect'. From a recent interview study of Senegalese political figures, Hartman (2010) suggests that ethnic and linguistic identifications remain insignificant in Senegalese politics. However, the situation with respect to Senegal's Sufi brotherhoods is visibly more complex in relation to a declared commitment to secularism, as we see below.

Since independence, Senegal has become known for the political stability of its multi-party democracy. While Senghor's successor was a political appointee, later presidents came to power through democratic elections. The elections of 2000 and 2012 also saw rotations in the political party of those in power. All the same, Senegal's democracy has sometimes seemed close to failing, with public protests over issues such as corruption, constitutional abuse, high taxes and youth underemployment spilling over at times into public unrest. Nevertheless, in the most recent presidential elections, transition of power from Abdoulaye Wade to Macky Sall did finally take place through the ballot box, leading US Secretary of State Hillary Clinton to applaud Senegal as a 'beacon of African democracy' (BBC News Africa 2012). Youth were extensively involved in the street protests which accompanied both the 2000 and the 2012 elections. Senegal's hip-hop culture and rapper groups such as '*Y'en a Marre*' *(We've had enough)* have been described as offering new spaces for youth politics, disrupting Senegal's 'strongly hierarchical age-power system' and 'gerontocratic traditions of public discourse' (Fredericks 2014:7). Despite its reputation as an exemplary African democracy, recurrent eruptions of youth protest are nevertheless suggestive of a culture that is resistant to change and where age relations remain important.

A further important dimension of Wade's presidencies was a more overt politicisation of Senegal's Sufi brotherhoods (Mbow 2009; Hartman 2010). While constituted as a secular democracy, Cruise

O'Brien (2003) points to their long-standing influence in political spheres, both during colonial rule and after independence. As shown above (Gaye 2015), the secular principles of Senegal's constitution remain a live issue, which makes the place of religion in the Senegalese nation-state particularly interesting, given the assumed separation of government and religion that can be supposed as part of secularism (Asad 2003).

In terms of religion, the great majority of the Senegalese population (94%) are Muslims, alongside a small percentage of Christians who are predominantly Roman Catholics (5%), and others who follow 'indigenous' beliefs (CIA 2014). Historically, Islam arrived in this region through Berber trade routes with North Africa, a Berber Muslim religious retreat reportedly having been established on an island on the Senegal River around 1040. Today, Muslims in Senegal mostly belong to four Sufi 'brotherhoods', these being the Qadiriyya, Tijaniyya, Mouride and Layenne. Two of these, the Tijaniyya and the Mouride, have had defining roles in the ways Islam is understood and practised in Senegal, as well as being influential in politics (Cruise O'Brien 2003).

Given their influential roles, the distinct histories and characteristics of these Sufi brotherhoods merit some brief elaboration. They are typically led by a holy man or *cheikh*. He is attributed saintly status by his followers, or disciples, who look to him for spiritual guidance and grace (*baraka*). The Qadiriyya originated in the eighth century in Baghdad and was the earliest brotherhood to appear in Senegal during the eighteenth century. The Tijaniyya also originated outside of Senegal, in Morocco. In contrast, the Mouride originated in Senegal, having been founded in Touba in 1880 by Cheikh Amadu Bamba (Cruise O'Brien 2003; Diouf 2002). The Layenne are a much smaller sect, more localised in an area to the north of Dakar. They are known for their highly syncretic form of Islam that combines Sufism with animist practices (Laborde 1995).

The influence of the Sufi brotherhoods in the economic, social and political spheres in Senegal has also been significant in both the past and the present. The Mourides in particular were central in the development of groundnut farming, supported by the organised labour of the brotherhood's *talibés* (a Wolof word for *disciples*). Mamdani (1996) writes of a notable Mouride *cheikh* having a thousand *talibés* working for him. When in the latter years of colonial administration the French moved to a dual legal system, the Mourides were favoured intermediaries between colonial administrators and local peoples (Cruise O'Brien 2003; Diouf 2002; Harrison 1988). Cruise O'Brien (2003:193) suggests that this allowed the Sufi brotherhoods in Senegal to provide 'an unusually effective link between state and society'.

Ethnically, the Senegalese population is diverse. The main ethnic groups in Senegal are Wolof (44.5%), Pular (or Peul, this being local name for the Fulani, a group that spans West Africa, many of who are nomadic) (25.2%), Serer (13.8%) and Diola (5%) (Diallo 2010). Wolof is the first language of around two-thirds of the population and the second language for a further quarter. This means that those speaking Wolof extend well beyond the group who would claim a Wolof ethnic identity. Although spoken by only around 20% of the population as either a first or a second language, Senegal retained French as the official language of government (Diallo 2010). This has been contested at different times but retained in the interest of not privileging one language group over another. In general, Senegalese society has not been marked by significant regional tensions or violence. Cruise O'Brien (2003:166–167) attributes this to the influence of the religious brotherhoods, whereby turning to local religious leaders (*marabouts*) was a more likely response when identities came under pressure, in ways that led to a blurring of ethnic divisions. Ethnic and religious boundaries do not necessarily intersect, so while ethnic groups such as the Wolof or the Lébou are largely Muslim, others such as Serer or Diola include both Christians and Muslims.

Historically, Senegal's education system followed a French model. After completing primary school and middle school, pupils who successfully gain the *Brevet de Fin d'Etudes Moyennes* (Certificate of Lower Secondary Education) then attend secondary school (or *lycée*) for 3 years, preparing for the Baccalaureate. This is required for higher education entry (International Bureau of Education 2010).

Although the right to education is enshrined in Senegal's 2001 constitution, and primary and lower secondary education is supposedly free and compulsory, IBE (2010) points to the Senegalese authorities' open acknowledgement that they cannot provide this to all children. Alongside the public education system, there is an expanding private education system, in which 14% of pupils are enrolled (UNESCO 2014). These include Catholic schools which are recognised for their high success rates. There are also different forms of Koranic schools, some of which are seen as being responsible for the numbers of child alms-seekers in the streets of Dakar, *les talibés* being the term used to describe them. Although this means 'disciple' in Wolof, the French term for them is debased to *mendiant* (*beggar*). For primary education, Senegal's gross enrolment rate (GER) was 86% for 2011, which is the ninth lowest in the world (UNESCO 2014). Moreover, only 60% of those enrolling reach the last grade of primary school. Educational outcomes are also very different for males and females, with the gap widening yet further between rich and poor. UNESCO (2014) report, for example, that only 20% of rural young women could read in everyday situations compared with 65% of urban young men. The youth literacy rate (15–25 years, 2005–2013) is the lowest of our four country cases at 56%—this being 61% for male youth, but only 51% for female youth (UNESCO 2016).

As elsewhere, Senegal's higher education system continues to expand, with two new public universities under construction in Dakar and Kaolack (Marshall 2015). With a capacity of 30,000 students each, these are intended to relieve congestion at the University of Cheikh Anta Diop (UCAD), the oldest university in Senegal, where many of the research participants studied. At the time of the research, UCAD had recently reopened, after a period of closure following a student's death during police interventions to quell student protests about non-payment of grants and overcrowding. Gender inequalities are also significant in tertiary education, with six women enrolled for every ten men (WEF 2015a).

In relation to gender, as a democratic republic, Senegal's constitution formally espouses the principle of equality for all citizens. It has been a signatory to the United Nations (1979) Convention on the Elimination of All Forms of Discrimination against Women (CEDAW) since 1980. However, it is ranked only 72nd out of 145 countries in the 2015 Global Gender Gap rankings (WEF 2015a). As noted above, it performs poorly in education, particularly in girls' education. Its WEF gender gap ranking is higher for political empowerment of women. In 2010, Senegal made it mandatory for men and women to be equally represented as electoral candidates. In 2012, women's representation was doubled, to 64 out of its 150 national assembly representatives (*députés*). However, the law was heavily contested and not fully observed. Sow (2014) notes, for example, that Touba's electoral list contained no women (this town is symbolically important, as the birthplace of the founder of the Mouride brotherhood).

After independence, Senegal also moved to reform the many different customary codes that were in place during the indirect rule of colonial times, aiming to create a modern, unified legal system for the nation. Nevertheless, Camara (2007) is highly critical of its 1972 Family Law. While overriding customary laws, she finds it anomalous in a supposedly secular state that Senegal's Family Law gave recognition to the Qu'ran for issues which were of a 'truly religious nature' (p. 788). She traces this to the need for politicians to take account of the views of the Sufi brotherhoods when developing the new legal codes. By introducing elements from both Shari'a law and French civil codes, she suggests that the reforms produced a more patriarchal legal system than before.

Overall, while Senegal's constitution holds a commitment to secular republican ideals, it seems clear also that the Sufi brotherhoods have been influential not only in shaping Senegal's religious culture, but also in socio-economic and political realms. While Senegal has a complex ethnic mix, the literature does not suggest ethnic tensions to be important. The opposite seems to be the case, however, in relation to gender, where significant inequalities are in evidence and where legislative attempts to address these have been openly defied in locations of high symbolic significance to Senegal's Muslims.

5.3 The Research in Senegal

The case study methodology was described in an overall way in Chap. 3. This section provides further expansions relevant to the Senegal case.

Table 5.1 The Senegal sample

	Male		Female		Total
	HE	Non-HE	HE	Non-HE	
Muslim	16	8	15	8	47
Christian	11	5	6	6	28
Total	27	13	21	14	75

A total of 18 focus groups and two individual interviews were conducted in November 2014 with 75 Muslim and Christian youth, as indicated in Table 5.1. Overall, 35 female and 40 male participants were involved, 47 Muslims and 28 Christians. All interviews were conducted in Dakar or its vicinity. Focus groups were arranged separately with males and females, Muslims and Christians, those in higher education and those not in higher education. This latter group included some who were still in school and a smaller number who had left school, these being a mix of employed and unemployed youth. As reported in Table 3.2, the Senegalese sample therefore consisted of 64 youth in education and 11 out of education. The numbers in the focus groups ranged from one to six. As noted in Chap. 3, the educated status of Christians contributed to the relatively lower representation of Christian youth outside of higher education. Two focus groups (one male and one female) were also conducted in Yoff, an area to the north of Dakar with strong associations with the Layenne brotherhood. These were all Muslim participants and included higher education students and school pupils. The local contacts who arranged these two focus groups felt that no Christians lived in that area.

Acronyms are used to attribute quotations from the different focus groups, these being FMH, FCH, MMH, MCH, FMnH, FCnH, MMnH and MCnH. These acronyms indicate the gender, religion and education status of the participants, in that order. In other words, M and F at the start of the acronym indicate male and female; Muslim or Christian religion is indicated by the second character; and finally, H indicates higher education participants and nH those not in higher education. This last group (27 in total) was mostly in school, although a smaller number had left school and were in employment (6) or were unemployed (5). Two focus groups for each category were conducted, and this is indicated by the numerals 1 and 2 at the end of the acronym. Thus, FMH1 indicates the first of two focus groups with female youth who were Muslim and in higher education. MCnH2 indicates the second focus group with Christian males not in higher education. The two sex-segregated focus groups conducted in Yoff involved a mix of participants who were Muslim in different stages of their education, and these are indicated by FM Yoff and MM Yoff.

The interviews drew on the interview guide described in Chap. 3, which was translated into French. Each interview began with a review of the information sheet, as described in Chap. 3, and a request to the participants to complete the bio-data sheet. These data were analysed to develop the depiction of the participants presented below.

In relation to participants' age, it was important to accommodate local understandings of the concept of 'youth' and participants' self-identifications with this as a social category. In other words, if after being approached by the research assistants they agreed to take part, this was understood to imply their self-identification as a youth. The mean age across the participants was 24; this included a small number of participants (4) who were in their thirties. The age range was 16–35, so all fell within the African Union (2006) definition of youth (see Chap. 2).

The majority of participants were approached through two higher education students who were known to Barbara from her previous research in Senegal. These research assistants were both female Muslims in higher education in Dakar. Both had family connections with Casamance, a region in the south of Senegal, and were of Diola ethnicity. Both spoke French and Wolof. They drew on their personal networks to identify relevant participants and also sought out new contacts. Interviews were conducted over a period of 2 weeks, during which they devoted an extensive amount of their time to the research. The two focus groups conducted in Yoff were arranged and hosted by the local leaders of a youth cultural exchange organisation.

In terms of participants' origins, approximately half reported they were from Dakar, with a further quarter from Ziguinchor or Casamance, the area that the research assistants were from themselves. Other locations cited included St. Louis, Thies, Kaolack, Fatick and Touba. The bio-data sheet also asked for participants' religious sect or brotherhood. Forty of the 47 Muslim participants identified a brotherhood; none identified a sect (i.e. Sunni or Shi'a). Half of the 28 Christian participants identified a sect, all being Catholic. In a context where Catholicism is the predominant Christian sect, but a minority religion, an internal differentiation within Christianity is likely to be less salient than that of Muslim versus Christian. There was much more differentiation among the Muslim participants with respect to their brotherhood affiliations: 15 were Mouride, 20 Tijania, 4 Layenne, and 1 Ibadou. As for ethnicity, 17 reported this to be Wolof, 13 Sérère, 12 Diola, 8 Lébou and 7 Mankagne, 5 Peul, with the remainder being Manjack, Mandang, Socé, Toucouleur, Bainouk, Creole or Halpulaar. Overall, this was a highly diverse set of participants therefore, as one might expect in a capital city which has seen significant rural–urban migration, as well as having Senegal's oldest and most reputed university. No focus group was homogeneous with respect to brotherhood or to ethnicity, which may have contributed to a flattening of reported differences—we will also see below how different respondents invoked the principles of secular republicanism, which typically eschews recognition of particularities, that is to say, ethnic, religious, gender or other differences.

While no claims are made about how representative this might be, analysis of the biodata showed a substantial level of religious homogeneity across the families of the participants, for both Muslims and Christians. At the same time, marriage between Christian and Muslims was not impossible, there being three instances of this across the participant group. Of these, two participants (one Christian and one Muslim) had taken the religion of their mother. Another had followed the father in adopting Christianity. There was also some fluidity in the Sufi brotherhood one might belong to when compared to parental affiliations. So five Muslim participants (12.5% of those who identified a brotherhood) had espoused a brotherhood that was not that of their parents. Different brotherhood affiliations between the parents were also reported for a further eight participants (20% of those identifying a brotherhood). Overall, while brotherhood affiliations were clearly significant markers of identity for many Muslim participants, these affiliations were dynamic, rather than normatively ascribed.

The biodata entries for parental ethnicities also showed 21 instances of inter-ethnic marriage (28% of the 75 participants); all but three of these participants identified with their father's ethnicity. Ethnic boundaries seemed to have a varying degree of porosity with respect to the association of religion and ethnicity. For example, while the Wolof, Lébou and Peul were entirely Muslim, other ethnic groups such as Diola and Sérère were a mix of Muslim and Christian. Fifteen different languages were reported across the participant group as a first or second language, with Wolof as the majority first language (55 of 75 participants, or 73%). Only two participants did not identify Wolof as a first or second language. French was spoken by 6 participants (8%) as a first language (five of these being Christians) and by 59 participants (79%) as a first or second language.

Most interviews were conducted mainly in French, although Wolof was predominantly used in interviews with Muslim participants not in higher education. The two research assistants provided valuable support in interpreting between Wolof and French, and particularly where Wolof was the preferred language, were largely responsible for the conduct of the interviews. They also provided valuable expansions upon issues raised in the interviews, both within the interview conversations, in debriefs after the interviews, and more generally our working together during the two weeks of the fieldwork. The majority of the interviews were recorded, transcribed and translated into English by a Senegalese translator who also spoke Wolof and French. The contact through whom the two focus groups in Yoff were arranged translated those into French and transcribed them. Excerpts from these two interviews were selectively translated into English by the case study researcher, Barbara Crossouard. Both translators and transcribers also provided helpful expansions on events and personalities identified in the focus groups.

We now turn to our analysis of the Senegal case study data, beginning with the discourses through which youth constructed their identities in relation to nation, then turning to religion, followed by gender. We do not imply through this structure that these discourses are discrete and separate from each other. We point throughout to their intersections and will explore when turning to gender in particular how their intersection may compound difference and disadvantage, at the same time as being a critical site of contestation.

5.4 Imagining the Nation: New Formations of the Secular

Overall, a sense of Senegalese nationality and belonging had much significance for the Senegalese youth participants. It was the most frequently identified aspect of their identities in the bio-data sheet, being the first descriptor used by 30% of male participants and 37% of female participants. Moreover, when the second descriptor is taken into account, their national affiliations figured in the top two identifiers for 60% of females and 42% of males.

Youth's affiliations to Senegal as a nation were at one level a matter-of-fact issue of having been born in Senegalese territory and having Senegalese parents—an unremarkable part of one's being, a 'naturalized facticity' (Butler 1990). When encouraged to expand on different aspects of their national belongings, and the markers of difference from other nations through which their sense of nationhood was constructed, youth took up this discussion with enthusiasm and many spontaneous expressions of pride, which would have been intensified because they were responding to a non-Senegalese outsider and by the circulation of these affects within the focus group.

> I feel very proud to be a Senegalese. It creates in me a feeling of love for this country [..] it's our homeland. Everything we have, we have it here, so we fight to help the country to move forward. (FMH1)

Across the interviews, being Senegalese was bound up with a sense of distinction. The Senegalese were described as being admired by other nations, for example as '*superior*' or '*more intelligent*'. Particular characteristics were recurrently invoked in an imagined ideal of the Senegalese. These included being tolerant, peace-loving, pious, respectful, well-disciplined,

5   Senegal: Muslim Youth Identities in a Secular Nation   141

hard-working, well-educated, community-minded, hospitable and open to others—Senegal was above all the country of *'teranga'*.[1] The counterpoint of this ideal—its 'other'—readily emerged, however, when participants shared aspects of the Senegalese character of which they were not proud. This included the ease with which this Senegalese superiority was assumed, the weak work ethic of the Senegalese and a propensity to look for easy profit, including by those in public office:

> [The Senegalese] have a tendency to think that they are superior to others, that a misfortune [such as the Ebola outbreak] will never happen to them […] they often like spending the whole day idling, eating a good "Thièbou diène", the national dish, taking tea and saying 'God is good', 'God is good', the miracle will come. But it is said that 'God helps him who helps himself', you have to work to earn something. (FMH1)

> … the great majority of Senegalese want to earn money without working. And it often happens; we often hear it on the radio, about embezzlements; people who have positions of responsibility, but who confuse national interests with their own pockets. (MCnH)

Similar concerns were also voiced about corruption in public office, most frequently in relation to politics, but also in the military and the police:

> What I deplore most in Senegal is corruption. Corruption in every domain… politicians who are corrupt, the military, the police. That is really painful for me. (MMH1)

The constitutive 'others' against which Senegalese superiority was constructed were also evident in participants' depictions of how one would recognise a Senegalese. Although sometimes described as difficult to portray, this was readily related to range of embodiments, for example Senegalese ways of dressing, their language and their manners, and especially their *'correctness'* in comparison with other African nationalities, or groups who were characterised as *'niakk'*, a term that was recognised by a female Muslim as *'very discriminatory'*:

'Niakk', that's the Ivoirians, other nationalities.. Burkinabe…everything that's a bit in the sub-region, all that is Ghanaians, Nigerians, Burkinabe, etc. Maybe, well, not Malians.. and Gambians also. (FMH1)

When probed about the meaning of *niakk* (a Wolof word), this was someone who lived in the bush, beyond the pale of civilisation, indeed someone '*who was not civilized*'. A further term that reflected more internal as opposed to external ethnic hierarchies was '*Ndring*', which was explained as a derogatory term directed towards the Peuls and the Toucouleur. The construction of Senegalese distinction depended then upon this hierarchical positioning against others, both external and internal. Some participants critiqued these ethnic stereotypes and the paradoxes that this gave rise to within the national imaginary, for example how they sat in contradiction to claims that the Senegalese had a strong sense of community solidarity, or to Senegal's claim to speak for the peoples of Africa as one people, which we elaborate upon more below. As one female Muslim put it:

… we talk about African unity but yet there is discrimination between us. (FMH1)

These were the more elite participants however. It was not always the case that the participants showed awareness of these paradoxes, as shown below when we explore youth's responses to questions about ethnicity.

When prompted about what language(s) distinguished the Senegalese, their way of speaking both Wolof and French was cited, including by those whose background was from other ethnicities such as Diola. As Diallo (2010) suggested, Wolof has become strongly associated with being Senegalese, and its use extends beyond its ethnic group. However, it is only one of many local languages, raising questions about the positioning of the speakers of other minority languages. While French is spoken by a minority, it remains the language of power and distinction. That French was cited as a marker of distinction points to the elite, highly educated status of many of the participants.

5 Senegal: Muslim Youth Identities in a Secular Nation

At the same time, while 'Frenchness' could sometimes be recruited as a marker of distinction in youth's discourses of national identity, it was also a powerful counterpoint *against* which youth defined their national imaginary. Thus, a defining historical event for both Muslims and Christians was Senegal's independence from France. The importance of this is also reflected by the identification by both Muslims and Christians of the first president, Leopold Senghor (a Catholic Christian of Serer ethnicity) as an important national figure for the part he had played in realising Senegal's independence from France. Very few national heroines were identified. This invariably required some prompting, while one participant explicitly commented *you have to know that women didn't have a major role to play in the history of Africa* (MCH2). However, a notable exception was a female leader (Aline Sitou Diatta) who was singled out by both Muslims and Christians for her resistance to French colonisation and agricultural reforms.

The identification of these figures shows that the struggle of Senegal against its colonial rulers clearly remained important in the collective history of the nation held by these youth. Furthermore, Senegal's significance as leaders in the struggle against colonial powers was often extended in the attributions of both Christian and Muslim youth to an imaginary which encompassed (West) Africa and 'black culture' more generally:

> … it's a country which has distinguished itself throughout history, mostly the history of black western Africa. I think of slavery, I think of colonization and the role our country played in all these processes. And also when resisting anti-globalization and neo-colonialism and all that follows, my country hasn't always been an easy ground for the colonists. [..] Knowing that our leaders of that period were the great architects of independence in West Africa. We are proud of that, we are proud of the role we play in the African Union, that's it, this republican spirit. (MCH2)

In addition to this association of Senegal's distinctiveness with republicanism (see also below), youth's narratives often portrayed Senegal as a leader of Africa in ways that foregrounded resistance to hierarchical

North–South relations and the supposed superiority of the Global North:

> He [Senghor] went to Europe and he represented us well, he was the first of his kind in that respect, and who showed, contrary to what people tend to think, that Africa is not always lagging behind, so that we can sit round the table and be proud to be African. (FM Yoff)

Senegal's leadership in organisations such as the Francophonie (an international commonwealth of French speaking countries) or the African Union was also recruited to claim distinction, both in contemporary times and historically. Leopold Senghor and Cheikh Anta Diop, in particular, were cited for developing new understandings of African history, so that Africans no longer had to accept history as written by *'white people [who] had said what suited them'*:

> They fought to make black people and Africans believe that you can become emancipated by yourselves, that you don't need the white men. Between us, we are strong enough; we are intelligent, we are capable enough to make things work. [..] They fought for the recognition of a black cultural identity. (FMH1)

The concepts of negritude and '*Africanité*' (Pan-Africanism) were invoked with pride, asserting a positive, shared vision of black/African cultural identity. This implies that the national imaginary involved both a construction of distinction in opposition to other African countries and the construction of Senegal as a leader of pan-African sensibilities, positions that are not without inherent tensions. Unsurprisingly, these positions were reconciled differently by different respondents. For example, while speaking French well could be recruited as a marker of distinction (FMH1), another participant (MMH1) criticised Senghor for having privileged French over local languages, while another (MMH2) saw Senegal's commitment to the Francophonie as misplaced.

A further important aspect of Senegal's distinction was youth's pride in its successful democracy—even if a counterpoint to this was the frequent concern across all groups about political corruption and poor

5 Senegal: Muslim Youth Identities in a Secular Nation

governance described above. However, both Muslim and Christian participants pointed to the stability of their country, contrasting this with other African states.

> It's especially the stability there is in this country that makes us proud to be Senegalese [..] it is a country that really stands out for its democracy. (FM Yoff)
>
> ... we don't have coup d'états, we don't have genocides, we don't have the kinds of civil wars that are destroying Africa – we've been spared that until now, that's something we should be proud of. (FMH1)

Youth were also proud of their defence of their constitution during the recent 2012 elections:

> What makes me most proud to be Senegalese has to be June 23 [..] when the whole population turned out in the streets to defend the constitution, to defend their rights. [..] all the Senegal people stood up to say no to a third term by the President. I was proud that young people could go into the street to say no for democracy to prevail. (MCH1)

Some specifically raised the republican character of the Senegalese constitution, articulating this as part of their pride in being Senegalese, for example *to have a nation and a republic and to be proud, and to belong to it* (MCH2). Another pointed to the influence of the French constitution on the Senegalese constitution, recruiting this with pride in the construction of her national affiliations. The concept of secularism was also invoked in some interviews, although in ways that suggested tolerance or co-mingling of different religions, rather than a banishing of religion (Badran 2009), as in the following response to the question of how one might distinguish between Muslim and Christian Senegalese:

> ... you cannot recognize the Muslim and the Christian here in Senegal, because we have the same type of dressing, because Senegal is a secular country. Meaning Muslims and Christians have blended everything, together with the animists. [..] There is no differentiation. (MMnH1)

Another female Muslim participant drew on the concept of secularism to explain why she would relate more readily to a Senegalese Christian, rather than a Muslim abroad:

> … with the secularism which prevails currently in Senegal, we see that there is really a perfect harmony. (FMH2)

A sense of the need for some separation of religion and politics was occasionally articulated, by Christians and Muslims. For example, when a male Christian identified the founder of the Mouride brotherhood as an important national figure, another youth in this group objected to this, pointing out that that he was a religious rather than political leader (MCnH2). While many Muslim participants identified religious leaders as significant national figures (see below), some Muslim participants constructed a boundary between religion and politics. For example, when asked if being Muslim made a difference for being Senegalese, this female student responded:

> … being a Senegalese it's not the same as a religious identity. There is actually a difference. We are religious, I am Christian or Muslim, I practice like everybody else, it's good. But that doesn't stop me from being Senegalese, that doesn't stop me from having ambitions, to do my projects and all that. (FMH1)

She also expressed criticism of the influence of the religious brotherhoods in Senegal's elections. When asked whether her objections related to any formal constitutional principle, she related this instead to a principle of equality of all citizens:

> We have preconceived ideas that it is the constitution, whereas it's not the case. But normally, to my mind, the religious power or guides must not be implicated. Because, certainly they are religious guides, but they are citizens like the others before all. They must not have an influence in the decisions to be taken, in principle. (FMH1)

With respect to religion and republican principles of equality, the term 'secular' was sometimes explicitly invoked in the interviews. However, this sat well for Muslim participants with their religious identities:

> [Being Muslim], it's about humanity, really universal values, democracy. Because Islam, contrary to [inaudible], it is an open, tolerant religion, which inculcates values such as sharing, like respect, like democracy. (MMH2)

With respect to ethnicity and republican understandings of equality, ethnic differences were not identified as a cause of friction. Indeed, at times, questions about differences between groups, such as by nation and ethnicity, were resisted. For example, one male Muslim participant from an elite background stated *it doesn't matter the colour, the nationality, the sex*, preferring instead to consider himself a *citizen of the world*. As discussed in Chap. 2, claims to cosmopolitan citizenship often reflect a relatively privileged social class position (Calhoun 2008). However, participants often could not say what ethnic group key Senegalese figures belonged to, suggesting that this was relatively unimportant for them. On the whole, ethnic relations were described as being good-humoured, with potential tensions flattened in favour of national unity:

> There is also the sense of solidarity in the country which allows a friendly banter between different ethnic groups and which consolidates peace. I think peace is important. (FM Yoff)

Questions on what ethnicity one might want or not want nevertheless prompted much laughter, and some particularly sharp comments about the Peuls, for example as '*wicked and racist*' (FCnH) or as '*herd robbers*' (MMH). These comments did not necessarily demonstrate the same level of critical awareness as those discussed earlier, where participants were able to identify themselves the contradictions between the imaginary of the nation and the invocation of ethnic stereotypes as 'others' using terms such as '*ndring*' and '*niakk*'. This hierarchical othering would seem to sit in some tension in other words with the claim that the Senegalese people lived in peaceful harmony.

We revisit now the ways the national imaginary related to participants' religious identities. The significant national figures and events identified by Muslim youth included political figures such as Senghor, but very often involved religious leaders, with the founder of the

Mouride brotherhood most frequently singled out. The excerpt below shows how this Sufist religious icon was bound up with this Muslim participant's national identity:

> Serigne Touba, the great marabout of Touba, was a defender of the rights of the Senegalese people. At the same time he was a religious guide, but he also defended the Senegalese people culturally speaking. Because he didn't want Senegalese people to get confused with the modernity European people tended to instil in us. And he defended himself, but peacefully. He did not use arms, and yet he was harmed. He was forced to go into exile in Gabon for 8 months. He came back to Senegal, but during this entire struggle, he led a peaceful struggle. (MMnH2)

An important constitutive element in this narrative is the positioning of the religious leader as a leader of local opposition to the violence of the colonial period, and its particular form of modernity—while the (modern) language of rights is taken up in the excerpt above, this is turned against the injustices of the colonial powers. As Chatterjee (1993) pointed out, in its emergence as a nation, the writing of a national culture is central, in opposition to the culture of the colonial power. A key part of the Muslim brotherhood's significance was therefore in having produced a particularly African version of Islam, which was central to the definition of the nation in a relation of opposition to the previous colonial power and its understandings of modernity, as well as in a relation of difference to the Islam of the Middle East. The particular characteristics of this are explored more in the discussion of religious discourses below.

However, somewhat in contradiction to Chatterjee (1993), who describes nations emerging from colonisation as trying to emulate the economic, scientific and technological prowess of the West, past and contemporary Mouride religious leaders were also praised for the particular ways they had contributed to economic and industrial development of the nation—a contemporary Mouride leader being described as a billionaire, with significant investments in agriculture and mining, who employed *'thousands of youngsters'* (FMH1). So for many Muslim participants, these leaders were central to the collective imaginary of the nation, having contributed in a significant way to its delineation as it emerged from French colonial rule. The assertion of the nation involved an assertion of its difference from France, and intrinsic to this was the significance of Islam—in particular its own version of 'African Islam'—within the national imaginary. The conjoining of religious discourses with discourses of national identity was not without tensions, however, particularly in relation to gender. As one female Muslim pointed out, when arguments were made for change in gender relations, this could readily be equated with anti-religious and/or pro-Western sentiments. We discuss this in more detail when addressing the intersections of gender with nation and religion below.

In conclusion, youth discourses of their nation reverberated with notions of distinction, sometimes in comparison with other African nations, but also as their leader in opposition to the ex-colonial power, or more widely in opposition to *les blancs,* and their particular ethos of modernity. However, modernity was also embraced in many youth narratives, with Senegal's democratic values and practices being held up as markers of distinction, in some cases associated with the particular secular or republican character of the Senegalese constitution. Ethnic and language differences were recognised, but were mostly constructed as involving good natured 'banter', and were not represented as a source of internal tension in the focus groups. Internal unity across ethnic groups was privileged instead. It was also clear that in its distinctive, local, 'African' form, Islam was integral to the imaginary of the Senegalese nation for Muslim participants.

5.5 Being a Young Senegalese Muslim: Rejection of the External Other

We now turn to consider youth's construction of their religious identities. Religion was the most important aspect of their identities for the great majority of participants, being identified as such in the closing questions of the interview by 80% of female and 70% of male participants (75% of the total). A further 5% could not place one aspect of their identity over another, and in all these cases, religion was implicated.

Both Islam and Christianity were described by their followers as religions of peace and love. However, Muslim youth recognised how this conflicted with the ways Islam was constructed elsewhere in contemporary times:

> Being a Muslim it means harmony, peace in the world. Because the main message of Muslim religion is solidarity, sharing, peace; the entire inhabitants of Earth are our brothers, are our sisters. Currently it's not very easy to identify ourselves as a Muslim, to talk about the Muslim religion, because we are the victims of some doctrines, of certain influences, of a lot of disastrous things that happen now in the world. But anyway, Islam is peace, love, sharing. (FMH1)

> The Christian religion is a religion of tolerance; I don't say that the others are religions of conflict. But the Christian religion is a religion of tolerance, of respect of the other, of acceptation of the other and of forgiveness and all. We are inculcated values that I consider very important. For me, being a Christian is, have the faith, follow the good way and live in peace. (FCH1)

Youth's emphasis on the importance of peace and harmony also led to some criticisms being voiced about conflict-affected contexts elsewhere, as in this comment on the Palestinian situation from a female Christian participant:

> … it's a country which has a link with the Muslim religion and the Christian religion. I think that they should give the good example there compared with the other nations. Look at Rome, Italy over there people do not fight. The Christians go there to venerate the Saints who are there, but despite.. how can I say, people do not create tension there. Whereas, in Palestine they are always in conflict, yet it was the country which should give the best example in the world. (FCH2)

This provoked a strong reaction from one of the female research assistants, who was more informed about Palestine's history. Nevertheless, only exceptionally was the West's involvement in wars against Islamic countries a focus of youth critique. One Muslim participant did declare that he did not want American nationality as the USA was responsible for '*sowing terror*' and making war on Islamic countries. In contrast to such critique, Americans were often admired by both Muslims and Christians, for being a stable, well-disciplined, hard-working people, with a strong sense of national and moral purpose. These affiliations seem likely to be influenced by the numbers of Senegalese—particularly Mourides—who migrated to the USA after crop failures and economic downturns faced by Senegal in the 1970s and 1980s. As a result, there is now a flourishing Mouride diaspora there and elsewhere which retains strong connections to its homeland (Diouf 2002; Mbaye and Nadhiri 2010).

The respect for an ethos of strong discipline and hard-work may have contributed to the relatively privileged position of the Christian minority in Senegal. Many of the Christian respondents spoke of the value of their education, including both the education of the home and the school, within the private education system. This Catholic education inculcated strong discipline and achieved better results than public schools.

> Catholic private schools are more serious, there is more rigour, more results, more discipline, less disturbances [..] even Muslims say it, and they have a great respect towards that religion. (MCH1)

These views also had some acknowledgement from some Muslim participants. As described above, French was more often a first or second language for Christians. Both HE and non-HE Christian focus groups were conducted in French, whereas non-HE Muslim focus groups drew extensively on Wolof. We indicated earlier how French is the language of education and of government, and although the language of the previous colonial rulers, it has remained associated with distinction by some Muslim participants, as well as with being Senegalese. Despite being a minority religion, therefore, Christian participants had a sense both of the importance of respect for others and of being respected.

When asked about being a Christian minority, one Christian participant replied that he did not feel any burden from this:

> Yes, we constitute a minority here in Senegal, but that minority is not felt, it doesn't prevent us from expressing ourselves loudly, it doesn't prevent us from saying what we think regarding the development of this country, it doesn't stop us from taking responsibilities at the highest level of the state. (MCH2)

In the same focus group, there was a hint of the sense of the superiority of Christian values; for example after lamenting the high levels of corruption in Senegalese politics, this Christian male implicitly attributed this to an absence of Christian values:

> we were talking about corruption just now, I think that if we become impregnated with those Christian values, I think that we would not be able to act in that way. (MCH2)

Being a minority religion appeared to have an effect of intensification on Christians' religious practice and its use as a reference point. While seeing the overall principles of Christian religion as universal, Senegalese Christians' religious practices were reported to be more faithful to Christian codes than those of Christians elsewhere. For example, attending mass on Sunday was compulsory (MCH2) and couples living together before marriage was prohibited, even if practiced by Christians in other countries such as Nigeria (FCH1). Young Christians in Senegal were also reported to be much more present in churches than elsewhere—it was felt that youth in France hardly went to church (MCH2). One Christian participant also found the religious observation of Christians in Senegal more assiduous than that of its Muslims (MCnH2), although this provoked a strong response from the Muslim research assistants. On the whole, however, Christians clearly had space to practice in Senegal and did not feel othered or marginalised within its society.

We turn now to consider the 'others' of the Muslim youth. As the Christians had, the Muslim participants pointed to the universality of the message of their religion. Distinct differences were identified, however, between Senegalese Islam and Islam elsewhere, sometimes involving Islam in other parts of Africa, but especially Islam practiced outside of Africa. The previous section discussed how Senegal's Muslim brotherhoods were central in defining the nation. This was in part associated with their development of a distinctively Senegalese version of Islam, which now had followers around the world. For example, the annual 'Magal' held at Touba, the birthplace of the founder of the Mouride brotherhood, was described as drawing thousands of believers from around the world, as well as emptying the streets of Dakar. Senegal's Islam was described as Sufi Islam, which was explained as being:

> very spiritual, where we meditate a lot, there are lots of incantations, where people really try to be in communication with God, so really a very mystic branch of the Muslim religion (MMH1)

As noted above, no participant identified with either Sunni or Shi'a Islamic sects, although most declared a brotherhood affiliation. Being a Muslim for many was described as involving scrupulous observation of the five pillars of Islam, that is to say recognition of there being one god (Allah), the ritual of daily prayer, alms-giving, respecting the holy month of Ramadan and the Hajj, or pilgrimage to Mecca. Beyond this, religious observance was described as being open to individual interpretation, in ways that seem to resonate with the concept of ijtihad (Mamdani 2004)

> No one can create unanimity on one thing, one single thing [..] Who will be able to say it is this, this is Islam? Every time researchers will add something more, at any moment everybody will take the right to interpret the religion in their own way. It's through this way and in this optic that we should know now what religion is, try to understand the religion, and then to try practice it. (MMH1)

Being a good Muslim primarily seemed to involve individualised work on the self, that is to say what Mamdani (2004) describes as greater jihad, in which an individual's rights to their beliefs should be respected.

For example, in the excerpt below, a female Muslim talks of having rebuked another Muslim for discrediting other faiths in an online discussion (some participants were active users of social media, others were resistant or dismissive of this). For her, Islam demanded that one showed respect for an individual's religious beliefs:

> You are Muslim, you have your religion, you believe in what you believe, but it's not a reason to discredit the others or to hurt their beliefs. I told him religion, it's the heart, it's not based in reason. So, you have to control what you're saying, if not, you might hurt others. Because each one has their beliefs. Also it is said that in the Muslim religion that you have to be reserved, that is to say, you believe in what you believe, someone believes in what they believe, ignore him, don't be there discrediting him. (FMH1)

The biodata analysis presented earlier also suggested some level of individual responsibility with respect to what brotherhood one could belong to. The interview data were rather more contradictory—while one participant spoke of being a Mouride because his parents were Mouride (MMnH1), another saw this as a more individual issue:

> I am Mouride and my brother is Layenne, while our parents are Tidianes. Everyone has their different ambitions and beliefs. (MM Yoff)

Differences in the practices of the different brotherhoods were acknowledged, as was minor disputes between them, but these were not felt to be significant by most Muslim participants. Rather than stressing their differences, a more prevalent message was the importance of the founding brotherhood leaders in leading Senegal's conversion to Islam. The peaceful ways they had done this were described as being formative for its successful democracy:

> Regarding the Senegalese people, [the brotherhood leaders] didn't spread Islam through war. But it was through their messages, miracles, etc, that they convinced all the Senegalese, or the majority of Senegalese to be

Muslims [..] and this is what makes the strength of Senegal, because since our independence we have never had coup d'états. (MMH2)

Differentiations between the brotherhoods (as internal others) are flattened here. Instead, the peaceful ways the brotherhoods collectively spread Islam are articulated as one of the distinguishing unifying characteristics of the nation and its democracy.

Representations of the message of peace and tolerance of Senegalese Islam involved much more external differentiation against religious 'others', as opposed to internal differentiations between Senegal's brotherhoods. For example, Senegalese Islam was set in contrast to the '*diabolized*' Islam of other contexts, where the message of peace of the Prophet was being ignored, or Islam where '*jihad*' was being pursued:

> … today currently we see people who claim to be representatives of Muslims, whereas basically they are not Muslims, basically they are really not practicing properly. Basically, they are not here to bring the message of peace the Prophet was carrying at the beginning, they rather spend their time talking about things that are not even part of the Holy Koran, that are not part of Sharia. And that's what is leading to conflicts in some regions (inaudible/overlapping voices)…Islam is diabolized…with the Islamists in Mali, all that. (FMH1)

> Senegalese Islam is not forced [..] you adopt or you drop it. But on the other side, the Islam.. if I take the example of Nigeria, we've seen the two hundred kidnapped women, people forced them to get veiled, people forced them to have husbands. And also, when we take the example of the Islam of the East, that is to say the Middle-East, their Islam, it is forced Islam. [..] they are currently saying that they are doing jihad [..] there is a domination of the Jewish. So in this case, they are going to establish a (inaudible), therefore, do jihad. That's the reason why they are doing kamikazes and other things. [..] they are spreading Islam, or to really fight against discrimination against Islam. (MMH2)

> … we take the Mouride model which says that it's the cult of work, and we go to Afghanistan or we go to another country, the cult of those countries is the jihad; it's different. We do not kill on behalf of religion, but we feed ourselves on behalf of religion. (MMnH2)

The articulation of 'proper' versus 'improper' Islam re-emphasises the message that Senegalese Islam is a religion of peace and constructs Islam that involves conflict as 'inauthentic', as an external other. This external religious 'othering' was echoed by Christians and provoked some strikingly broad chains of association and equivalence. For example, when a group of Christian males was asked what nationality they would not want, the dialogue that ensued conflates national and ethnic categorisations, as well as constructing equivalences across groups associated with 'hard-line Islam' and terrorism.

> R1: Yes for me the Arabs, that stuff in Afghanistan…that terrorist stuff, for me I do not want to be of Arab nationality. […] what I don't like is their ideas, how they see life and how they want to change the world, you see. They have ideas a bit far from people, because they say that they live for God, they practice the hard-line Islam like the stuff of.. their.. how to say it?
>
> R2: Bokko Haram
>
> R1: Bokko Haram and their, how to say it, their sect, how to…
>
> R2: Terrorists
>
> R1: Yes terrorists.. (MCH1)

So while we have critiqued the ways discourses of the West often present homogenised depictions of youth and of Islam, there were points in the research where youth discourses themselves demonstrated some strikingly broad and undifferentiated associations between different social categories and across different contexts in their construction of the 'others' against which they sought to define themselves.

A key differentiation that distinguished more or less strict forms of Islam was their enforcement of particular ways of dressing, with women's dress coming under particular scrutiny. Often the reference point here was the external other, rather than an internal other. Female Muslim participants recognised Senegalese norms of dressing as being relatively free in comparison with other Muslim countries, one suggesting that *in a country like Indonesia, Iran or Pakistan, I would be killed if I went out dressed like this* (FMH1). However, another participant (FMH1) commented on the Ibadou having a stricter dress code than other Senegal brotherhoods, for example banning women from wearing hair tresses and requiring them to wear a veil—she was wearing hair tresses herself, and like the great majority of female respondents was not veiled. In a later focus group, the only Ibadou participant (MMH1) was indeed highly critical of the '*immodest*' ways that women in Senegal dressed. The policing of women and their dress is discussed further below.

The distinctiveness of Senegalese Islam was differentiated regionally, but this seemed to be valued rather than othered. Religious leaders were recognised as important in allowing this differentiation, because they spoke local languages and so could mediate their followers' relationship with their religion. Many Muslim respondents also described the interweaving of local ethnic (animist) practices with Islamic practices, particularly the Diola and the Lébou participants. This syncretism seemed to sit happily alongside upholding the universal values of Islam. Only occasionally was the accommodation of local, situated understandings described in ways that hinted at a hierarchy between more or less 'pure' versions of Islam within Senegal:

> … the Diola maybe practises the Muslim religion, but there are cultural and traditional diversities which appear all the time. [..] we do not make a dichotomy but we mix the two together, religion, tradition and other. [..] Compared with the Muslims of the north, they do not have those kinds of diversities, those kinds of sacred practices, they simply practise. (MMH2)

Mostly, however, participants were not defensive about the syncretism of their Islam. Indeed, two participants pointed to the thinking of Senghor to justify the ways that traditional beliefs had been maintained by the different ethnic groups in Senegal. One quoted him as saying '*know your own roots before opening your culture up to others*'.

Both Muslim and Christian groups spoke at length about valuing their respective religions, and they were also proud of the ways both Muslims and Christians lived peacefully together throughout Senegal.

There were accounts from both of sharing each other's festivals, from Muslims and Christians, particularly in Ziguinchor, in the south of Senegal:

> ... there's a cohabitation between Christians and Muslims in the neighbourhood. [..] During the Eid festival, at home, we cook and give to the Christians. We slaughter the sheep, we take the meat and give it to the Christians. They come and eat in our home. During Christmas and Easter holidays, they invite us to eat with them in their homes. (FMH1)

In keeping with this, even if religion was often identified as the most important aspect of their identities, almost all Muslims reported they felt closer to Senegalese Christians, than to Muslims outside Senegal and vice versa. This was because they were part of their community and they were neighbours whom they lived with on a daily basis. In some instances, the extended family included both Christians and Muslims. This depended to some extent on participants' ethnic groups; the Wolof and Lébou were described as being entirely Muslim, while the Diola and Sérère were a mixture of Muslims and Christians. As also suggested by Cruise O'Brien (2003), ethnic boundaries seemed to intersect to some extent with religion, but often were not sharply defined.

In summary, youth's constructions of Muslim and Christian religions saw them both as peace-seeking and respecting of others, including respecting each individual's right to their religious beliefs. The dominant representations of both religions sat well with modern ideals. Senegal's brotherhoods were important to Muslim youth for having authored a distinctively Senegalese, or African form of Islam, that had accommodated local traditions. The brotherhoods had also been significant in the formation of the nation-state, being greatly admired for their peaceful resistance to colonial powers as significant external others. While differences between the brotherhoods were acknowledged, their role in realising Senegalese independence meant that their unifying characteristics rather than their differences were privileged in participants' narratives. Their shared characteristics—in particular their message of peace—also meant that Senegalese Islam was generally constructed as the other of *'diabolized'* or jihadist Islam, which was associated with external others—these being other African countries, such as Mali and Nigeria, or more broadly with the Islam of the Middle East or 'Arab' Islam.

In contrast, the predominantly Sufist Islam of Senegal was generally described in ways that suggested work on the self, an inward- rather than outward-looking transformation, a construction which might be understood in terms of *greater jihad*. Both Muslims and Christians stressed their mutual tolerance and the extent that they lived peacefully together. It was also striking that although a minority religion, Christians seemed to be highly respected in Senegalese society. They seemed able to access elite forms of education that gave them command of the language of power and government. Finally, delineations of Senegalese Islam consistently invoked gender differences in the positioning of Muslim women and men. This was largely accepted in some focus groups, although contended in others, particularly by some of the Muslim female youth in higher education, as discussed further below.

5.6 Gender as Trouble: Impossible Positions?

As discussed in Chap. 2, gender is understood as performative, as constantly being brought into being through discourse and discursive practices. Rather than being viewed as a binary of male and female, gender involves the doing of different forms of masculinity and femininity which are read as intelligible and legitimate in context-specific ways, as well as potentially involving different modes of subjectivation (Mahmood 2012). Throughout the previous sections of this chapter, we have pointed to significant gender dimensions in youth's constructions of their national and their religious identities. We also pointed to the ways in which youth's national and religious identities intersected, as well as how these identities were constructed against colonial powers, or the West more generally. We will begin by considering the intersection of gender and nation in youth's narratives, before turning to the ways that these narratives were also bound up with religion, and the conflicting modes of subjectivation that would seem to be implicated (see our discussion in Sect. 2.6).

In relation to national imaginaries, Chatterjee (1993) suggested how the modernising postcolonial nation constructed its national identity by accepting reforms in the public sphere as well as science and technology, but preserved their uniqueness against the West through its distinctive culture. Thus, a nation's identity narratives became strongly associated with differentiation and distinction in spiritual/cultural (and emotional) domains, processes which he described as a 'defining feature' of postcolonial nationalisms in Africa and Asia. We discussed the gender implications of this in Chap. 2, given that the responsibility for nurturing these dimensions fell primarily on women. It meant, for example, that women's bodies became crucial sites on which the markers of 'imagined community' of the nation were inscribed. This in turn rendered the policing of the nation's women and their bodies essential in the maintenance of the national imaginary (Mayer 2000).

In constructing their national identities, youth articulated strong gender binaries. These reflected a regime of compulsory heterosexuality where marriage was assumed as the norm, associated also with strong divisions of labour for both males and females. When identifying the characteristics of the ideal (male) Senegalese, for example, Senegalese masculinity was constructed in terms of becoming a responsible breadwinner and head of household:

> … to be seen as an ideal man, first of all, you have to be someone who is very responsible, someone who is ready to strive, someone who knows how to take charge of his life, who is not always there expecting others to do something for you. Also the marriage side matters a lot. At a certain age, if you are not married, you are considered—excuse me for the term I am going to use, as a pervert [..] even if they don't say it to you, they're there talking behind his back, but why isn't he married? He's not a responsible person, he doesn't want to have children. (FMH1)

Similar values were expressed in Christian and Muslim narratives, male and female. These accounts often stressed how ways of dressing were bound up with traditional Senegalese moral values, although mostly this focused on women's dress:

> Senegalese customs do not allow a certain number of behaviours. [..] the Senegalese dress in ways that they think a decent way. For example we have to cover the body, even if we are not veiled, cover the body with very decent clothes. [..] But also from the point of view of education, our moral code wouldn't want... There are terms we often use, for example the '*soutoura*', the fact of hiding, '*soutoura*' is a Wolof word that is about hiding certain things, bashfulness, discretion. (FCH1)

While this Christian participant associates this way of dressing with Wolof culture, for many Muslim participants, what was proper (or *correct*, in the sense of appropriate) was also defined by religious sensibilities, so that policing of national identities intersected with policing of religious identities:

> ... so our dressing must first be correct, secondly to have a good behaviour, try also to copy our elders. Because today, we see outrageous things in the country. We should be correct, dignified, respectable, and also be pious, because we are a Muslim country. (FMnH1)

A Senegalese women's sexuality was also sometimes articulated within this self-policing. As one Muslim female put it, *as Senegalese women, we take pride in ourselves, control ourselves until we have a husband* (FMnH1).

A strong division of public and private or domestic spheres was salient. Although there were some challenges to this, particularly from some of those higher education (see below), a division of labour where the ideal Senegalese woman worked in the home and looked after the family was identified in all focus groups, as in this depiction from a female Christian participant:

> ... the Senegalese woman stays at home to do the household, cook, takes care of children, and the Senegalese man goes to work to look for what to bring home to feed the family. (FCnH1)

This was echoed by a male Christian respondent:

> ... in Senegal one cannot compare the man to the woman. They will always tell you that the man is superior to the woman, he's the head of the household [..]. The right of the woman is, to love her husband, to respect him, to abide by him, to take care of his children and mostly to take care of her family in law. (MCH2)

At the same time, women could be greatly respected within these boundaries:

> ... in Senegal the woman occupies a very important place. Because if we see in the home it is up to the woman to educate the children. And this is really important. And also the fact that she is given the power, she's the one who cooks. So we can say that we are in a country where matriarchy is very important. (MCH2)

A key example of the centrality of woman's work in the symbolic imaginary of the nation was the gendered assumptions embedded in the concept of *'teranga'*, a Wolof word meaning 'hospitality'. When discussing Senegalese nationality, Senegal was described as the country of *teranga* in all focus groups, male and female. However, this involved gendered power relations. With many accounts asserting a strongly gendered domestic division of labour, the promise of hospitality might be made by the male head of household, but the servicing of *teranga* fell to the woman within the ideals of the national imaginary. The excerpt below demonstrates a strong sense of masculine entitlement in this Christian male participant's elaboration of the concept:

> ... when we talk about teranga, it means that the woman, she is open.. welcoming. If we go into the houses, that is to say us personally, when we go somewhere we expect that hospitality, we expect that she welcomes us. (MCnH1)

The few exceptions to the confinement of women to the home were some ethnic groups where women also worked in the fields, and men were described as typically *'sitting with their arms folded under the tree'*, or modern life in Dakar, where a woman could also go out to work.

However, although more women were now working in professional fields, it was pointed out that women could have more rather than less onerous lives because of this. Women also had to fight their corner when moving into public domains that men had previously dominated. This female Muslim reported having to rebuff a challenge from three male youths about her taking a leading role in a youth association and having to fend off this question:

> actually, how come you are a woman, the others are men and you become the President? You lead both women and men? (FMH1)

She had refused to be '*abused*' and in the end had faced off their challenge. However, the difficulties faced by women in overcoming gendered divisions of labour were also illustrated in a discussion of new legislation giving women the right to paid maternity leave, where a Christian male reflected on the difficulties this presented for the promotion of women. His logic found it right not to promote women, because they would need to be absent from work, and to ensure instead that the importance of women's reproductive role was acknowledged:

> So sometimes Directors of Human Resources do not give many responsibilities to women in general. And I do think that there is no dishonour in this, because there is no more gift more wonderful than giving birth. So they don't need to feel disadvantaged for that. It's the opposite. (MCH2)

We turn now to the ways gender and religion intersected. While at one level both men and women could construct themselves as being equal before God within both Christian and Muslim religions, women's lesser status in Islam compared to that of men was also somewhat contradictorily cited across many interviews. For example, women could not lead prayers, they could not attend burials, and a woman's ascent to heaven depended on her husband. As Velayati (2016) explained, men's power within religious institutions has in many instances led to assumptions of them being God's 'vicegerents', embodying his authority on earth. This is particularly the case in contexts where sacred texts had to be mediated through another language, for example in the translation of the Q'uran into French or in this case into local Senegalese languages. Christian participants also identified differences in the relative status of Muslim men and women. In some interviews, Christians claimed that no such differences existed in Christianity, although after prompting, they recognised similarities, for example how women could not be priests. Contradictory discourses about women's supposed equality are also evident in the quotations from Christian participants above, which construct women's place as being in the home.

Discussions of gender relations often took up recent legislation which had attempted to create gender parity in Senegal's National Assembly. Although contended, in one reading, this demonstrated the multiple discourses through which women's subordination could be maintained, which variously recruited national, religious and ethnic discourses. From another reading, the discussions illustrate the tensions that could arise from the contradictory values embedded in two different modes of subjectivation—the ideals of secular national government and the pillars of Islam. Turning first to nationality, discussion of Senegal's gender parity law produced assertions about men's superiority and, in this male Christian focus group, the construction of women's rights as being to know her place in the home:

> ... in Senegal you cannot compare a man to a woman, it's not possible. They will always tell you that the man is superior to the woman, he's in charge of the house. [...] The right of the woman is to love her husband, to respect him, to abide by him, to take care of his children. The ideal woman in Senegal is [..] she who is submissive (soumise), who is attentive, who respects her husband. (MCH1)

While the notion of submission is often associated with Islam, we can see from the focus group above that male superiority could also be intrinsic to Christian ideals of a Senegalese woman. Conversely, Muslim men sometimes argued for gender equality and contested the concept of submission. Nevertheless, it was on questions of gender equality that tensions between secular state policy and religious imaginaries were most explicit. For instance, in a male Muslim focus group, one participant was arguing for gender equality, rejecting the notion of submission as implying women's '*annihilation*'. However, disagreement ensued:

> R1: The man and the woman, it's different; more particularly in Senegal if you take the religious domain. In the Muslim religion they say that the woman is created from the man. So, the woman must always stay inferior, the woman must always be submissive (soumise) to the man. […]
>
> R2: Because in the Koran, as a Muslim, what is said is that the woman must submit. It's the husband who must give the orders. [..] so when he talks about submission, I agree. But it is not a total kind of submission, like slavery you know. (MMH1)

Yet another male drew on Diola ethnic traditions to contest gender parity and argue for woman's submission. So national, religious and ethnic discourses could all be recruited and invoked in relation to the contended issue of the position of women. Moreover, the complexities of the concept of 'submission' became evident when the same male participant went on to praise Aline Sitou Diatta for being submissive while also recognising her as a national heroine for resisting colonisation. As we discussed earlier in Sect. 2.6, and in concert with Mahmood (2012), this illustrates that submission in Islam does not necessarily imply an absence of women's agency. Furthermore, Velayati (2016) makes the important point that submission before God should not be conflated with submission before men.

In other discussions of this law in another Muslim male focus group, religious and wider cultural norms were mobilised together against gender parity:

> Wade [the previous president] wanted to push forward the issue of parity, as he had seen white people do. Really, above all, as a Muslim one should base everything one does on one's faith, and there is very specific place for women in religion, that is to say, the family home. (MM Yoff)

The parity law is constructed here as an undesirable import from an alien culture, in a way that recruits colonial or neo-colonial traces to other and resist it. In another focus group, the parity law was similarly associated with '*the arrival of modernization, and the western influence*' (MMH2), although, in this particular case, this was not necessarily seen negatively (see also below in relation to changes in family structures). However, the earlier excerpt citing Cheikh Bamba's resistance to '*the modernity European people had a tendency to instil in us*' suggests how Western forms of modernity could be constructed as something against which Senegalese national identity was defined.

It was suggested earlier that the intersection of gender and religion could make it doubly difficult for women to contest a subordinate positioning. As a female Muslim youth pointed out, attempts at gender reforms could readily be blocked through these being constructed as attacks on religious or traditional values. The examples above show how multiple discourses could be recruited and intersected to construct women in '*second place*'. However, women's regulation also worked through women's agency, as in the example below. Here, a female Muslim had been contesting interpretations of the Koran which saw women's ascent to heaven as depending on her husband:

> R1: But is this is it said in the Koran? Because sometimes there are people who add things, that are not part of the Muslim religion. [inaudible]
>
> R2: …it's something crucial in the Muslim religion…
>
> R1: Sometimes there are exaggerated interpretations. It's true that they scare people, but in reality they don't exist in the Holy Koran.
>
> R2: We're going to cast doubt the texts of Islam.
>
> R1: No, we are not casting doubt on them [inaudible] were those texts written by the Prophet? No, by men, the '*Sahabas*'? [Mohammed's disciples] - I don't know, who wrote that? (FMH1)

The inaudible sections of the transcript indicate the affective intensity of the discussions, when several participants were contributing simultaneously with great animation. The argument seems to take up the strictures within Islam against contending the Prophet's words in public (Krämer 2013) and shows how they remained powerful in this context, and for at least one of those in this group closed down the possibility of debate on gender issues.

The discussion also demonstrates how women themselves do 'border-guard' work, rather than only men, as well as illuminating points of resistance to dominant gender norms. In general, this resistance came mostly from female Muslim youth in higher education, who pointed to changes in women's role in Senegalese society, the emergence of an agenda around women's emancipation and the appearance of more women in public positions. Family relations and marriage practices were also identified by some female Muslims as a site of some change, associated with modernity:

> now, with modernity, people tend to get married, to live alone with the husband, and children. [..] It's part of the changes in the couple, with the children. (FMH1)

Other female participants suggested, however, that any changes were mainly confined to professional, rather than domestic life, and were occurring in urban rather than rural contexts. Some youth also spoke of ICTs and new media as bringing change in their lives, opening up new ways of thinking and awareness of differences in how different people lived in other contexts. However, this was not necessarily viewed positively and was sometimes actively resisted. For example, a female Muslim described having been propositioned on Facebook by another woman, whom she had immediately 'blocked':

> I could not believe that a person would have the audacity to make advances to someone of the same gender but that happened to me. That was of course a big shock to me. (FM Yoff)

Without being prompted about how this related to religious norms, she reflected on homosexuality being unacceptable within Christianity as well as Islam. There were no indications in the data to counter this. On the contrary, one Christian male (MCH1) spoke of his respect for Christians in the USA because of their strong stance against both abortion and homosexuality.

Contestation where it occurred was principally over the subordinated place of women in society. However, the ways that multiple discourses could be recruited against gender equality suggest that significant tensions lay between the formal ideals of the secular Senegalese nation-state and the gender relations that were sedimented in its society. We have already highlighted how gender hierarchies are intrinsic to the modern imaginary and critiqued its inherently masculinist ideals in Chap. 2. We stress then the additional complexities faced by those female Muslims who were attempting to contest gender inequalities in Senegal.

5.7 Conclusion

In the Senegal case, there was a recognisable national imaginary which was strongly embraced by youth. Their Senegalese identity was one of distinction, recruited in contradictory ways against other African nations, but also as leaders of Africa. The national imaginary drew on a shared history with France, as well as defining itself in an oppositional way against French colonial rule. However, the ways that 'Frenchness' could still be recruited as a marker of distinction meant that the Christian minority did not feel marginalised. On the contrary, they could contribute at the highest level to Senegalese society.

Senegalese national values sat harmoniously with religious values. Indeed, its religious leaders were integral to the national secular imaginary, at least for Muslims. This was traced to the importance of Senegal's Sufist brotherhoods, who authored a distinctly African form (or forms) of Islam and were also central to the emergence of the independent nation, although using pacifist rather than aggressive forms of opposition. Their work in unifying the nation against the colonial other was a dominant discourse and contributed to a flattening of both ethnic differences and differences between the brotherhoods themselves.

Both Muslim and Christian understandings of religion were important in allowing the co-habitation of their different communities. Both were constructed as tolerant, peace-loving and above all a question of individual work on the self, in ways that sit well with modern ideals. The emphasis on Islam as a religion of peace also meant that Muslim participants' identities were defined in opposition to the *'diabolized'* Islam that was portrayed as being practised in other contexts, such as Mali, Nigeria or the Middle East, which was seen as illegitimate, as not *'proper'* Islam. The processes of defining African versions of Islam had also opened many possibilities for its fusion with traditional ethnic customs and beliefs, allowing Islam to take root in multiple syncretic forms across Senegal. Its distinctiveness and 'Africanity' were valued, however, rather than being seen as an 'inauthentic' form of Islam. Across the focus groups, participants stressed the peaceful cohabitation and sometimes interpenetration of Muslim and Christian communities, fused with traditional animist customs and beliefs in some regions. Local attachments with 'others' of whatever faith were always more important than transnational associations with those of the same religion.

The Senegal case contradicts many of the assumptions that see Islam as being incompatible with a modern, secular and nation-state. Senegalese youth's understandings of religion sat to a large extent in harmony with their national ideals. However, it is in relation to gender that tensions appear within and between youth's discourses of nation, religion and ethnicity. In a context where modernity was embraced by some youth, but could also be constructed as an undesirable imposition, each of these discourses (nation, religion and ethnicity) could be recruited individually to justify unequal gender norms. Their power is intensified when they are recruited together and conjoined with potentially negative associations with modernity, as an imposition from the Global North. The promises of equality that are supposedly at the heart of republican values here prove evanescent. Instead, from the perspectives of these youth, the national, religious and ethnic imaginaries seemed to depend largely upon gender relations which assume women's subordination. Women might be highly respected and valued, but this respect depended on an acceptance of (submission to) powerful gender hierarchies, rather than starting from any assumption of equality. Challenges to these gender hierarchies punctuated some focus groups, more especially those involving females in higher education.

Overall, the case suggests the contradictory and always situated nature of the discourses through which youth's identities are articulated and performed with respect to nation, religion, ethnicity and especially gender. Importantly, the case demonstrates an imaginary of a secular democracy which is tolerant of religion, which is in part related to an imaginary of Islam which might be understood to privilege *greater jihad*, and which participants set in opposition to Islam that pursued jihad '*as a cult of war*'. It also demonstrates the continuing salience of national belongings to youth in this context, even if these are entwined with the circulation of global norms, such as those associated with different world religions or human rights discourses (Beck and Levy 2013). There would seem to be no superseding of the national by the kinds of supranational cosmopolitanism envisaged by Held (1995). Instead, the enactment of youth's identities is infused with local colour tessellated with many different cultures. It may rather involve the confrontation of 'native' with 'global' modernities, giving rise to different forms of 'vernacular cosmopolitanism' (Diouf 2002). This recognises and gives value to the infusion of the local by the global, without assuming any hegemonic form of global governance rooted in Western modern values, or the necessary imposition of any particular faith—which in its intolerance of difference has been seen as a form of counter-cosmopolitanism by those espousing more normative perspectives of cosmopolitanism (Appiah 2006). However, as we discussed in Chap. 2, Appiah's normative framework has little traction in relation to gender. As shown in the Senegal case, gender remains a site of significant inequalities, which seem better unpacked through poststructural theorisation which is attentive to difference in the production and articulation of our identities.

Note

1. At the time of the fieldwork, billboard posters were on display in Dakar to promote an upcoming summit of the Francophonie. These posters activated the concept of *teranga* in its construction of a national imaginary. They portrayed a young woman and a girl, accompanied by the text '*Women and young people of the Francophonie: vectors of peace, agents of development. Welcome to the country of teranga*'.

References

African Union. (2006). *African Youth Charter*. Banjul: African Union Commission.
Appiah, K. A. (2006). *Cosmopolitanism. Ethics in a world of strangers*. London: Penguin.
Asad, T. (2003). *Formations of the secular. Christianity, Islam, modernity*. Stanford: Stanford University Press.
Badran, M. (2009). *Feminism in Islam: Secular and religious convergences*. Oxford: Oneworld Publications.
BBC News Africa. (2012). US Secretary of State Clinton hails Senegal democracy. Retrieved July 21, 2015, from http://www.bbc.co.uk/news/world-africa-19073601.
Beck, U., & Levy, D. (2013). Cosmopolitanized nations: Re-imagining collectivity in world risk society. *Theory, Culture & Society, 30*(2), 3–31.
Butler, J. (1990). *Gender trouble. Feminism and the subversion of identity*. London and New York: Routledge.
Calhoun, C. (2008). Cosmopolitanism in the modern social imaginary. *Daedalus, 137*(3), 105–114.
Camara, F. K. (2007). Women and the law: A critique of Senegalese family law. *Social Identities, 13*(6), 787–800.
Central Intelligence Agency (CIA). (2014). *World factbook—Senegal*. Retrieved March 22, 2015, from https://www.cia.gov/library/publications/the-world-factbook/geos/sg.html.
Chatterjee, P. (1993). *The nation and its fragments: Colonial and postcolonial histories*. Chichester: Princeton University Press.
Conklin, A. L. (1997). *A mission to civilize. The republican idea of empire in France and West Africa, 1895–1830*. Stanford: Stanford University Press.
Cruise O'Brien, D. (2003). *Symbolic confrontations: Muslims imagining the state in Africa*. London: Hirst & Company.
Diallo, I. (2010). *The politics of national languages in postcolonial Senegal*. Amherst, NY: Cambria Press.
Diouf, M. (2002). The Senegalese Murid trade diaspora and the making of a vernacular cosmopolitanism. In C. A. Breckenridge, S. Pollock, H. K. Bhabha, & D. Chakrabarty (Eds.), *Cosmopolitanism* (pp. 111–137). Durham and London: Duke University Press.
Fredericks, R. (2014). "The old man is dead": Hip hop and the arts of citizenship of Senegalese youth. *Antipode, 46*(1), 130–148.

Gaye, M. (2015). What would Senegal have become had President Wade been re-elected in 2012? *Pambazuka News*. Issue 718. Retrieved March 19, 2015, from http://www.pambazuka.net/en/category/comment/94241.

Harrison, C. (1988). *France and Islam in West Africa, 1860–1960*. Cambridge: Cambridge University Press.

Hartmann, C. (2010). Senegal's party system: The limits of formal regulation. *Democratization, 17*(4), 769–786.

Held, D. (1995). *Democracy and the global order: From the modern state to cosmopolitan governance*. Cambridge: Polity Press.

International Bureau of Education. (2010). *World data on education* (7th ed. Revised Version). Geneva: UNESCO-IBE.

Krämer, G. (2013). Modern but not secular: Religion, identity and the *ordre public* in the Arab Middle East. *International Sociology, 28*(6), 629–644.

Laborde, C. (1995). *La confrerie layenne et les Lebou du Senegal: Islam et culture traditionnelle en Afrique*. Bordeaux: Centre d'étude d'Afrique noire, Institut d'études politiques de Bordeaux.

Mahmood, S. (2012). *Politics of piety: The Islamic revival and the feminist subject*. Princeton, NJ and Oxford: Princeton University Press.

Mamdani, M. (1996). *Citizen and subject. Contemporary Africa and the legacy of late colonialism*. Princeton, NJ: Princeton University Press.

Mamdani, M. (2004). *Good Muslim, bad Muslim. America, the Cold War, and the roots of terror*. New York: Pantheon Books.

Marshall, J. (2015). Two new universities in 2016 to increase student capacity. *University World News*. Retrieved April 5, 2015, from http://www.universityworldnews.com/article.php?story=20150108160654484.

Mayer, T. (2000). Gender ironies of nationalism: Setting the stage. In T. Mayer (Ed.), *Gender ironies of nationalism: Sexing the nation* (pp. 1–24). London: Routledge.

Mbaye, L., & Nadhiri, A. (2010). Contextualizing "Muridiyya" within the American Muslim community: Perspectives on the past, present and future. *African Journal of Political Science and International Relations, 4*(6), 231–240.

Mbow, P. (2009). *Secularism, religious education, and human rights in Senegal, Institute for the study of Islamic thought in Africa (ISITA)*. Working Paper Series. Institute for the study of Islamic thought in Africa. Evanston, IL: Buffett Centre, NorthWestern University.

Sow, F. (2014). Secularism at risk in sub-Saharan secular states: The challenges for Senegal and Mali. *Open democracy 50:50*. Retrieved March 22, 2015, from https://www.opendemocracy.net/5050/fatou-sow/secularism-at-risk-in-subsaharan-secular-states-challenges-for-senegal-and-mali.

United Nations. (1979). *Convention on the elimination of all forms of discrimination against women (CEDAW)*. New York: United Nations.

UNESCO. (2014). *EFA global monitoring report. Teaching and learning: achieving quality for all.* Paris: UNESCO.

UNESCO. (2016). *Global Education Monitoring Report.* Paris. Retrieved May 10, 2016, from http://en.unesco.org/gem-report/node/6.

Velayati, M. (2016). Gender and Muslim families. In *The Wiley Blackwell encyclopedia of family studies* (pp. 1–5). London: Wiley Blackwell.

World Bank. (2014). *Senegal overview*. Retrieved March 22, 2015, from http://www.worldbank.org/en/country/senegal/overview.

World Economic Forum. (2015a). *Global gender gap report*. Geneva: World Economic Forum. Retrieved May 10, 2016, from http://reports.weforum.org/global-gender-gap-report-2015/.

World Economic Forum. (2015b). *The human capital report 2015.* http://reports.weforum.org/human-capital-report-2015/economies/#economy=NGA.

6

Nigeria: Muslim Youth and Internal Others in a Multi-religious Nation

Abstract This chapter presents an analysis of the ways that Muslim youth from Northern Nigeria construct, assert and navigate their identities. It locates this analysis within the contested social and political landscape and the complex distinctiveness of the population. Importantly, this contextualisation includes reference to the colonial history and its significance to the formation of the Nigerian State. The data gathered largely through focus groups discussions were used to explore how youth understood and articulated their sense of belonging in national, ethnic, religious and gender terms as well as their sense of difference and distinction from others. Despite the strong sense of national allegiance and pride, many Muslim youth expressed dissatisfaction with democratic and government processes. In their identity narratives religion was a dominant discursive axis of belonging and of differentiation. While as Muslims they were keen to distance themselves from extremism, terrorism and the actions of Boko Haram, they constructed Christians as the 'internal other'. This discursive Fracturing of the nation revivified the birth scars of the Nigerian state and its uneasy historical emergence as a postcolonial, multi-religious democracy. At the same time a conflation of region and religion (Northern

Muslim—Southern Christian) worked to flatten local ethnic differences. As region and religion did not map neatly on to one another, Northern Muslim youth invested considerable effort to 'other' their Muslim compatriots from the south. This was accomplished through the derision of Southerners including Muslims for their westernisation and loss of culture, in opposition to the superior and more 'pure' Islamic identity and practice of Northern Muslims. Turning to gender, the lack of an explicit reference to this within youth narratives of identity stood in stark comparison with the way it structured everyday life. Gender relations were an important symbol of religious identity. These conjoined with dominant masculinities to find expression in projections of subservient, modest femininities although these were at times resisted by some female youth. Finally, this case study illustrates the importance of the local context to the ways that young people try to produce themselves as intelligible subjects, and the significance of the complex political and geographical histories of nation-state formation as the backdrop to the youth identity narratives.

6.1 Introduction and Context

This chapter presents the Nigerian case study. It starts by providing an overview of the national context that draws on the history of colonialism, the formation of the Nigerian State, the contested social and political landscape and the complex distinctiveness of the population. This is followed by a section on the approach to the case study research which has also been described earlier in Chap. 3. The chapter then turns to an analysis of the ways that youth construct, assert and navigate their identities. It is a focused exploration of Muslim youth in the north of Nigeria and the ways they understand and articulate their sense of belonging in national, ethnic, religious and gender terms and how in this process they variously connect and distance themselves from local, national and global 'others'.

Nigeria in West Africa is bounded by the Gulf of Guinea to the south, Benin to the west, Niger to the north, Chad to the north-east and Cameroon to the east (See Fig. 6.1). It is renowned for being the most populous country in Africa, with claims that one in four Africans are Nigerian. According to the 2006 census, the population has reached over 140 million (National Population Commission (NPC) 2010), and it is currently estimated to be in excess of 160 million (Humphreys with Crawfurd 2014). The population growth rate is reported at 2.45%. With a median age of 18 years and population estimations that approximately 61% are under 25 years; 19.3% between 15 and 24 years (Central Intelligence Agency (CIA) 2015) and 42% under 15 (UNICEF/UIS 2012), issues of the youth are clearly significant to economic growth, welfare, equity and development in Nigeria.

Over recent years, Nigeria has achieved an 8% per capita annual growth in GDP (Litwack et al. 2013) and has overtaken South Africa as the largest economy in Sub-Saharan Africa. Oil and gas revenues contribute to its economic success even though the majority of the population are engaged in agriculture and, in common with many other countries worldwide, the country has seen a decline in manufacturing and a growth in the service sector (United Nations Development Programme (UNDP) 2009). Nevertheless, the majority of Nigerians (54%) still live in poverty (UNDP 2009; Litwack et al. 2013) and 42% of children are malnourished (British Council 2012). Nationally, there are significant general health concerns related to malaria, malnutrition, maternal and child mortality and HIV/AIDS (Boston University Center for Global Health and Development with Initiative for Integrated Community Welfare in Nigeria (BUCGHD 2009; Humphreys with Crawfurd 2014).

Nigeria gained independence in 1960 and became a federal republic in 1963. The establishment of Nigeria as a nation-state, however, has been built on a history of colonialism as well as on territorial, religious and ethnic differences and conflicts. Its territory of over 910,000 km^2 was established when the British amalgamated the Northern Protectorate and the Southern Protectorate and the Lagos Colony in 1914. By 1939, three regions, North, South-East and South-West, comprised Nigeria, and these remain the territorial basis of the federal system of government and the development of the national constitution leading up to independence and afterwards (Nwabueze 1982; Falola and Heaton 2008). Before and since independence, Nigeria has experienced multiple conflicts, notably those against the British colonial administration, attempts at secession by the south-eastern region in the Biafran War, inter-ethnic conflict in the Niger Delta, Plateau State, Kaduna State and Kano, coups, attempted coups, military regimes and the insurgencies of Boko Haram with a 'state of emergency' declared in some Northern states. Despite this history, the 2015 democratic elections saw the government of Goodluck Jonathan of the People's Democratic Party (PDP) peacefully hand over the power to Mohammadu Buhari of the All Progressives Congress (APC). Jonathan, a Christian from the South, handed power to Buhari, a Muslim from the North who had previously been part of the military government of Olusegun Obasanjo before democratic rule was re-established in 1999. This was the first time in Nigerian history that an opposition party has taken up power democratically from a ruling party and an incumbent president (Al Jazeera 2015).

The foundation of the independent federal state of Nigeria was set up under the British administration, and the colonial legacy continues to mark the social, economic and political landscape in Nigeria. Each of the three regions that comprise Nigeria is powerful in its own right, and this has resulted in fluctuating allegiances and commitment to the central federal government. Nwabueze elaborates that '… the three-state structure had created an attitude of self-sufficiency, of separatism and of intolerance among the regions' (Nwabueze 1982:148). To add further fragility, each of the three regions was also identified by a majority ethnic group, namely Hausa-Fulani in the north, Yoruba in the west and Igbo in the east. Along with English, the respective languages of these groups, Hausa, Yoruba and Igbo became the official languages of Nigeria. Given that there are estimates of up to 500 ethnic groups and languages in Nigeria (Osaghae and Suberu 2005), disputes and conflicts over minority rights, territory and representation continue to date. Perhaps in partial recognition of the range of ethnic distinctions within Nigeria, the three regions established in 1939 are now governed in 36 states and the Federal Capital Territory of Abuja (See Fig. 6.1). These states are arranged in six geo-political zones,[1] three in the North

6 Nigeria: Muslim Youth and Internal Others in a Multi-religious ...

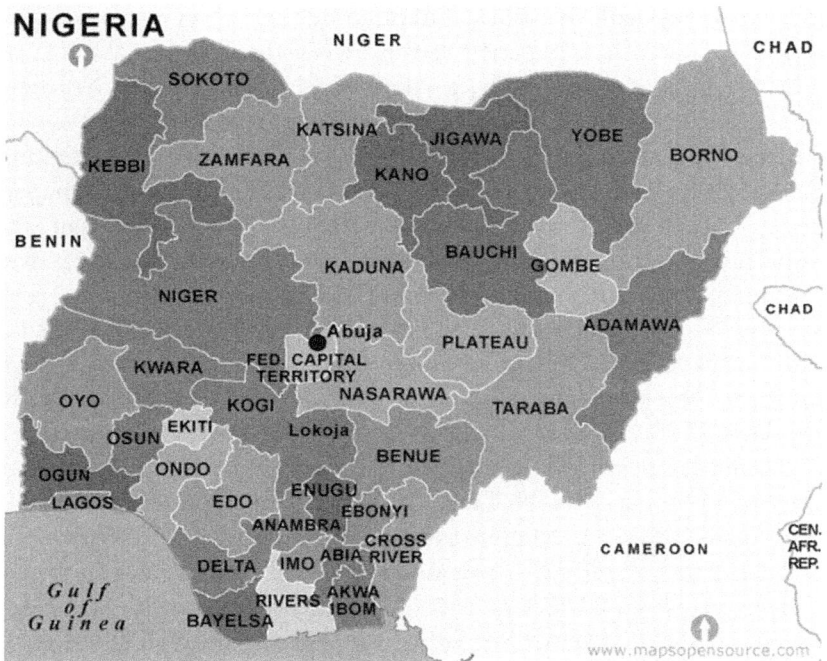

Fig. 6.1 Map of Nigeria.
Source http://www.mapsopensource.com/nigeria-map.html

(North-West, North-Central and North-East) and three in the South (South-West, South-South and South-East) (Ukiwo 2005).

There have always been distinct ethnic and linguistic differences within and between the three main regions of the Federal Republic of Nigeria. The largest group, the Hausa–Fulani from the north, comprises about 29% of the national population. They are followed by the Yoruba at 21% who originate from the south-west, then by the Igbo from the south-east at 18% (CIA 2015). The Southern regions are more densely populated than the north with Lagos reaching over 10 million people (NPC and ICF Macro 2009). While Nigeria may be described as a multiparty democracy and a secular state, religion plays a significant part in the political process and in the lives and identities of its population (Sampson 2014), with Sunni Islam identified with the north and Christianity with the south. Although neither ethnicity nor religion has been included in a Nigerian census, it is estimated that about 50% of the population are Muslim, predominantly living in the Northern states, a further 40% are Christian, residing mostly in the south, with another 10% practising traditional religion (CIA 2015). The religious/regional segregation is however a gross oversimplification (Onapajo and Usman 2015) as there are Northerners who are Christian and Southerners who are Muslim, ethnic groups of both religions, as well as internal migration and resettlement, such that Muslim indigenes from the North can be found living in the predominantly Christian South and vice versa. This leaves many regions and cities across Nigeria with a mix of ethnic and religious populations. Adamawa State in the north-east, the location of much of the fieldwork for this case study, is commonly described and assumed to be predominantly Muslim but is estimated to have a 40–45% Christian population (Dunne et al. 2013).

The introduction of religion to the different regions of Nigeria was closely tied to trade links. Islam was introduced into the northern part of Nigeria between 1100 and 1400 AD and associated with the development of trans-Saharan trade routes. It was not until much later, in 1804, that the Sokoto Caliphate was created and it effected the spread of Islam beyond the ruling elites to ordinary people. Similarly, from 1450 onwards, coastal trade links with Europeans, which included the transatlantic slave trade, were the precursor of specific attempts to bring Christianity to Southern Nigeria in the 1840s (Nwabueze 1982; Falola and Heaton 2008). At independence and through British manipulation of the boundaries, the northern region included 75% of the total land and comprised 60% of the population (Nwabueze 1982). Indeed, the current religious and ethnic tensions in Nigeria have been traced back to lobbying and favouring of particular groups and regions by the colonial administration:

> … relations between both religious groups in Nigeria also shows that there have been mutual feelings of marginalisation and fear of domination between them, which clearly has a relationship with the way religion has been instrumental to the promotion of political interests in the country. (Onapajo and Usman 2015:109)

There have been attempts to deal with the suspicion between the religious groups through an extra-constitutional rotation of the presidency between a Muslim Northerner and a Christian Southerner. This itself caused some tensions when Goodluck Jonathan ran for election in 2011 and again in 2015 after a three-year period as Vice-President (2007–2010) and then as Acting President in 2010 after the death in office of President Umar Yar'Adua who was a Northern Muslim. The election of Muhammadu Buhari in 2015 saw a return to the unofficial rotation of power that is likely to have calmed some tensions and anxieties, especially among Muslims.

Outbreaks of ethnic and religious violence and conflict nevertheless persist in Nigeria. The rise of Boko Haram with the explicit aim to Islamise Nigeria has fuelled fear within the Christian population and deepened religious tensions even though killings and violence have been perpetrated against both Christians and Muslims (Salaam 2012). While there certainly have been agreements and compromises between the religious factions, for example, in the operation of three systems of law: customary law, shari'a law and English common law (Sampson 2014), the possibility of extra-national allegiances to the *ummah* among Muslims is seen to threaten both Nigerian Christians and the imagined 'secular' nation (Anderson 1991; Asad 2003; Last 2008; Sampson 2014). However, discussion and analysis of the motivations of Boko Haram and of ways to deal with the threat they represent to the lives of Nigerians, security and national stability suggest that:

> … Boko Haram is not only about rejecting Western education *per se*; it is a judgment about the failure to provide opportunities for better lives, and thus becomes an instrument for mobilising and radicalising the unemployed, unskilled and poverty-ridden youths to join its cause and dislodge the secular controlled state, as an alternative and plausible answer to their misery. (Salaam 2012:151)

It is evident that despite rich natural resources and positive economic growth, the majority of Nigerians live in poverty and this is most acute in Northern Nigeria. Measures of human capital using education and employment statistics show that Nigeria is ranked 120 of 124 countries and below average for its income group across all age categories (World Economic Forum (WEF) 2015b). Similarly, the composite Education Development Index ranks Nigeria at 103 of 113 countries (UNESCO 2015). These data certainly draw a dismal picture of the largest economy in Africa. The obvious social, educational and economic inequalities together with the evident religious, ethnic and political tensions nevertheless are the context within which young Nigerians grow to understand their social position and identities, which is the focus of the empirical work in this chapter.

Poverty, especially in rural areas, more adversely affects women, and this is manifest in regional differences that show much poorer economic, health and educational outcomes for women in Northern Nigeria (British Council 2012). Despite a population with a roughly equal gender split, there are slightly more males than females (1.04:1.00), and males comprise 81% of household heads, with higher proportions of female-headed households in rural than in urban areas (NPC and ICF Macro 2009). At the same time, although women make up over 60% of the rural work force in Nigeria, at best they own 10% of the land and as little as 4% in the North-East. In common with many other national contexts, women earn less, occupy less formal sector roles and are under-represented in senior public service roles, as organisational executives and as political leaders (British Council 2012). The wide gender gap in Nigeria has left it ranked 125 out of 145 countries (WEF 2015a). In terms of education, women have fewer years of formal schooling and have higher rates of illiteracy than men. In a survey of parents and guardians, around 55% were literate, but these figures show wide variation by age, with older people less likely to be able to read; by location, ranging from 48% in the rural areas compared to 76% in urban areas; and by geographical zone, with 39% in the North-West and North-East compared to 75% in the South (NPC and RTI International 2011; Humphreys with Crawfurd 2014).

Notwithstanding the importance of education for individual social and economic prospects and for equitable national growth, Nigeria is recorded as having both the largest number of children out of school and very large educational and gender disparities between the north and the south. With an estimated 39% of school-aged children (5–14 years) engaged in some form of labour (Federal Office of Statistics (FOS)/ International Labour Organisation (ILO) 2001; BUCGHD 2009), distressingly there has been a slight decline in primary school enrolments over the past decade. These remain at about 60% nationally with lower attendance for those children in rural areas, in poorer households, in the north and in those who are nomadic, disabled, girls or Muslim (Humphreys with Crawfurd 2014). In terms of gender, statistics show that the net enrolment for girls (60%) is significantly lower than for boys (71.2%) (UNICEF 2015). A survey of school-aged children reported that 31% had never attended formal academic school (Western education) although an estimated 8.7 million in the North attend Qur'anic school which traditionally only taught the Qur'an (Hoechner 2011). There is evidence that those who do attend school may be in a formal academic school or a Qur'anic school or both (NPC and RTI International 2011). More recently, IQTE (Integrated Qur'anic Tsangaya Education) schools have been developed which integrate parts of the formal academic curriculum with the traditional concentration on the Qur'an.

Gender disparities have been observed in all levels of formal education across Nigeria. Although the balance has shifted towards girls in one or two southern regions, in broad terms the educational participation of girls is lower than that of boys in access, retention and completion of basic, secondary, further and higher (Bakari 2009; British Council 2012; Humphreys with Crawfurd 2014). There are significant economic, governance, social and especially gender implications of less than 10% of women and 14% of men having attended more than secondary school (NPC 2014) and with only 8.1% of 18- to 35-year-olds participating in higher education in Nigeria (Agboola and Ofoegbu 2010). There have been a range of reasons suggested for the lower rates of female participation in school that include those related to household poverty such as direct school costs, opportunity costs, the need for child labour in income generation or in the home, hunger and ill health. Other factors include community views of schools and Western education as un-Islamic, early marriage, pregnancy and early childbirth, and poor sanitation, all of which particularly affect girls in northern states. These and a range of school quality factors which concern the environment for learning, poor or absent teachers, a lack of resources, gender stereotyping, corporal punishment and sexual violence negatively affect the education of both girls and boys (British Council 2012; Humphreys with Crawfurd 2014). Gender discrimination, harassment and violence have been cited as a significant factor to the educational experience and female dropout in higher education (Pereira 2007; Bakari and Leach 2008; British Council 2012).

This overview has provided some background on the geographical, political and social context in Nigeria. It presents insights into the social conditions and complexities within which young people interact and develop social relations and networks that help them to begin to understand their own identities and the ways they are socially located within the nation and more globally. The emphasis in the above has been an historical and contemporary account of the interweaving of nation, ethnicity, religion and gender within Nigeria to provide the basis for exploring how these interplay for the Nigerian youth who participated in the study. In the next section, we briefly describe the sample and approach to the research which has already been outlined in Chap. 3.

6.2 The Research in Nigeria

The approach to the Nigeria case study was consistent with that used in the other three country cases elaborated in Chap. 3. It comprised a series of focus group discussions (FGDs). The fieldwork for the study was completed in early 2014, and initial drafts of the research instruments were trialled as early as 2011. With research interests in Muslim youth identities, the initial design focused on two northern states in Nigeria: Plateau in North-Central and Adamawa in North-East. It also included some interviews with Christian as well as Muslim youth as a means to provide critical insights into the ways that religion interplayed with national, regional and gender identities. The sample was designed to include roughly equal proportions of females and males and where possible to include youth from different socio-economic backgrounds.

Nigerian researchers from both locations were involved in the data collection. They were all inducted into the conceptual framing of the research; the instruments, which some researchers were involved in shaping; the research protocols that were focused on youth respondents' voice and views; ethics; permissions; and confidentiality. In addition, they were trained in the more technical procedures of data collection, including recording, transcribing and providing personal reflective insights after each interview. In total, nine research assistants worked across the two locations. They encouraged the FGD respondents to discuss the questions in their preferred language which involved code switching between Hausa, English, Pidgin and other vernacular languages. Each interview was transcribed and translated into English, and these together with a bio-data sheet completed by each participant and the researcher reflections are the data analysed in this chapter.

Given the ongoing community tensions, violence and bombings in Nigeria, the use of two research sites was a practical measure in case of the upsurge of violence or any emergent safety issues or ethical difficulties arising in either location. Jos in Plateau State has witnessed ethnic and religious tensions since at least the turn of the century which have sparked violence and bombings (Jonah and Igboeroteonwu 2014). The Islamist insurgent group Boko Haram has been implicated in the violence in Jos, Plateau State, and in Adamawa State (Hjelmgaard 2015). On the basis of the escalation of Boko Haram insurgency in 2013, President Goodluck Jonathan declared a state of emergency in Adamawa (Tran 2015). The recent influx of refugees in Yola, Adamawa State, trying to escape violence in neighbouring Borno State indicates that the insurgency continues to disrupt communities in the North-East (Mark 2015). The continuing threat and perpetration of violence and the declaration of a state of emergency produced conditions in which it was difficult to conduct research. This led to a reduced set of FGDs in each context.

Due to the safety concerns and time constraints, it is only in Adamawa that interviews were conducted with Muslims and Christians. The four Plateau State FGDs were conducted with Christians only, but they comprised two with youth who had studied at higher education level and two with non-elite youth who had not received postsecondary education. Given the prevailing circumstances in Adamawa, it was decided that interviews with non-elite youth might have put the interviewers at risk. All Muslim respondents were from Adamawa, and all had studied either in a teacher training college or in a university. It was through these higher education institutions that respondents were accessed in Adamawa, whereas in Plateau State, it was through personal contacts and snowballing that respondent groups were brought together. After unsatisfactory trials with mixed sex groups, all the interviews used in this analysis were conducted in segregated groups by gender and religion.

In total, 19 focus group discussions took place, but two were lost due to technical recording problems. Nine of these were with females and eight with males; nine were with Muslims and eight with Christians. In total, 78 Youth participated, of whom 58% were Muslims and 56% were female. They were aged between 18 and 36 years with an average age of 24 years. In regional terms, 76% were based in Adamawa in the North-East and 24% were in Jos, Plateau State, in North-Central. To facilitate discussion, interviewers were matched to the youth respondent group by gender and religion as far as possible. In only four cases, the interviewers were not the same gender as the respondents, and in three of these cases, it was female researchers interviewing male respondents. In another two cases, a Christian researcher interviewed Muslim respondents (Table 6.1).

The analysis of the data began with discussions with the researchers about the conduct of the focus groups, their feelings about the way the discussions had developed and the key issues that had emerged. This was followed by several readings of the interview transcripts and at times reference to the audio and/or the interviewer with respect to the interview data. The interview transcripts were then coded by hand with reference to the key concepts of 'nation', 'religion' and 'gender'. These were extended by codes for 'ethnicity', 'internal other' and

Table 6.1 The Nigerian sample

	FGDs	Individuals	Gender		Location	
			Female	Male	Adamawa	Plateau
Muslim	9	45	27	18	45	0
Christian	8	33	17	16	20	13
Total	17	78	44	34	65	13

'external other'. As described earlier, the nine focus group interviews with Muslim youth were the main focus of the analysis that is reported on in this chapter. Each FGD was given a code that denoted religion, gender, location and an ordinal interview number (1–17). So a code of MMA15 refers to an interview with Muslim Male Youth in Adamawa State that was 15 out of a total of 17 FGDs in the whole sample. A code of CFP9 is an interview with Christian Female Youth in Plateau State that was the ninth FGD of the sample. To protect anonymity, the FGD participant's names have been substituted by a number, for example Participant 1—P1 and Participant 2—P2, that are consistently associated with their specific contributions and further identified within their FGD code.

6.3 Youth Identities—Initial Views

All youth respondents were asked to complete a bio-data sheet which was a short questionnaire asking respondents to describe themselves in terms of age, gender, education level, nationality, religion, ethnicity, language, region and location. The sheet also included questions about their parents' religion and ethnicity. These initial nominal identifications were also part of the introductory sequence of the FGDs.

According to the completed bio-data sheets, the Muslim respondents were all from northern Nigeria and had undertaken third-level education. This does mean that this is a case study of rather elite Northern Muslims. As described earlier, despite a more expansive research intention, the prevailing conditions militated against interviews with Muslims from less educated backgrounds. As a group, the respondents came from nine different ethnic groups with over one-third describing themselves as Fulani who used Fulfolde (the language of the Fulani) at home. A further quarter were ethnically Hausa although as many as 44% spoke Hausa at home. It is both an official national language and dominant in the north. All respondents spoke Hausa and at least one other language. Claims to ethnicity drew on parental heritage, with as many as 62% of parents coming from the same ethnic group. Where parents came from different ethnic groups, all respondents claimed the ethnicity of their father. There was only one exception in the case of a Christian father, and in this case, the religion and ethnicity of the mother were claimed.

At the start of the FGD as a form of warm-up to focus on identities, respondents were asked to introduce themselves and say who they were. They usually responded with between two to four descriptors, for example, 'I am a Nigerian, a Muslim from Adamawa State' and all were included for this analysis. The data presented below provide a summary of these initial responses about the youth identities using data from all the interview transcripts as a means to facilitate regional, religious and gender comparisons (Table 6.2).

As a whole, the four highest identity markers for all youth in rank order were home location, nationality, religion and ethnicity. The range was from well over a half referring to their home Local Government Area (LGA) or State to about one-third referring to religion. Clearly, there is a need to exercise caution given the small and unbalanced sample, but the regional comparison is of interest and signals spaces for further research. In this respect, we can see a much stronger reference to a religious identity in Yola which is more than double that in Jos. Exploration of the responses showed a very stronger identification with religion (80%) among Christian females in Yola. In contrast, reference to home location in Jos is much stronger, which may be related to the respondents' experiences of protracted periods of ethnic and community violence in comparison with Yola. Given the importance of gender in this study, it is worth pointing out how few respondents referred to

Table 6.2 Initial youth identifications by region in Nigeria

	Age	Location	Nation	Religion	Ethnicity	Gender	Occupation	Individual attribute
All (n = 80)	4	46	38	29	22	6	20	14
All (%)	5%	58%	48%	36%	33%	8%	25%	18%
Adamawa (n = 67)	4	37	31	26	18	6	20	12
(%)	6%	55%	46%	55%	27%	9%	30%	18%
Plateau (n = 13)	0	9	7	3	4	0	0	2
(%)	0%	69%	54%	23%	31%	0%	0%	15%

this identity marker with none at all in Jos. Although just under one-third referred to occupation in Yola, again this was not mentioned by the youth in Jos.

The data in Table 6.3 have been disaggregated by religion. It shows a very strong reference to national identity by the Muslims compared to the Christians. The importance of national identity was reflected equally in both female and male responses. This is interesting given the Nigerian Christians' suspicion of stronger extra-national than national allegiances of Nigerian Muslims (Asad 2003; Last 2008; Sampson 2014). While religion ranked third for both Christians and Muslims, there was an interesting pattern of difference in the claims to a religious identity between the two groups. Muslims tended to directly state this in descriptions of themselves, specifically 'I am a Muslim … ', while Christians often referred to 'God', his inspiration and his guidance as significant to their identities.

It is also worth noting that it was only the Muslims who explicitly referred to their gender and by contrast only Christians who referred to their personal individual attributes in responding to the question about who there were. Given the historical links between Christianity, colonialism and capitalism in the formation of Nigeria, it is tempting to connect the youth responses with the 'modern' subject and the project of the self in new individualising neoliberal times (Giddens 1991; Beck 1992; Kalberg 1997), but the data here are too limited although it may signal an avenue to explore in a larger study.

Table 6.3 Initial youth identifications by religion in Nigeria

	Age	Location	Nation	Religion	Ethnicity	Gender	Occupation	Individual attribute
All (n = 80)	4	46	38	29	22	6	20	14
All (%)	5%	58%	48%	36%	33%	8%	25%	18%
Muslims (n = 47)	2	26	30	16	15	6	11	0
Muslims (%)	4%	55%	64%	34%	32%	13%	23%	0%
Christians (n = 33)	2	20	8	13	7	0	9	14
Christians (%)	6%	61%	24%	39%	21%	0%	27%	42%

Table 6.4 Initial youth identifications by gender in Nigeria

	Age	Location	Nation	Religion	Ethnicity	Gender	Occupation	Individual attribute
Females (%)	2%	49%	46%	36%	11%	2%	13%	25%
Females (n = 45)	1	22	21	16	5	1	6	9
Males (%)	9%	69%	49%	37%	49%	11%	40%	17%
Males (n = 35)	3	24	17	13	17	4	14	6

The data on gender in Table 6.4 show that the main differences were with males explicitly using their home location and ethnicity as identity markers. They also referred to their gender more than the female respondents who tended to refer to personal attributes in reference to their identities. This does resonate with gender differences in which males refer to explicit public categories and personal status, while females refer to softer more interpersonal qualities. The latter, however, was not found among Muslim females. Again, these small-scale data cannot lend massive support to these observations although this tendency was notable in the discussion transcripts.

This introductory section of empirical analysis has provided some preliminary insights into the differential ways the sample of Nigerian youth construct their identities by drawing on a range of identity categories. In the following three sections, we move to a more nuanced analysis of their discursive entanglements in their struggles for intelligibility.

6.4 Nation and External Others

A very strong sense of national pride reverberated across the youth responses. Different elaborations of national superiority dominated the early parts of all the discussion groups, and these tended to be expressed as self-affirming rallying calls. There was only one of the 78 respondents, a Christian male, who was unhappy to be a Nigerian and wanted to change his nationality. The expressions of national pride circulated around essentialised personal/national characteristics, collective behaviours as well as descriptions of the national territory. The uniformity with which this was expressed across the different focus group discussions irrespective of the gender, religious and regional configuration indicates the strength of the national myth and the use of these descriptions, in Butler's 1990 terms, as naturalised 'facticity'. Depictions of national character included proud, confident, and intelligent as well as a range of other attributes such as kind, generous, hospitable, friendly, honest and smartly but modestly dressed which were further supplemented by claims that Nigerians were hard-working, peaceful and resilient. Culture and food were consistently referred to in positive and more generic ways alongside which references to the land, oil, mineral wealth and agricultural productivity were all also incorporated into the might of Nigeria and Nigerians.

> P4: I really thank God for making me a Nigerian because it is something of great priority for me to be a Nigerian because as compared to other countries in Africa or in the world at large, Nigeria is actually a peaceful country. So, I am very happy and thank God for that. (MMA16)

Several youth highlighted a sense of African belonging which in some FGDs shifted into a reference to a global hierarchy of developed and developing countries. Across the FGDs, the introduction of national comparisons fed through to claims of Nigeria as the 'lion of Africa'. The more emotive expressions of national pride similarly drew on more technical measures of hierarchical position at the individual level, for example Nigerians as among the most highly educated in Africa as well as the actions of the Nigerian State in other African nations especially by the armed forces. It was these multiple threads of discourse that were used to claim and substantiate the superiority of Nigeria and Nigerians, especially in Africa.

> P3: When I say I am a Nigerian, I define myself as somebody who is from a part of the African continent where every other black person looks up to as in other countries in Africa they look up to Nigeria for a lot things that's why they seem to call us the giant of Africa so when I say I am a Nigeria it carries a lot of weight. (CFP9)

P2: ... aahh, one of those things that made Nigeria distinctive is the role that the Nigerian government has played in terms of peacekeeping and emancipating other African nations from colonial dominations, from apartheid regime and contributing in terms of other nations to stabilize economically. So ... other nationalities in Africa [to] see Nigerians as big brothers and sisters ... at the level of governance [that] Nigeria has actually contributed more than any other African nation to the liberation of other sister nations. (CMP8)

Peace and peaceful co-existence of the large ethnically and religiously diverse population was offered as a point of contrast from other African nations. This was also expressed as a form of soft secularism (Last 2008) in which respondents referred to the freedom to practice any religion. We will return to this point in the next section. Here, we continue by exploring first how positive notions of the nation were tempered by discussions that took up the issues of governance and the state and second how this was reflected on the ways that Nigeria was positioned with a global context.

Dissatisfaction and disappointment with the workings of the Nigerian State haunted the positive youth imaginaries of the nation.

P1: ... they don't bring out money to help people, like bad roads, schools are not equipped, hospitals too they are not well equipped, there are some operation we Nigerians we have to go outside to have that operation, why can't we have it in our own country. They are eating money. (MFP13)

P3: The people in power say they are doing their best but people at the grass root don't actually see the benefit. Because things actually gets worse, costs are getting higher, the common man, the common salary he earns is not enough to even take care of his family. (MMA17)

P1: ... lack of social amenities, pipe borne water, electricity—we have the money—poor roads, pot holes here and there, people are dying, accidents and you know they keep promising us that they will do this they will do that after four years, four good years nothing to show so I am not happy over it. (CMA4)

The poor local amenities and infrastructure were raised in all the FGDs, and the responsibilities were laid squarely in the hands of political leaders. This led to discussions about deepening social inequalities within Nigeria, poor local and national development, and an absence of morality and accountability of political leaders despite election promises.

> P2: We have all that it takes for us to be (developed), you know a developed nation but because of mis-governance we are where we are today and that is never a good thing. (CMP8)
>
> P1: Especially the poor people suffer a lot and the government is not taking care of them. They do not even care about who is poor they just take care of themselves and their children. … almost all of the leaders are corrupt. Actually, that makes me feel bad of being a Nigerian. (MMA15)

The impacts on youth were highlighted.

> P3: And some youths are drug addict.
>
> P1: Because of drinking, smoking Indian hemp?
>
> P2: Its because of the frustration Ma, they are not given what is due to them, that' why they go on taking what they take. …
>
> P3: What makes them to be poor is that the government is not given them what is due to them.
>
> P6: Also lack of employment. (MFA13)

There were extensive descriptions of the forms of corruption by public officials and leaders and its impacts. The obvious frustrations with abuses of public office were tinged with a sense of inevitability and youth impotence in changing these practices. The contagion of state corruption was used to describe its penetration into wider social norms:

> P5: The leaders are terrible, that is the leaders are corrupted and even we the Nigerians, it's not just the leaders, we the citizen we are corrupted because of the leaders. (MFA14)

P3: …corruption is in all levels in Nigeria, not only our leaders, from the grass root there is corruption. (MMA15)

P2: …when people are in Nigeria they behave lawless in the sense that they don't obey rules and they don't follow laws. (CFP9)

According to the youth respondents, forms of corruption included opportunism of officials with any gatekeeping power to extort cash by eliciting 'gratuities' in return for special favour in the normal course of their official duties. Several examples were provided in relation to job-seeking which not only affected them individually, but also led to the appointment of under-qualified and incapable staff in a range of public service roles. Bribery and clientelism were seen as part of a spiral of corruption and state failure that appeared to them difficult if not impossible to address. In these discussions, they did not see themselves or other youth as either agents of change or resistance.

P2: There are some instances that when you go to look for work somebody may tell you that you must give him bribe before he gives you that appointment he is not supposed to be there and you are looking for something to earn a living and they insist on bribe which is very bad. (MFA13)

P4: (Interrupts) even police recruitment they will ask you to give 100,000 Naira to get appointment. (MFA13)

P1: … there is nothing that is done or given on merit any more, you go to school, for you to get admission you have to know somebody, you go to find a job you can't get a job on merit you have to know somebody you know that it's so discouraging so you find people in places where they don't even merit that place they don't belong there but because they know somebody who is there so they are placed there so things can't just go right. (CFP9)

In contrast to the earlier generally positive views of Nigerians, it is these latter negative depictions that they thought dominated the views of Nigeria and Nigerians from outside.

P3: … most of the countries view about Nigeria is that Nigeria is the most corrupt country. (MMY15)

P2: I think people outside they see Nigerians as dishonest, insincere people from the government down to the people and they don't believe that there is any good person in Nigeria. (CFA9)

P2: … no country would like to be like us. (CMP11)

P1: If you go to Saudi Arabia for example, they call Nigerian 'Mujurum' Nigeria Mujurum (laugh!) Meaning Nigerians are thieves. (MFA14)

As we noted in Chap. 2, several authors point to the divide-and-rule strategies of colonial powers as having encouraged relations of patronage. Mamdani (1996) and Kabeer (2002) both highlight, for example, how indirect rule through local intermediaries was widely exploited by colonial rulers and gave particular local groups arbitrary power over others, in ways that fostered and embedded clientelism in local power structures.

The list of negative attributes associated with Nigeria by other countries also included prostitution and child-trafficking as well as a more global phenomenon in which they described all Muslims being regarded as terrorists. Despite the multiple problematics the youth associated with Nigeria and Nigerians, the vast majority expressed and sustained their strong sense of national pride and belonging to Nigeria. It is interesting to observe that within these broad-level discussions, the youth positioned themselves neither as agents of change nor as a particular direct threat locally or nationally. At this point, we turn from these wider level concerns to consider youth perspectives on the internal dynamics of the nation taking up religion as an axis of differentiation.

In advance of this exploration, it is important to reiterate that this case study of youth in Nigeria provides a different social, political and demographic context from the previous chapters on Pakistan and Senegal. Although Nigeria with approximately 50% Muslims may be described as having a majority Muslim population, it is constitutionally a secular state with a multi-religious and multi-ethnic population. In this particular form of secularity (Burchardt and Wohlrab-Sahr 2013), the national imaginary has therefore to offer some discursive cohesion, and the state has to try to provide some operational and political balance. The commonalities of the youth constructions of the nation above, the legitimated use of different legal codes and the notional alternation of presidential office by region/religion attest to some forms of cohesion and balance even if these are contingent and fragile. As we note in Chap. 2 however, this also creates parallel traditions of citizenship with contradictory boundaries of belonging, the fragilities of which are often particularly exposed when it comes to questions of women's rights (Kabeer 2002; Nash 2012).

In the next section, we explore the more striated discourses of the nation through an exploration of youth perspectives on the internal dynamics and the ways that identity structures interweave and diverge. Consistent with the main threads in this book, we emphasise the views of Muslim youth within the multi-religious and multi-ethnic social context. However, we use the voices of Christian youth respondents as a counterbalance to the hegemonic (re)construction of internal others within the predominantly Muslim north of Nigeria.

6.5 Religion and Internal Others

The complexities of the Nigerian case produce multiple structural and discursive intersections that youth navigate in order to shape their own identities. In this section, the exploration flows from affirmations of national unity across its religious communities to issues of ethnic belonging and division within a nation of some 500 ethnic groups. Driven by youth claims that ethnicity has less contemporary significance to them, the discussion traces the predominance of region as a key signifier of belonging and difference. This is followed by a more direct exploration of youth identifications with religion and Islam as well as the ways this intersects with national and ethnic belongings. This section moves from a beginning that exemplifies youth claims to national uniformity and uniqueness framed against external 'others' to divisions within the nation that are used to describe internal 'others', which are also bound up with religious identifications. This provides the space to explore the more fine-grained, local and personal construction of youth identities through their various appropriations of discourses available within their social sphere. The final part of this section links back from the local to wider concerns as the youth, while expressing 'thick' attachments in their belongings, recognise how religious identity and division have been used and deepened to manipulate the population for specific political purposes.

A Religious Nation

The shift to discussions of diversity and difference within Nigeria precipitated youth reaffirmations of a sense of allegiance to the nation and claims to a national unity. In all youth FGDs, a sense of unity and freedom in Nigeria was portrayed. The only exception, was related to issues of gender and gendered freedoms, which were raised and questioned in one Muslim female group discussion in particular. We will return to this in Sect. 6.6.

For the Muslim youth, this sense of unity referred predominantly to the importance of religion to most Nigerians:

> P7: To me I am proud to a Nigerian because Nigerians are very religious people, in terms of their faith, either Muslims or Christians, they are very religious. (MMA16)

> P5: 70 percent of Nigerians they have their religion in their heart. (MFA12)

> P4: Nigeria is different from other countries because of peaceful co-existence. Despite the fact that we practice two major religions in Nigeria but we live in peace because we actually live as brothers … (MMA15)

In addition, youth expressed pride in the Nigerian State's tolerance of different religions:

> P3: My nationality as Nigerian permits me to practice any religion and to practice my culture the way I like it … (MMA15)

The enshrining of religion as essential to Nigeria contradicts a key characteristic of modernity, which eschews tradition and religion as the antithesis of progress and development (Weber 1947, 1976; Parsons 1977;

Berger 1999; Hermann 2005; Vorster 2013) and demonstrates a form of 'soft' secularity which embraces religious expression and diversity (Last 2008; Burchardt and Wohlrab-Sahr 2013).

For the youth, it was the portrayal of peaceful co-existence of Muslims and Christians that was most significant. Their affective attachments (Ahmed 2004) were in the entanglements of nation and religion which they articulated through exemplifications of their local everyday context as well as through wider comparisons to the conditions in other nations.

> P.3 ... both Muslims and Christian students do things together, they eat together, they share ideas and sometimes if the Muslims are going to mosque the Christians do say 'pray for me', while when ... Christians are going for their own service they'll say they should pray for them. (MMA15)
>
> P.2 ... in America anywhere you see a Muslim he is just seen like terrorist but here in Nigeria you find out that, a Christian, maybe his best friend is a Muslim and they are living, he will advise him, eat with him, talk to him, many things. (MMA15)

It is striking within the predominantly Muslim north of Nigeria that there was a consistent defence against the links between Islam and terrorism and a claim that tensions between Christians and Muslims did not characterise daily life in Nigeria.

> P4: Say your neighbour here is a Christian and he helps you and another fellow a Muslim who is in Saudi Arabia which one will you prefer.
>
> P6: No your neighbour is your neighbour even if it is a pagan.
>
> P1: Excuse me according to the teaching of Islam even our prophet was a guardian to a Christian he had his times in Saudi when he ran away. Where did he run to? He ran to the King of Johe a Christian—your neighbour is your neighbour even a Christian. (MFA13)

Such reaffirmations of the importance of nation, a religious nation, were predominant within all the youth responses. In the Muslim youth FGDs, there was a celebration of both diversity and national unity.

> P3: There is one big thing that makes me proud being a Nigerian. That thing is unity. … Nigeria is blessed with different multi-ethnic groups … despite our diversity, we are able to unify ourselves and achieve a kind of development. [MMA16]

While this idealisation was echoed by northern Christian youth, their accounts of their experience within the Muslim-dominated north betrayed a sense of feeling somewhat marginalised.

> P2: There is no peace especially in this northern part. … if you come here, even to communicate even in the school … if you are not a Muslim …
>
> P1: We are suffering from corruption, discrimination.
>
> P4: I don't know why they discriminate like that but since you are not the Muslim. Even when you are about them you just feel like you are nothing. [CFA5]

Religion was a key identity marker and social distinction in Nigeria. However, the discussions of youth identity, diversity and internal others precipitated discussions of other social divisions that included language, ethnicity and location (see Tables 6.2, 6.4). In this section, we will illustrate the overlap and complex intricacies of social distinctions which are riven by narratives of tradition and history as well as by the workings of power and politics. With the exception of intermarriage, gender was rarely explicitly brought to bear in discussions of identity and social relations. The embedded patriarchy (Mouffe 1992) was constantly evident in the ways that both female and male respondents made reference to an assumed masculine subject.

Religion and Ethnicity

Beyond identification with nation, home location and ethnicity were among the four key identity markers used by youth in their initial identifications (see Tables 6.2, 6.3). Reference to ethnic identity was much more common among male than among female youth. Ethnic diversity was used also to substantiate the idea of Nigerian national unity and cohesion. This was largely accomplished through broad comparison with ethnic conflicts in other African countries such as Sudan, Congo and Somalia and also contrasted with the local stories of peaceful co-existence among different ethnic groups in Nigeria.

> P3: ... we have more than 20 tribes and we are living peacefully. We don't have this problem of this ethnic... I am from Kilba, I am from Bachama. You can go to a house and find out that this room is a Kilba, another one is Bachama, another group is Fulani and they are living peacefully, their children are eating, playing and doing everything together. (MMA15)

When youth were asked about belonging to ethnic groups other than their own, discussions opened up around the particularities of ethnic differences. Initially, these focused on local, northern ethnic groups as illustrated in the above FGD extract. Comments ranged from descriptions of commonalities between some ethnicities to distinct differences with respect to traditions and cultural practices. Although 38% of the respondents had parents from different ethnic groups, they recognised that:

> P1: Marriage is what brings about a conflict about ethnicity. (MFA14)
>
> P7: ... when it comes to marriage they don't consider you being a Christian or your being a Muslim but they consider which tribe are you? Where are you coming from? (MMA16)

This is significant in Nigeria where religion and ethnicity do not map directly onto one another and where the religious and ethnic mix, especially in the urban areas, has been influenced by internal migration. Importantly, just as people of the same ethnicity could be either Muslim or Christian, members of the same family could also follow different religions.

> P1: (interrupts) yes, ethnicity and religion now, In our own place as I am telling right now, I have brothers, step brothers, step mothers that are Christian while I am a Muslim, yes, we marry each other. (MMA17)

Across the FGDs, however, youth provided a sense that the importance of ethnicity was receding. This was discussed in terms of both intergenerational difference and cultural loss.

> P2: It was only the parents that saw the difference between the ethnicity. Why, simply because the parents were adhering to their forefathers, that's their ancestors. They want a continuity in their culture. The young Nigerian is not looking at that. (MMA15)
>
> P1: But the youths there do not believe with these traditions nowadays. So you can see that our parents believe in traditions while we believe in western civilization and the rest. (MMA16)

This youth seems to embrace a movement away from traditional ethnic customs towards practices that are seen as 'Western'. However, later in our analysis, particularly in relation to religious practices, the epithet of 'Western' is used differently, to symbolise rejection of practices that are seen as being imposed from the outside (Krämer 2013). Change was also contended. For example, there were several accounts of the ways that questions of marriage were subject to parental authority with strongest objections to prospects of marriage outside both ethnic group and religious affiliation. These differences were readily recruited to articulate regional distinction. In the next extract, a Hausa youth, a northern Muslim describes the parental encouragement of marriage to a northern Muslim of different ethnicity (Fulani) and emphatic refusal to even consider marriage to a Christian from an ethnic group originating in the South-East (Igbo).

> P4: It's my mother that proposed one Fulani girl for me, so, I told her that I cannot marry a Fulani especially those in Yola and the mother of the girl is in Yola, she told me to go and see the girl. I told her that I am not interested in marriage. She directed my brother to ask me, I told him that there is one Igbo girl that I want to marry, he told her (my mother), she said that over her dead body. So, I just stopped talking about it. (MMA15)

The Igbo are one of the three major ethnic/language groups predominant in South-East Nigeria. They are known as successful business people who have migrated to many parts of Nigeria. They are predominantly Christians remembered for the Biafran War when they sought secession from post-independence Nigeria and garnered support from the Catholic Church in these efforts. The Igbo were often cited by the research respondents as the most reviled ethnic group and the least favoured alternative ethnicity. Across the FGDs, youth recruited ethnicity to demarcate regional differences that reflected the forging of the nation-state in which the north dominated by Hausa/Fulani Muslims amalgamated with the Christian south comprised largely of the Igbo in the South-East and the Yoruba of the South-West who though largely Christian Protestant also included some Muslims.

> P3: … we are forced to live together. Originally we are not identical in any way whatsoever, by culture, religion and what have you. … After the amalgamation we also had a breakdown during the military regime—coup, counter coup which finally led to a civil war. (MMA16)
>
> P2: … our forefathers have inculcated in us an element of hatred between that north and the south and there is no respect if you see an Igbo man here, he will be first identified as an Igbo not as Nigerian. (MMA16)

Regional Distinction

The regional differences were much more strongly present and sharply described than ethnicity in the youth discussions of internal others. Sanusi (2007) argues that this flattening of ethnic affiliations and distinctions has emerged as a result of investments in northern religious leaders, during the British administration, which encouraged an emphasis on religious identity. Christian missionary intrusion and the British administration in the South did not operate in this way such that in the South, ethnicity plays a more prominent role in the local social and political landscape (Peel 2003; Otayek and Soares 2007; Sanusi 2007). As exemplified below, in the narratives of regional distinction, northern Muslim youth selectively invoked religion, threats to national unity and cultural difference to sustain regional mistrust despite more than 50 years of national independence.

> P3: Actually there are a lot of problems between the North and South. It is in the history that since the Biafran war the southerners have it in mind that they are non-Nigerians up till now. They regard themselves and citizens of Biafran country because at this particular point in time,

especially during this democratic period, the Northerners do not want the Southerners to rule them while the Southerners do not want Northerners to rule them. This is because of the regional differences between us. So my own observation, we are living like the 'yam and palm oil' (a Hausa saying used in describing a distrustful relationship), we are living together but our minds are not clear. More especially during this insurgency, if you go to the South they think you are Boko Haram. They will call you Boko Haram straight forward. (MMA16)

P4: … if something like violence comes up in Nigeria, so, the Igbos are the first target. The Northerners will attack on Igbo's property in the North, and likewise in the South, if something happens there… for instance just recently, there was a bomb blast in Kano. So, the Igbos… because the people that were killed are Igbos, so, the Igbos that are in the Southern part of Nigeria retaliate towards the Northerners that are living there. (MMA15)

P1. Southerners view people from the north as people that are not educated. They don't want to go to school. They feel that the Northerners prefer to go to farm and get married and get two or three wives and give birth to kids and they feel that the Northerners have children on the street they only go and beg. The average Westerner [South-Westerner] almost all the children in the family must have first degree. Some of them may have two or three degree in the family, they may have two doctors among the children as compared to the Easterner [South-Easterner] where the average person or the average Igbo man is business inclined their own view of good life is for one to get established with a business and just forget about anything else. And an Igbo man feels he is very wise. Any slight opportunity he will try to trick you in to believing that which is not. (MMA17)

The reference to a regional identity was clearly important to the youth despite the mixed population in most regions and cities of Nigeria. Further, regional identity was mapped onto and articulated largely through religion which was used to bolster an authenticity of the religious practices of the Northern Muslims. This precipitated an internal hierarchy in which Muslims in the South and especially Yoruba Muslims were not quite 'proper' Muslims:

> P5: A Muslim from Yoruba land is different from Kano or other (northern) state ...
>
> P4: ... they value culture more than religion it's just ignorance of religion before it was like that (in the north) now it is changing.
>
> P5: Yoruba's follow Islamic teaching while if it comes to culture they do their real culture.
>
> P4: ... this is what I said they value their culture more than the religion. (MFA13)

As region and religion were not mutually inclusive categories, the idea of a 'proper' or a received form of Islam (Mamdani 2004) was used to reassert the regional difference by 'othering' not only the Yoruba Muslims but also other Muslims living in the South.

> P3: If Abdul (a Muslim) is from southern part of Nigeria, if he comes to north ... some Muslims do not accept them as good brothers and sisters. .... some northerners will think that your religion is not as perfect as his (northerner) religion. (MMA15)

Regional identification was conflated with a notion of a more 'proper' religious identity in ways that overshadowed and trumped ethnic identity for all Muslim youth (see Tables 6.2, 6.3). This produced exclusions in which the Muslims in the south as well as the Christians in the north occupied a somewhat marginal position (or were even absent) in the national imaginary and in this regional factionalism.

'Pure Islam'

The reference to a received or 'proper' Islam was constructed in contrast to syncretic or 'impure' forms of Muslim practice in which local cultural practices were interwoven with the formal received Islamic doctrine and practice. The youth's ideas of 'proper' Islam were infused by their awareness of Islamic practices in other national contexts which had been facilitated by the use of information and communication technology (ICT):

P3: We do know how we practice Islam, why Saudi Arabia is practicing Islam but in the olden days we only knew that we are Muslims. We were not practicing the religion as a religion. (MFA14)

The youth claimed that their observation of other Islamic contexts and communications with youth from elsewhere had influenced their social and cultural relations and produced shifts especially with respect to a religious consciousness and practices. This contributed to a sense of a 'proper' practice against syncretic or more hybrid forms of Islam. This was most evident in the performative space of the FGD which was used by Muslim male respondents who competitively engaged in correcting their fellow participants on the history and teachings of the Prophet. These were expressions of a singular masculinist certainty (Butler 2013) that invoked a hierarchy of practice through reference to an implied 'proper', transnational form of Islam. This was notionally important as a means to guard against, or expunge any syncretic or 'impure' forms of practice. The reference to a 'proper' Islam was constantly used to reiterate and substantiate regional difference which remained significant to their production of, and distinction from, internal others in Nigeria. The central identity claim for Northern Muslims within the nation pivoted on the achievement of religious distinction either from Christians or from other Muslims practising syncretic forms of Islam including Yoruba and many other Nigerian Muslims. The ideal of a pure, received Islam was the imagined foil against which they expressed their identifications as Northern Muslim youth.

It is interesting to highlight that the FGDs were an arena in which the youth respondents also played out and performed their identities. While youth respondents made efforts to exchange ideas and to produce coherence across the multiple layers of identity, the spectre of a pure, received Islamic practice haunted the FGDs. The discursive register of this identity narrative invoked a hierarchy and a superiority over internal others based on the efforts to expunge syncretic forms of Islam. Within FGDs, a number of contradictions and tensions were raised, and in some cases, this led to airing of different perspectives and disagreements which were largely mutually acceptable except with respect to Islam. The male youth respondents in particular used reference to 'proper' Islamic practice to 'trump' any argument or disagreement and usually to effectively halt discussion. It was an available resource with which to proclaim victory within the verbal exchanges of the FGD and beyond.

A small number of male respondents further contributed by accentuating the significance of religion, as illustrated in the following extracts. The first describes the potential of religion to erase other structures of difference, and the second highlights the personal importance of religion above regional or national belongings:

> P6: Religion can shape any other thing, you forget about ethnicity when you are religious, you forget about gender when you are religious, you forget about anything if you are 100 percent or 90 percent religious or even 80 percent. (MMA16)
>
> P1: Based on my perception sir, I'd rather be closer to somebody that is staying at the end of the world, if he is a Muslim. (MMA17)

In contrast to these purist notions of Islam, however, the majority of Muslim youth participants had observed Islam across the globe (for example in Pakistan, Indonesia, Saudi Arabia), and they recognised the ways culture and poverty had contributed to variations in religious practices. Interestingly, their understandings of the influence of national/ethnic culture on religion in foreign contexts elsewhere did not influence or soften their views about their fellow nationals but internal 'others', the Yoruba Muslims. The reference to international Islamic contexts did provide the basis for them to acknowledge their own moments of religious, ethnic and cultural conflict and compromise, for example, in accepting hospitality like drinking alcohol when visiting relatives. It was clear that while religion certainly worked as a 'matrix of subject formation … and a mode of belonging and embodied social practice' (Butler 2011:72), it did not operate in a straightforward or consistent way. Indeed, notwithstanding the complex configuration of religion, region and ethnicity as well as insights from Islamic communities elsewhere, the Muslim youth sustained a strong identification with the nation.

> P4: I prefer being with Christians in Nigeria than Muslim from other country because the Christians in Nigeria, they happen to know my tradition, do's and don't's, what I need and what I don't want without me telling them. (MMA16)

This expression of the sustained importance of national belonging was a shift away from a reference to a received, 'pure' form of Islam to an acknowledgement of variations at its intersection with local traditional cultures that produce hybridity or syncretic forms of religious practice. The above quote echoes the claims to national unity described at the start of this section which throughout the FGDs tended to refer to neighbourliness within the same locality across the Muslim–Christian divide. It was rarely extended to breach the regional differentiation which was largely expressed in terms of Northern Muslim and Southern Christian. Relations between Northerners and Southerners in Nigeria were consistently articulated in religious terms and used to restate the mutual suspicion (Onapajo and Usman 2015). In the following extract, a Northern Muslim male describes the basis of the suspicion of the North from a Southern perspective:

> P2: First, we outnumbered them. So, they are looking at the Muslims [in the north] using their Islamic agenda to achieve their… their political interest or something like that. (MMA15)

Political Manipulation

Although the youth were very proud of their national identity, discussion of internal 'others' was frequently used as a cue to reflect on the history and contemporary viability of the Nigerian nation-state. This turned to issues of corruption and state failure explored at the end of the Sect. 6.5 as well as to a broad recognition that wider politics and politicking since pre-colonial times had used and manipulated religious and other differences in the pursuit of political power:

> P1: ... there is concept of divide-and-rule that our leaders introduced to us, your blood brother who happens to be a Christian will hate you because of what is introduced to him by politicians, so that is what makes me feel bad. The kind of leadership being practiced in Nigeria is what is making very sad about being a Nigerian. (MMA2)
>
> P5 ... now as we're approaching this election a lot of text messages in churches and in Mosques, religious leaders campaigning to their followers to go to their fellow faithful and that is what is going on here.
>
> Interviewer: So to vote along religious lines?
>
> P5: Yes. (CMA4)
>
> P4: Democracy divides the nation. It is only politicians and the media that are propagating this thing. But in normal Nigeria, there is nothing, there is nothing like a Southerner or a Northerner. (MMA15)

The disillusionment with the divisory tactics in democratic processes in Nigeria compounded youth dissatisfaction with the operations of the State. In all the Male Muslim FGDs, this led into a more global commentary that specifically pointed at 'Western' influence as a catalyst for the demise of traditional and religious ways of life. In the extract below, a male youth respondent describes the potential of religion to reconfigure various axes of social difference which he describes as arbitrary Western constructions.

> P3: ... religion can shape morality can shape anything, you've done away with these gender, ethnicity, nationality and what have you because we learnt from religion that we belong to the same earth. All these demarcation of countries, continents is just being programmed by the western world. (MMA17)

Interestingly, resistance to 'Western' cultural influences was used to valorise religion and to illustrate the weakness of the culture and religion of internal 'others' specifically in the denigration of Southern Nigerians.

> P1: If you refer to the other part of the country [in the south], whether a Muslim or Christian or whatever tribe in the south, they compete in responsibilities because of the culture and western influence. (MMA16)

> P1: Currently our Nigerian Muslims are imitating the white people. So, as of now you can't differentiate them, more especially, Yoruba people [Southerners]. (Laughs) (MMA17)

Inter-regional differences were somewhat more ambiguous in youth discussions that moved away from religious comparisons to issues of social, educational and economic development. The lower and slower economic progress in the North is used to describe a sense of inferiority which is at the same time essentialised to Muslim Northerners rather than contextualised within the political histories and contextual geographies of the region.

> P4: … they [Southerners] are highly industrial, they are highly educated and they are highly westernized you see that these three things make us to believe that they are better than us and are good in their entire life. That's what makes us to be weak and lazy, Northerners don't struggle, Allah will provide. (MMA17)

In this section, we have considered the ways that religion plays a part in the construction of the particular versions of Muslim youth identities in Nigeria. Following from Sect. 6.4 that described how Northern Nigerian Muslim youth constructed the uniqueness of their national identity, here we have focused on the ways that youth use religion in particular to distinguish themselves from Nigerian national 'others' including other Muslims. As a starting point, it was made clear by both Muslim and Christian youth that religion was a central characteristic of the secular Nigerian State. Their preferred vision of their nation was both religious and modernising. Their discussion showed that, while projecting a sense of national unity especially against external 'others', in this particular form of secularity, religion was a persistent subtext to their social lives and views. Although at times somewhat contradictory, they appeared to value neighbourliness within local areas, irrespective of religion, and they regarded local ethnic differences as of minimal or reduced significance to their social networks and relations. The main axis of internal 'othering' was that of regional difference. Issues of national history, ethnicity and religion were all accumulated to reassert the North–South divide.

It is important here to highlight the ways in which greater global interconnectivity impinged upon the youth and the ways they framed internal 'others', shaped their sense of belonging and navigated their identities (Beck and Levy 2013). Access to Muslim communities across the globe had clearly had an influence that worked in uneven ways both to shape aspirations to a received and pure form of Islam and to understand how Islam intersects within different geographical and cultural locales to produce variation. The reference to a unilateral, transnational Islam was used most strenuously in emphasising their difference from Southern or especially Yoruba Muslims, as a means to sustain the North–South distinction. Significantly too, it was used by male Muslim respondents who adopted a masculinist tone of doctrinal certainty that imposed a sense of absolute authority in opposition to the discursive flow within the FGDs. A similar phenomenon was observed among Christian males who often spoke of their religion in definitive and almost evangelical tones. For the Muslim youth, the insights through ICT had provided a sense that there was authentic Islamic practice behind their claim to be Northern Nigerian Muslims. It was a resource to draw upon to bolster the position of the North within the nation and to resist the cultural and political ravages of the Christian South and the multi-religious secular state.

Finally, while the youth expressed thick affective attachments to their national and religious identities, they were also aware of the multiple ways in which such attachments and identifications had been, and continue to be, manipulated for political purposes. On the one hand, this was used to reflect on state corruption and failure across the nation and especially for the youth, and on the other hand, it was recruited to further demarcate regional distinction in which the internal 'others' in Southern Nigeria had been penetrated by the west in their religion, education and culture. Resistance to the west was constructed as a symbol of cultural and religious strength with most of the debate circulating around the social relations of gender and the position of women, which we now turn to in the next section.

6.6 Gender

As discussed in Sect. 6.1, the economic and educational underdevelopment in Nigeria as a whole is more acute in the North and this is particularly evident with respect to women. Embedded patriarchy and the widespread subordination of women have become normalised and somehow neutralised in most local and global contexts. Consistent with this, cursory observation in Northern Nigeria will show that within everyday life, gender is a clear and evident axis of social differentiation. The naturalisation of gendered hierarchies and subjectivities within social 'normality', however, makes gender identity more difficult to 'trouble'. This was reflected in the ways that gender was rarely referred to by the youth for self-identification (see Table 6.4) and in how their ethnic identities, with only one exception, were claimed through the paternal line. Nevertheless, gender was heavily drawn upon and symbolically important to distinctions in the dominant axes of region and religion.

Male youth tended to refer to gender far more than females in ways that were worked into regional and religious comparisons between Northern Muslim women and Christians or Southerners. The issues of appearance and the embodiment of Islamic femininity were the starting points:

> P2: Ok, a typical Nigerian Muslim supposed to be wearing Hijab always. … all her body is supposed to be covered. (MMA15)

The comparative descriptions of differential dress codes by region and religion focused only on females. The following extracts specifically refer to the female body, the moral significance of dress as well as explicit forms of gender/sexual regulation that all underline the symbolic significance of the feminine to religious and regional identities and distinction.

> P4: (interrupts) we Northerners are very good even in terms of mode of dressing. … especially females you will identify her by her dress. If she (a

> Southerner) dresses, you will know that this is not a Northerner because they expose their body and sometimes they can walk naked … half naked. … They think if people see them like that, they will look attractive and it is not like that. According to our custom even though you cover every part of your body and put that veil, a woman puts a good dress, she will look so good and there is no way you do bad dress and then bad people will not contact you. But if you do good dress and appear very well there is no way bad boy will come … (MMA15)
>
> P1: If you see a Muslim woman that is Yoruba by tribe, you can't compare her with Hausa woman. They (Yoruba) will wear trouser, mini skirt, spaghetti shirt … and we don't normally allow our women to appear like that. They like exposing their body parts so that they will look attractive. (MMA2)
>
> P2: If a Muslim woman wears trouser in my place, they will see you as a prostitute. (MFA13)

Notwithstanding these comparisons across religious groups, it was interesting to note that a number of Christian females living in the North had adopted modest forms of attire that mimicked the dress codes of Muslim females including wearing veils and full-length dresses. Muslim males also used descriptions of social inter-relations between females and males to highlight the distinctions between the two religious traditions:

> P4: … if I was a Christian … hugging, chatting, blending with girls, I can do. But as far as I am not a Christian, I can't do that. It is restricted to me because my religion told me that it is not good. But if I am a Christian … it is not restricted to them, more especially in terms of doing Zina (fornication). (MMA17)

When male youth were asked specifically about gender differences, they drew on and embellished myths of biological or essentialised difference to support and justify gendered practices. Their explanations were always based on binary notions of sex, gender and sexuality (Dunne 2008).

P3: there are a lot of things that can differentiate a man from a woman. Because man, even from history, God created a woman from the ribs of man, you cannot compare a man and a woman because man is very strong and women are not strong. They are very weak. (MMA2)

P6: … the IQ of a man, under normal circumstances should now double that of a woman. (MMA16)

P2: Yes, Islamically, being a Muslim man differs from being a Muslim woman. Being a Muslim man means a man is more complete than a lady because in a month there are days a Muslim lady will not perform the act of ibada, the act of worship. That's a difference, that's one that's their monthly period. Also when she gives birth and … I think that's when she'll be limited to follow some of her duties as a Muslim. (MMA15)

This framing of women as essentially and necessarily weak, unintelligent and incapable of practising 'proper' Islam fully was elaborated by Muslim males. They extended their characterisations of women to describe and rationalise everyday familial relationships, discrete gender social spheres and a male-dominated gender hierarchy across society.

P4: Women in Nigeria, most of them are house wives. Most of them are restricted to domestic roles. More especially here in the North. (MMA17)

P1: Responsibilities also differ. The man is said to be the head of the house and he's the one that is supposed to provide all the necessary things for the woman at home and the woman will be at home to take care of the children… you understand… she is only allowed to be out on condition … Conditional circumstances. She is always at home but the man is said to be out to get some things to bring home. (MMA15)

P3: … the man is the head of the household so, whenever a woman is going out, she has to look for permission from her husband… (MMA16)

P2: … yes, he is in-charge he gives the instructions, so the woman obeys the husband even in terms of divorce, it is hard for the woman to divorce (Laughs). And you can marry more than one wife … but the woman is not allowed to marry more than one husband. (MMA15)

Similar gender views were articulated by Northern Christian males:

> P3: No, no, no, women ... are meant to be home makers, you know a man cannot just go and be washing dishes cooking here and there ... [according to] our culture in Nigeria a woman should be under a man's control ... A woman cannot sit down no matter how rich she is, she cannot be ahead of her husband so a man is always a man and a woman is always a woman. (CMP11)

A Nigerian man ...

> P1: ... doesn't take nonsense from a woman, he is always a man and he always deserves the respect that should be accorded him.
>
> P2: ... would always want to be a breadwinner in the family ... and has ultimate responsibility as the head of the household.
>
> P3: ... does not compromise his position no matter what ... the Nigerian woman [who] is at the back seat. (CMP8)
>
> P2: Any man that is not the bread winner of his family is considered a woman. (CFP10)

Female Muslim respondents confirmed these social and domestic conditions which they justified through reference to the Qu'ran and Islamic practice rather than an essentialised and subordinate female character. As the following extracts illustrate, however, the female youth highlighted the problematics in the ways that the gender aspirations for 'proper' Islam intersected with local practicalities and experiences of everyday life:

> P4: ... for the Muslim men they have too many wives while the women just one husband, and the Muslim men are to go outside and look for what to take care of the family, while the women you're going outside without your husband permission is totally unacceptable. (MFA14)
>
> P5: You see in Qu'ran they tell woman to stay indoors, but the main problem the Muslim women are having they don't agree, if they do that

> ... for the men when they are not capable of doing that, it brings problem to their lives. (MFA13)
>
> P3: Ok, for the men, you know in Islam is permitted for you to marry four wives you have to treat them equally. But now they take it as you just marry somebody and neglect the other one. (MFA13)
>
> P3: You are only permitted to marry four wives, that is, if you are capable. Some of them they don't have anything and if you ask them they will say that Prophet Mohammed (SAW) did that. They want to do it, they won't practice other things that the Prophet does only that marriage site. (MFA12)

Despite these challenges, an idealised gender positioning within Muslim Northern Nigeria was drawn into discussions to highlight the tensions between Muslim doctrine and those condoned by secular state policy:

> P1: My religion instructs that I should not interact with my female counterpart who is not my legal wife. The society or my country allowed it. We interact in the market, in the school, everywhere, sometime you have doctors who are females they might have to look at your private part to give you medicine, although the religion permits it under certain circumstances, but that thing is painful. Like what the federal government is now saying that we should have birth control and also about equal rights between men and women, that women should be allowed to participate in the administration of the nation. (MMA15)
>
> P1: ... I cannot allow my wife to go out in public without a reasonable excuse that is allowed by my religion. I do restrict her despite the fact that they said women absence is also a right. I cannot allow her to work in a public institution; my religion denied me that, so I cannot expose her to such level. ... the law is saying that women should go out and participate in politics, this is against my religion. (MMA16)

Gender equality and female participation were framed as symbolic of Western influence and oppositional to a pure, received Islamic practice. This was observed even in Saudi Arabia which was the most revered nation outside Nigeria for the majority of Muslim youth.

> P2: Most people like Saudi because they are religious, but the problem is that they are beginning to copy the western world recently they are deciding how to put women in their government and if you see the real teaching of Islam, woman supposed to be not in government and now they are deciding to put women in their government so they are not religious. (MFA12)

It was in the same vein that Nigerian State policy on gender equality as well as demands from women for greater inclusion in governance were actively rebutted by both female and male youth as against their religious principles:

> P1: … in Islam it is not accepted for a woman to become a leader … they (men) are more economical, they control our economy. We women we do as women we are just there to guide them and help them they have the powers—they rule us. (MFA13)
>
> P1: Another thing is that we don't allow our women to participate in politics in Nigeria compared to other nations especially in the north. (MMA17)
>
> P3: … a lady may have something to say but because of her sex, you deny her from saying. (MMA17)

The misogyny, explicit regulation of women and their exclusion from public participation highlights deep fissures between the national and federal aspirations of a future Nigerian nation and those expressed, often very personally, by the Muslim youth respondents (Nagel 1998). The above-described female embodiments, gender relations, female subordination and their exclusions tended to be valorised. Certainly, within the public space of the FGDs, these gender norms were problematised by only a few Muslim females. It is significant that in these cases, female contestation of the norms was on the basis of Islam rather than invoking national gender equality legislation. Resonating with Mahmood's (2012) analysis, we point to these as examples of women's agency exercised within the codes and practices of Islam. Nevertheless, the representations of women described above were symbolically important and used as a discursive vector of differences in religion, region and ethnicity

(Mayer 2000). The naturalisation of gender was also critical to the production of Muslim youth masculinities. This worked to solidify male power and authority and reciprocally to bolster the aspiration to notions of a received 'pure' form of Islam.

6.7 Conclusions

In this chapter, Muslim youth identities were explored largely through qualitative inquiry supplemented by some quantitative data and analysis of their initial identifications. While the main focus has been on Muslim youth, the contributions of Northern Christian youth have been selectively incorporated to provide some nuanced comparisons of youth expressions of belonging and difference. With only one exception, all youth expressed enormous pride and a strong affective attachment to their national identity. The acknowledged problems associated with their national identity and especially its association with corruption appeared not to shake their allegiance to the nation-state. We return to the continuing significance of youth's identifications with the nation in the concluding chapter, particularly given the contemporary significance often attributed to transnational, post-national or more 'cosmopolitan' forms of citizenship. Discussions of how external 'others' viewed Nigeria also precipitated expressions of dissatisfaction and disappointment with successive national governments, the electoral system and local governance processes. While state failure, especially with respect to youth, was provided as an explanation for the Islamic extremism of Boko Haram, there was no sympathy expressed for their cause and strategies. The stronger tendency was for Muslim youth to distance themselves from terrorism and defend themselves against the accusation.

As the FGDs moved on to relations with their compatriots, strong lines of internal social differentiation were discussed. Although not mutually inclusive, religious differences between Muslims and Christians were conflated with regional distinctions to form a region–religion dyad. This was a dominant discursive axis taken up by the youth to frame their identities and solidify a position as Northerners. It also worked to reduce the significance of local ethnic differences which were recognised, but rarely used to demarcate internal 'others'. Whether from the north or the south of the country, ethnicity was always submerged within the respective regional affiliation. The regional fracturing of the nation revivified Nigeria's birth scars and its uneasy historical emergence as a postcolonial, multi-religious democracy. However, as region and religion do not map onto each other exactly, considerable discursive space and effort were taken up in forging a rift between Northern Muslims and their Muslim brothers (and sisters!) from the south. This rift is produced by suturing Northern Muslim identity to a notion of a received, 'pure' Islamic identity and practice. Facilitated by ICT, Northern Muslim youth had access to transnational Islamic communities and individuals from across the globe. For some, this had transformed their Muslim identity from an internal, regional and political belonging to one associated with principled forms of practice and connection beyond the national landscape. The reference to a received, 'pure' form of Islamic practice, however, was used largely to re-invoke the same distinctions that they claimed separated northern from Southern or Yoruba Muslims. In other words, the recruitment of more 'universal' religious practices that transcend national boundaries and so can be equated with more 'cosmopolitan' or post-national forms of citizenship (Calhoun 2008; Eliassi 2014) was inseparable from the construction of the internal 'others' of the nation and integral to its reimagining (Beck and Levy 2013).

Internal 'others' were further derided in their loss of culture and their adopted Westernisation. Within the FGDs, some male youth employed the apparent imperatives of a received form of Islam in the performance of authoritative masculinities that quickly closed down conversation or debate on matters of religion. This was by no means universal as many Northern Muslim youth, especially females, recognised the moderating effect of local cultural traditions on aspirations to a 'pure' Islamic practice. In the discussions of internal 'others', gender was rarely claimed or named as a structure of identity. This invisibility within the youth narratives stood in stark comparison to the ways that everyday life was highly gendered and the male-dominated gender hierarchy was assumed. Despite this, it was a key axis for comparison with the internal 'others' and a critically important symbol of religion, religious identity and religious purity. Projections of subordinate and modest femininity were vital to the masculinist images of strength, control and superiority. Many male youth framed their own gender identities through a convergence of dominant masculinity with 'proper' forms of Islamic practice which were articulated through reference to subservient, modest femininities. This convergence of religion and masculinity implied that a softening in either masculinity or religion indicated a softening of both. It was from this convergence that male youth, both Muslim and Christian, drew authority and expounded on 'proper' religious practice in ways that were rarely demonstrated by female youth. However, some female youth could identify and be critical of the contradictions between certain Islamic codes, such as rules relating to marriage, and their lived realities, in ways that male respondents rarely did. This suggests females taking up agentic space within norms of Islamic religious practice in ways described in Mahmood's (2012) study. Further systematic ethnographic research could usefully elaborate upon female agency within Islam which we were unable to explore through focus group discussions.

This exploration of Muslim youth identities in Northern Nigeria in this chapter is the third of four country case studies. It is part of a theoretical and empirical thread of the book that explores how youth construct their narratives of belonging within Muslim-majority populations in specific geographic and national locations. The effort has been to trace how youth appropriate, configure and navigate locally available discourses of identity to position themselves locally, nationally and globally. The case of Nigeria as a multi-religious secular state offers a particular set of social circumstances that contrast with the very high Muslim populations in the Islamic state of Pakistan and the secular state of Senegal. The specific circumstances for the emergence of Nigeria as a postcolonial nation, its multi-religious yet secular state as well as its enormous ethnic and linguistic diversity provide a complex historical and geographical backdrop within which young people are trying to make sense of themselves and frame their identities. While all Nigerian youth articulated strong attachments to the nation, the emphasis in this case study on region and religion (Muslim and Christian) as axes of difference from internal 'others' reflects the enormous diversity within the state. The fracturing of the state by religion (and region/geography) is taken up further in the next country case of Lebanon. The dominant focus on Lebanese Shi'a Muslim youth is set within a context in which state boundaries include Christian and Sunni Muslim populations. The focus on Shi'a youth identities and their connection to historical and contemporary narratives in Lebanon, especially between Muslim groups, holds an important place in this series of case studies and is a significant final case in our explorations of Muslim youth identities.

Note

1. For a map of Nigeria showing the geo-political zones, please see http://3.bp.blogspot.com/-yWnFva-e7EI/TiyjIWbSScI/AAAAAAAABOM/18Qbfn53CXA/s1600/Naija-GeoPolitical-Map.jpg.

References

Agboola, B. M., & Ofoegbu, F. I. (2010). Access to university education in Nigeria: A review. http://20.132.48.254/PDFS/ED511051.pdf.

Ahmed, S. (2004). *The cultural politics of emotion*. Edinburgh: Edinburgh University Press.

Al Jazeera. (2015). Buhari secures historic election victory in Nigeria. Retrieved April 10, 2015, from http://www.aljazeera.com/news/2015/03/opposition-party-declares-victory-nigeria-election-150331135603507.html.

Anderson, B. (1991). *Imagined communities: Reflections on the origin and spread of nationalism*. London: Verso.

Asad, T. (2003). *Formations of the secular. Christianity, Islam, modernity*. Stanford: Stanford University Press.

Bakari, S. (2009). *Making gender sense in schools: Nigeria*. Unpublished report (2nd ed.) based on the commonwealth study for E. Page & J. Jha (Eds.), *Exploring the bias: Gender and stereotyping in secondary schools*. London: Commonwealth Secretariat.

Bakari, S., & Leach, F. E. (2008). 'I invited her to my office': Normalising sexual violence in a Nigerian College of Education. In M. Dunne (Ed.), *Gender, sexuality and development: Education and society in sub-Saharan Africa* (pp. 71–83). Rotterdam: Sense Publishers.

Beck, U. (1992). *Risk society. Towards a new modernity.* London: Sage.
Beck, U., & Levy, D. (2013). Cosmopolitanized nations: Re-imagining collectivity in world risk society. *Theory, Culture & Society, 30*(2), 3–31.
Berger, P. L. (1999). The desecularization of the world: A global overview. In P. L. Berger (Ed.), *The desecularization of the world. Resurgent religion and world politics* (pp. 1–19). Grand Rapids: Eerdmans.
Boston University Center for Global Health and Development with Initiative for Integrated Community Welfare in Nigeria (BUCGHD) (2009). *Situation analysis on orphans and other vulnerable children: Country brief.* Boston: Center for Global Health and Development, Boston University.
British Council. (2012). *Gender in Nigeria report, 2012. Improving the lives of girls and women in Nigeria: Issues policies action.* Nigeria: British Council/UK Aid.
Burchardt, M., & Wohlrab-Sahr, M. (2013). Multiple secularities: Religion and modernity in the global age—Introduction. *International Sociology, 28*(6), 605–611.
Butler, J. (2011). Is Judaism Zionism? In J. Butler, J. Habermas, C. Taylor, & C. West (Eds.), *The power of religion in the public sphere* (pp. 70–92). New York: Columbia University Press.
Butler, J. (2013, September 16–19). *Rethinking vulnerability and resistance: Feminism & social change.* Paper presented at the Women Creating Change, Istanbul workshop. http://www.institutofranklin.net/sites/default/files/files/Rethinking.
Calhoun, C. (2008). Cosmopolitanism in the modern social imaginary. *Daedalus, 137*(3), 105–114.
Central Intelligence Agency (CIA). (2015). *The world factbook.* https://www.cia.gov/library/publications/the-world-factbook/geos/ni.html.
Dunne, M. (Ed.). (2008). *Gender, sexuality and development: Education and society in sub-Saharan Africa.* Rotterdam: Sense Publishers.
Dunne, M., Humphreys, S., Dauda, M., Kaibo J., & Garuba, A. (2013). *Adamawa state primary education research: Access, quality and outcomes, with specific reference to gender.* Adamawa State Universal Basic Education Board: University of Sussex; Brighton: Yola.
Dunne, M., Durrani, N., Crossouard, B., & Fincham, K. (2014). *Youth as active citizens report. Youth working towards their rights to education and sexual and reproductive health.* Brighton: University of Sussex; The Hague: Oxfam Novib.
Eliassi, B. (2014). Nationalism, cosmopolitanism and statelessness: An interview with Craig Calhoun. *Kurdish Studies, 2*(1), 61–74.

Falola, T., & Heaton, M. M. (2008). *A history of Nigeria*. Cambridge: Cambridge University Press.

Federal Office of Statistics (FOS)/International Labour Organisation (ILO). (2001). *National modular child labour survey: Country report*. Geneva: ILO/SIMPOC.

Giddens, A. (1991). *Modernity and self-identity*. Cambridge: Polity Press.

Hermann, L. (2005). Religion and politics in processes of modernisation. *Totalitarian Movements and Political Religions, 6*(1), 53–70.

Hjelmgaard, K. (2015, April 14). Timeline: Boko Haram conflict. *USA TODAY*. http://www.usatoday.com/story/news/world/2015/04/14/boko-haram-timeline/25757989/.

Hoechner, H. (2011). Striving for knowledge and dignity: How Qur'anic students in Kano, Nigeria, learn to live with rejection and educational disadvantage. *European Journal of Development Research*. doi:10.1057/ejdr.2011.39.

Humphreys, S., & Crawfurd, L. (2014). *Review of the literature on basic education in Nigeria: Issues of access, quality, equity and impact*. Abuja: EDOREN.

Jonah, A., & Igboeroteonwu, A. (2014). Bombings kill at least 118 in Nigerian city of Jos. *Reuters*. http://news.yahoo.com/blasts-central-nigerian-city-jos-kill-10-174841877.html.

Kabeer, N. (2002). Citizenship and the boundaries of the acknowledged community: Identity, affiliation and exclusion. *IDS working paper 171*. Falmer: Institute of Development Studies.

Kalberg, S. (1997). Tocqueville and Weber on the sociological origins of citizenship: The political culture of American democracy. *Citizenship Studies, 1*(2), 199–222.

Krämer, G. (2013). Modern but not secular: Religion, identity and the *ordre public* in the Arab Middle East. *International Sociology, 28*(6), 629–644.

Last, M. (2008). The search for security in Muslim northern Nigeria. *The Journal of the International African Institute, 78*(1), 41–63.

Litwack, J., Joseph-Raji, G., Babalola, O., & Kojima, M. (2013). *Nigerian Economic Report no. 1*. Washington, DC: World Bank.

Mahmood, S. (2012). *Politics of piety: The Islamic revival and the feminist subject*. Princeton, NJ and Oxford: Princeton University Press.

Mamdani, M. (1996). *Citizen and subject. Contemporary Africa and the legacy of late colonialism*. Princeton, NJ: Princeton University Press.

Mamdani, M. (2004). *Good Muslim, bad Muslim. America, the Cold War and the roots of terror*. New York: Panthean Books.

Mark, M. (2015, January 28). Yola: The city where people fleeing Boko Haram outnumber 400,000 locals. *The Guardian*. http://www.theguardian.com/world/2015/jan/28/boko-haram-nigeria-yola-refugees-monica-mark-adamawa.

Mayer, T. (2000). Gender ironies of nationalism: Setting the stage. In T. Mayer (Ed.), *Gender ironies of nationalism: Sexing the nation* (pp. 1–24). London: Routledge.

Mouffe, C. (1992). Feminism, citizenship and radical democratic politics. In J. Scott & J. Butler (Eds.), *Feminists theorize the political* (pp. 367–384). New York: Routledge.

Nagel, J. (1998). Masculinity and nationalism: Gender and sexuality in the making of nations. *Ethnic and Racial Studies, 21*(2), 242–269.

Nash, K. (2012). Human rights, movements and law: On not researching legitimacy. *Sociology, 46*(5), 797–812.

National Population Commission (NPC). (2010). *2006 population and housing census. Priority table III. Population distribution by sex, state, LGA and senatorial district*. Abuja: NPC.

National Population Commission (NPC) and ICF Macro. (2009). *Nigeria demographic and health survey 2008*. Abuja: NPC and ICF Macro.

National Population Commission and RTI International. (2011). *Nigeria DHS Ed data survey 2010: Education data for decision-making*. Washington, DC: NPC and RTI International.

National Population Commission (NPC). (2014). *Nigerian demographic and health survey 2013*. Abuja: NPC.

Nwabueze, B. O. (1982). *A constitutional history of Nigeria*. London: Hurst Printers.

Onapajo, H., & Usman, A. A. (2015). Fuelling the flames: Boko Haram and deteriorating Christian–Muslim relations in Nigeria. *Journal of Muslim Minority Affairs, 35*(1), 106–122.

Osaghae, E. E., & Suberu, R. T. (2005). A history of identities, violence and stability in Nigeria. Centre for Research of Inequality, Human Security and Ethnicity (CRISE) Working Paper No. 6. Oxford: CRISE.

Otayek, R., & Soares, B. F. (2007). Introduction: Islam and Muslim politics in Africa. In B. F. Soares & R. Otayek (Eds.), *Islam and muslim politics in Africa* (pp. 1–24). Hampshire: Palgrave Macmillan.

Parsons, T. (1977). *The evolution of societies*. New York: Prentice Hall.

Peel, J. D. Y. (2003). *Religious encounter and the making of the Yoruba*. Bloomington and Indianapolis: Indiana University Press.

Pereira, C. (2007). *Gender in the making of the Nigerian University System*. Oxford and Ibadan: James Currey and Heinemann Education Books.

Salaam, A. O. (2012). Boko Haram: Beyond religious fanaticism. *Journal of Policing, Intelligence and Terrorism, 7*(2), 147–162.

Sampson, I. T. (2014). Religion and the Nigerian state: Situating the de facto and de jure frontiers of state–religion relations and its implications for national security. *Oxford Journal of Law and Religion, 3*(2), 311–339.

Sanusi, S. L. (2007). Politics and Sharia in Northern Nigeria. In B. F. Soares & R. Otayek (Eds.), *Islam and Muslim politics in Africa* (pp. 177–188). Hampshire: Palgrave Macmillan.

Tran, M. (2015, January 19). Boko Haram—The guardian briefing. *The Guardian*. http://www.theguardian.com/world/2015/jan/19/-sp-boko-haram-the-guardian-briefing.

Ukiwo, U. (2005). The study of ethnicity in Nigeria. *Oxford Development Studies, 33*(1), 7–23.

UNDP. (2009). *Human development report Nigeria 2008–2009: Achieving growth with equity*. Abuja: UNDP.

UNESCO. (2015). *Global monitoring report 2015: Achievements and challenges*. Paris: UNESCO.

UNICEF. (2015). *The state of the world's children: Reimagine the future*. Retrieved from http://www.unicef.org/sowc/.

UNICEF/UIS. (2012). *Global initiative on out-of-school children: Nigeria country study*. Abuja: UNICEF.

Vorster, N. (2013). Christianity and Secularisation in South Africa: Probing the possible link between Modernisation and Secularisation.*Studies in World Christianity, 19*(2), 141–161. Retrieved from http://dx.doi.org.ezproxy.sussex.ac.uk/10.3366/swc.2013.0049.

Weber, M. (1947). *From Max Weber: Essays in sociology* (H. H. Gerth & C. Wright Mills, Trans.). London: Kegan Paul, Trench, Trubner & Co.

Weber, M. (1976). *The protestant ethic and the spirit of capitalism* (2nd ed.) (T. Parsons, Trans.). London: George Allen.

World Economic Forum. (2015a). *Global gender gap report*. Geneva: World Economic Forum. Retrieved May 10, 2016, from http://reports.weforum.org/global-gender-gap-report-2015/.

World Economic Forum. (2015b). *The human capital report 2015*. http://reports.weforum.org/human-capital-report-2015/economies/#economy=NGA.

7
Lebanon: National Imaginaries, State Fragilities and the Shi'a Other

Abstract Lebanon, located along the eastern Mediterranean shore, has traditionally been an important cultural crossroads between East and West. However, despite its relative ethnic homogeneity (Arab), Lebanon has often been at the centre of Middle Eastern conflicts because of its geographical positioning and its distinctively complex religious composition. Unique in the Middle East, Lebanon has 18 officially recognised religious sects and no dominant religious group. Shi'a Muslims comprise a significant portion of the Lebanese population, and Shi'a make up the majority in South Lebanon, the Beqa'a Valley and the southern suburbs of Beirut. The sectarian complexity described above has only been intensified within the context of Lebanon's 'weak state', in which its governmental institutions are less powerful than many non-state actors. In particular, political movements and non-state paramilitary organisations organised along religious lines maintain considerable clout in the country (the most powerful being Shi'a-dominated Hezbollah). As a result, Lebanese politicians (and much of the population) view societal problems, politics and security issues through the lens of sectarian communal identification, while abstract notions of common Lebanese citizenship are destabilised. This chapter focuses on the ways that Shi'a youth in South Lebanon construct and negotiate their identities of nation, religion, ethnicity and gender within the local context of Lebanon's complex sectarian balance and within the broader context of contemporary regional conflicts. In particular, the chapter explores how male and female Shi'a youth understand themselves and live their lives both as members of the Muslim majority in Lebanon and the Middle East as well as Muslim minority 'others' in relation to the dominant regional paradigm of Sunni Islam.

7.1 Introduction and Context

With its geographical positioning on the shores of the eastern Mediterranean, its high literacy rate (Table 3.1) and its historic mercantile culture, Lebanon has traditionally been an important commercial hub for the Middle East, as well as an important cultural crossroads between East and West. However, in modern times, despite its small size and relative ethnic homogeneity (Arab),[1] Lebanon has often been at the centre of Middle Eastern conflicts because of its borders with Israel and Syria and its distinctively complex religious composition. Unique in the Middle East, Lebanon is a parliamentary democracy with 18 officially recognised religious sects and no dominant religious group (the largest religious groups being Muslim and Christian[2]). Unlike the other country contexts discussed in this book, Shi'a[3] Muslims comprise a significant portion of the population[4] (estimated to be approximately 30–40% of the total Lebanese population), and Shi'a make up the majority in South Lebanon, the Beqa'a Valley and the southern suburbs of Beirut.

This chapter focuses on the ways that Shi'a youth in South Lebanon construct and negotiate their identities of nation, religion, ethnicity and gender within the local context of Lebanon's complex sectarian balance and within the broader context of contemporary regional conflicts. In particular, the chapter explores how male and female Shi'a youth understand themselves and live their lives both as members of the Muslim majority in Lebanon and the Middle East as well asMuslim minority 'others' in relation to the dominant regional paradigm of Sunni Islam.

History and Geography

Lebanon, with an estimated population of five million (Table 3.1), is situated on a narrow coastal strip along the eastern shore of the Mediterranean Sea.[5] Geo-politically considered to be part of the Middle East, Lebanon, with an area of 10,400 km^2 (Table 3.1), borders Syria to the north and east and Israel to the south. Lebanon's history is long and rich, encompassing Canaanite, Phoenician, Egyptian, Roman, Umayyad, Crusader and Ottoman civilisations. Likewise, the Lebanese cities of Byblos, Beirut, Sidon (Arabic: *Saida*) and Tyre (Arabic: *Sur*) are among the oldest continuously inhabited cities in the world.

From the sixteenth century until the beginning of the twenty-first century, the land and people comprising what is now the state of Lebanon were part of the (Sunni-ruled) Ottoman empire (based in modern-day Turkey). Under Ottoman rule, Shi'a Muslims experienced both intense persecution and periods of 'unofficial tolerance' by state authorities (Winter 2010). This (at least partly) coincided with a period of powerful rivalry between the Ottomans and the (Shi'a-ruled) Safavid dynasty in neighbouring Persia (modern-day Iran), where Sunni Islam (along with other religions) was suppressed (BBC 2009).

After the fall of the Ottoman Empire, the Sykes-Picot Agreement (1916) partitioned the former empire's Arabic-speaking provinces into zones under British control and influence (modern-day Iraq, Kuwait, Jordan and Israel/Palestine) and those under the control and influence of France (modern-day Syria and Lebanon). Originally part of Greater Syria, the borders of Lebanon (centred around Mount Lebanon) were drawn by the French to carve out a Christian-majority country in the midst of the predominantly Muslim Middle East. This was intended both to provide a safe haven for the existing Maronite[6] Christian population of Mount Lebanon and to provide the French with a base of control from which they could exercise their power and interests in Syria. Territories to the north and south of Mount Lebanon, as well as the Beqa'a Valley and Beirut (largely populated by Sunni and Shi'a Muslims), were subsequently added to form Greater Lebanon, the precursor of the modern state of Lebanon. Both the boundaries of Christian enclave around Mount Lebanon and the later inclusion of

Sunni and Shi'a Muslims within Greater Lebanon produced fault lines of religious difference that remain significant in contemporary Lebanese social and political life. Greater Lebanon was officially put under French Mandate by the League of Nations in 1920, and the first Lebanese constitution (modelled after that of the French Third Republic) was promulgated on 23 May 1926 (Hakim 2013).

However, unlike the other country contexts discussed in this book, European colonial domination was short (lasting less than a generation) with Lebanon officially declaring its independence on 22 November 1943. At this time, an unwritten agreement divided parliamentary seats along communal lines as defined in the 1932 census, when the country had a (Maronite) Christian majority. No official census has been taken in the country since 1932, and Muslim groups have consistently demanded that political representation should reflect their increased proportion in the population. On the other hand, many Christians fear a Muslim majority, as (unique among country contexts discussed in this book) Christianity predates Islam in the region, with the city of Tyre (fieldwork location) being specifically mentioned in both the Old and New Testaments of the Bible.[7] This communal tension has been at the heart of most internal conflict in Lebanon ever since (Fisk 2001).

In 1975, sectarian tension in the country boiled over into a devastating civil war, which lasted for almost 16 years. Sometimes described as being 'Muslim versus Christian', the Lebanese Civil War was actually a multifaceted conflict in which there was nearly as much intra-sectarian violence as there was violence between religious groups. Starting in 1975, the war resulted in an estimated 130,000–250,000 civilian fatalities over the course of the next 16 years. Another one million people (approximately one-third of the population) were wounded, and thousands (mostly Christians) fled the country (Fisk 2001).

The conflict within Lebanon was intensified when neighbouring states used the internal instability within the country as a pretext for intervention. In particular, Syria, Israel and the Palestine Liberation Organisation (PLO) used the country as a battleground for their own conflicts and interests. Under the pretext of limiting the influence of the PLO in Lebanon (which had entrenched itself in the south of the country), Syrian troops entered Lebanon shortly after the war started, with Syria only ending its 29-year military presence in 2005 under international pressure after the assassination of former Lebanese Prime Minister, Rafik Hariri (BBC 2015). Also, under the pretext of ousting the PLO from Lebanon, Israeli troops invaded the country in 1978 and again in 1982, before pulling back to a self-declared 'security zone' in South Lebanon, from which they only withdrew in May 2000 (Fisk 2001). Israel still occupies territories in the south which are claimed by Lebanon, namely the mainly Shi'a 'seven villages' (*Tarbikha, Saliha, Malkiya, Nabi Yusha, Kades, Hunin* and *Ibal Qamh*), as well as the '*Sheba'a* Farms' (also claimed by Syria) (Kaufman 2006).

At the end of the Lebanese Civil War, the 1989 *Ta'if* Agreement, signed by surviving members of Lebanon's 1972 parliament, established a system of governance in Lebanon known as 'confessionalism', which attempted to fairly represent the 18 recognised religious sects in government. According to Article 24 of the Lebanese Constitution, the President must be a Maronite Christian, the Prime Minister a Sunni Muslim and the Speaker of the Parliament a Shi'a Muslim. This makes Lebanon's system of power-sharing extremely complex, as well as rigid. The confessional system has also constructed a unique legal framework in the country, which has resulted in an extreme case of legal pluralism. Lebanese are governed by a system of separate 'personal status laws', allowing the different historical religious groups in the country to apply their own laws to family affairs. While personal status laws exist alongside the country's secular civil law, there is no civil code covering issues such as marriage, divorce, inheritance, custody of children and spousal/child support, often placing women in particular situations of vulnerability. Moreover, in practice, there is little or no government oversight of religious courts (Tabet 2005).

Although the confessional arrangement was originally intended to deter further sectarian conflict, it has been a major source of tension and conflict within the country. This is because significant demographic changes have taken place within Lebanon since the last official population census in 1932, including a vast increase in the overall Muslim population (Sunni and Shi'a) mostly due to the emigration of large numbers of Maronite Christians and a higher Muslim birth rate. This has called into question the legitimacy of the current power-sharing arrangement. It has also led to ongoing feelings of mistrust between religious communities within Lebanon and worked to undermine the authority of the state.

In addition to experiencing major internal strife, Lebanon has also been embroiled in regional and international conflict. Arising from Israel's 1982 invasion and occupation of South Lebanon was the Iranian and Syrian regime-supported Lebanese Shi'a political and military organisation, Hezbollah (literal translation: 'Party of God', sometimes referred to as 'the Islamic Resistance'), which is widely considered to be the most powerful military force in the country. Since Hezbollah's foundation, there has been recurrent conflict with Israel, culminating in all-out warfare in July 2006. Since then, there have been intermittent armed skirmishes between Hezbollah and Israel, and Lebanon and Israel remain technically at war. The United Nations Interim Force in Lebanon (UNIFIL) remains in the country to patrol border areas with Israel and to monitor the cessation of hostilities. Although the UN has demanded the dismantling of all armed groups in Lebanon, including the military wing of Hezbollah (which controls much of southern Lebanon and the Beqa'a Valley), Hezbollah maintains that it needs to remain armed as a deterrent to further Israeli aggression. While Hezbollah is considered to be a terrorist organisation by several international governments, and some Lebanese consider Hezbollah to be a threat to the country's stability, it remains enduringly popular within the Shi'a community in Lebanon. This is partly out of respect for Hezbollah's considerable military accomplishments and partly out of appreciation for its charitable organisations, which provide much needed social service support in areas underserved by the Lebanese government (Saad-Ghorayeb 2002; Harik 2004).

Within the last few years, sectarian conflict between Sunni and Shi'a communities has increased throughout the region, culminating in all-out warfare in Iraq and Syria, with tensions spreading in Lebanon, Yemen, Saudi Arabia, Bahrain and countries further afield, such as Pakistan. Existing sectarian tensions within Lebanon have been exacerbated by Lebanon's long-term 'hosting' of 500,000 Palestinian refugees and recent 'hospitality' to 1.2 million Syrian refugees (both groups are overwhelmingly Sunni), with Syrian refugees alone comprising 25% of the total population of Lebanon. Lebanese politicians across the political and religious spectra are in agreement that permanent settlement of these refugees in Lebanon, imposed or voluntary, would devastate the Lebanese nation. This is partly because the naturalisation of such a large number of Sunni Muslims would upset the delicate sectarian balance carefully reconstructed in Lebanon at the end of the civil war (Fisk 2001). Recently, the neighbouring conflict in Syria has also spilled over into Lebanon, as Hezbollah has sent fighters across the border to support Syria's President Bashar al-Assad, a close ally of Shi'a-led Iran. On the other hand, Hezbollah's Sunni Lebanese rivals (supported by Saudi Arabia) have largely supported the Sunni-led rebellion against the existing Syrian government (BBC 2016).

The section below discusses the educational environment in which Lebanese youth learn about themselves and others.

Education

In Lebanon, the cycle of education consists of 6 years of primary education, 3 years of intermediate education and 3 years of secondary education. After secondary school, students may proceed to higher education (university, technical/vocational college) or employment. The languages of instruction in Lebanese schools are Arabic, French and English. Language of instruction depends on the type of education (public or private), level of education, subject being taught, affiliation of the school and the availability of teachers in rural areas. In general, Arabic is more widely used in public schools, at primary level, and for subjects such as history, geography and civics, while French and English are more widely used in private schools, at higher grades and for technical subjects such as maths and science.

The youth literacy rate (15–24 years) in Lebanon is nearly universal at 99%, and school life expectancy (13.8 years) is the highest of any country context discussed in this book (Table 3.1). Although Lebanon ranks quite low in gender equality overall (Table 3.1), and illiteracy among women over 40 years old is double that of men of the same age, there is near gender parity in education at primary level (0.93), and females outnumber males at secondary (1.01) and tertiary (1.09) levels (UNESCO 2016). Despite this, there are significant regional and communal inequalities. For example, the geographic distribution of quality schools tends to be concentrated around Beirut and the northern areas of the country, which are predominantly populated by Christians and Sunni Muslims. Moreover, illiteracy rates are higher in the Beqa'a Valley (14.45%) and South Lebanon (12.25%), which have predominately Shi'a populations (Frayha 2009).

A distinctive feature of the Lebanese education system is the predominance of private providers. The majority of Lebanese children and youth (approximately 70%) are educated in fee-charging private schools where the quality of education is relatively high, but attendance is contingent on families' ability to pay. On the other hand, 30% of Lebanese young people are enrolled in free but often poor quality public schools, which are largely dependent on donor funding and are often plagued by teacher shortages and infrastructure problems. This has resulted in the development of gaps between economically advantaged and disadvantaged youth in Lebanon (USAID 2015). The public/private divide is particularly acute in relation to higher education. While most of the oldest colleges and universities in the country were founded by missionaries and some, such as the American University of Beirut (1866) and the Université Saint-Joseph (1875), predated the establishment of the Lebanese State, many new private universities have been established in the last half-century, such as the Shi'a-affiliated Islamic University of Lebanon (1996). In contrast, the Lebanese University (1951) remains the only public institution for higher learning in the country.

Private education in Lebanon is generally segregated along religious lines, with religious communities of all denominations having the option to organise their own schools, control what is taught and choose their own textbooks (UNESCO 2014). The existence of parallel systems and diversified curricula have often been cited as contributing factors to ongoing divisions between communities and the propagation of sectarianism within the country. It has also challenged the development of a common national identity based on a set of shared social and civic values (Frayha 2009). Lebanon's history of communal conflict has particularly posed challenges for the teaching of history. As attribution for Lebanon's civil war remains unresolved and wounds between religious communities remain fresh, official history textbooks taught in Lebanese schools stop abruptly in 1943, the year the country gained independence. Although intended to avoid inflaming old hostilities, this has left many young Lebanese with unanswered questions about the civil war, as well as their communal past (Al Jazeera World 2011). Successive Lebanese governments have been unable to centralise the education system due to political and religious opposition. However, the Lebanese Ministry of Education and Higher Education (MEHE) has attempted to address this issue by insisting that all private schools be licensed and that all secondary school graduates pass the government baccalaureate examination. These regulations have (with varying degrees of success) worked to hold private schools to account and prevent them from diverting too far away from government curricula.

Conflict has had a tremendous impact on education in Lebanon. Since the outbreak of the civil war in 1975, the quality of public education in Lebanon has suffered, and the education system continues to face significant challenges. Most recently, the war in neighbouring Syria and subsequent refugee flow into Lebanon has overwhelmed the Lebanese education system, which has been called upon to support the local communities (including 40,000 out of school Lebanese), as well as to absorb the huge populations of school-age children (3–18 years) displaced from Syria (including 655,000 Syrian refugees, 16,000 Lebanese returning from Syria and 11,300 Palestinian refugees from Syria). This is in addition to the 53,000 Palestinian school-age refugees already resident in Lebanon (mostly educated through UNRWA[8] schools). This has resulted in mounting fiscal costs, schools operating in shifts to try and meet increased demand and a decrease in the quality of public education (UNHCR 2015). The current circumstances have also given rise to the recent proliferation of local and international NGO-run schools in the country (Shuayb et al. 2014).

Despite the high levels of youth literacy and school life expectancy in Lebanon, youth unemployment (22.1%) is the highest of any country context discussed in this book (Table 3.1). Moreover, Lebanon is located in the global region (MENA) with the world's highest rates of youth unemployment (ILO 2015) and the lowest rates of female labour force participation (IMF 2012). This means that education is not translating into employment outcomes for youth. Without employment prospects, the ability to transition into adulthood or marry (for males), many youth with financial means and/or personal networks are resorting to emigration from Lebanon in search of a better life (Rarrbo 2009). On the other hand, youth without the resources to leave the country are becoming vulnerable to socio-economic hardship and (particularly for males) possible recruitment into paramilitary organisations.

It is within this complex local and regional context that Shi'a youth in South Lebanon live their lives and work to negotiate their identities of nation, religion, ethnicity and gender.

7.2 The Research

This chapter reports on empirical work conducted with youth in predominantly Shi'a communities in the south Lebanese city of Tyre (*Sur*). Fieldwork for this study, built on previous extended research in the specific area and wider region, lasted approximately two weeks and was conducted in four private secondary schools and two universities. One school was owned and operated by a Lebanese Shi'a political organisation, one school had a strong Shi'a religious focus (although it was open to students from other sects), one school was officially and operationally secular with a mixed student body and teaching staff (but with a Shi'a majority), and one school had a strong Christian focus (but was open to students from all sects). Both universities in which focus groups were conducted were private and secular but had a majority Shi'a student population and faculty. Educational contexts were specifically chosen to reflect the broad range of Shi'a experience among youth within South Lebanon. Access to institutions was facilitated by the presence of gatekeepers known to the researchers.

Within the educational contexts mentioned above, eight single-sex focus group discussions (FGDs), four female and four male, and two mixed FGDs were conducted with a total of 58 youth (Table 3.2). Each focus group comprised approximately five students, aged 16–24, with the mean age of participants being 19 years. With the exception of the FGD conducted with Christian Lebanese youth at the Christian school, all students that were interviewed self-identified as 'Shi'a Lebanese'. Two students self-identified as 'Shi'a' in relation to group membership, although they considered themselves to be Communist and secular/atheist in terms of personal belief.

The country case study was led by a researcher and co-author (with experience living and researching in the area) within a team based at a UK university looking at youth identities. In order to comply with cultural norms, FGDs with female youth were conducted by the female lead researcher, and these interviews were conducted using a mixture of English, Arabic and French (both researcher and respondents having some competency in these languages). The FGDs with male students were conducted in Arabic by a male research assistant, a Shi'a and local to the area. When appropriate, the research assistant was accompanied by the lead researcher. FGDs were recorded where possible and, when needed, later translated into English. Each FGD was given a code that denoted the religion, gender and age of respondents. For example, a code of MM18 refers to an interview with a Muslim male, 18-year-old youth, and a code of CF20 is an interview with a Christian female, 20-year-old youth.

A reflective diary was kept by the researchers to record informal observations and responses to interview encounters.

The interview sample can be summarised in the table below (Table 7.1):

The next sections will discuss the themes that emerged from the research, mainly those of nation, religion, ethnicity and gender, and the ways that Shi'a youth negotiate and make sense of these identities within the context of life in South Lebanon.

Table 7.1 The Lebanon sample

	Male		Female		Total
	HE	School	HE	School	
Muslim (Shi'a)	6	16	13	17	52
Christian	0	4	0	2	6
Total					58

7.3 Nation and External Others

As discussed in Chap. 2 (Geographies of Identity), identity is not a singular linear narrative. Rather, all individuals bear multiple identities simultaneously, and at any given time, locality, race, ethnicity, religion, gender, class or generation (among others) can serve as the locus for identity, or for identity politics (Alexander 2002). Moreover, identities are not fixed. Rather, they are discursive constructions which are spatially and temporally situated. Individuals' attachments to identity positions are strategic and positional, and individuals form temporary attachments to specific subject positions based on the positions of perceived advantage (Bhaba 2004). In this way, identities are always in the process of shifting, transforming and 'becoming' in relation to changing life circumstances.

Attachment to the nation is one of the most important identity positions individuals can inhabit. National identity provides people with a point of origin, a space of collective belonging and a sense of rootedness. Moreover, when it is accompanied by state apparatus and institutions, it confers on individuals' important rights and responsibilities as 'citizens'.

As all nations are comprised of diverse individuals, the nation must be collectively 'imagined' through the construction of an 'authentic', shared culture and an official national memory. Moreover, at least some of these imaginings must be exclusive enough to distinguish one nation from another. In other words, it is through the concept of 'difference' between 'us' and 'them', and the erection of boundaries between communities, that nations are forged (Anderson 1991).

'The nation' is often imagined by communities through narratives of shared history, culture, language, religion and/or ethnicity. To some extent, narratives of shared history and culture are used by Shi'a youth in South Lebanon to construct the nation and notions of a distinct 'Lebanese' identity. For example, when asked what it meant to be 'Lebanese', a common response was 'we have thousands of years of culture'. Moreover, when asked how they recognised other people as being

'Lebanese', many youth offered up cultural signifiers such as shared language ('Lebanese accent') and cuisine.

However, several of the signifiers of 'Lebanese' identity mentioned by the youth are actually common to the region (Arabic language, Arab ethnicity, regional history and cuisine), thus problematising the notion of a distinct 'Lebanese' nation set apart from its Arab neighbours in the Levant. Moreover, some signifiers of Lebanese identity identified by the youth, such as cuisine, differ according to religious community. For example, some 'Christian' foods, such as escargot, are considered to be *haram* (forbidden in Islam) and are not eaten by Muslims. In this way, internal cultural segmentation works to challenge unified notions of 'Lebanese-ness' and to blur boundaries of the nation.

Because of Lebanon's geographical positioning in the Eastern Mediterranean, its historical role as a crossroads of civilisations and its uniquely complex sectarian composition, there are no strong or unified narratives of shared kinship (interethnic marriage is common), culture, lifestyle or religion among modern Lebanese. This lack of a clear, unifying and 'authentic' nationalist narrative has challenged social cohesion within the country and been at the heart of Lebanon's political fragility. On the other hand, it is precisely this ontological uncertainty, complexity and 'messiness' that has opened up spaces for the youth to construct notions of a distinct and shared Lebanese identity based on the narratives of pluralism and 'cosmopolitanism' ('citizens of the world') (Appiah 2006).

For young Shi'a in Lebanon, 'Lebanese-ness' is largely understood through cultural narratives constructed in relation to both 'East' and 'West' and perceived notions of 'tradition' and 'modernity'. For example, when asked 'what does it mean to be Lebanese?', youth often used traditional cultural values to construct both 'sameness' between Lebanese, and 'difference' between Lebanese and Europeans. As one female youth stated,

> Our traditions, generosity and hospitality to others. Family bonds do not exist among foreigners. Lebanese help their neighbours. We feel the pain and joy of our neighbours. (MF18)

On the other hand, cultural values of pluralism and modernity were also used by the youth to construct 'sameness' between Lebanese, as well as 'difference' between Lebanese and other Arabs:

> Our openness, acceptance of new things and modern life. We travel. We learn everything quickly. We are educated and love science more than other Arabs. All Lebanese are smart. We speak more than one language (Arabic, English and French). We are like Italians. They are stylish and dress to impress, like us. All the world love Lebanese and they imitate them. (MM17)

The construction of a shared 'pluralist' Lebanese identity was also evident when Shi'a youth were asked to decide which nationality they would like to take if Lebanese nationality was not open to them. To answer this question, the youth generally drew on narratives from both 'East' and 'West' and responded that they would like to take the citizenship of Iran (because of a shared 'way of thinking'), China (because of a shared respect for tradition and elders), Europe and America (because of a shared respect for science, commerce and human rights) and Japan (because of a shared respect for social cohesion and stability). Despite a short period of colonial rule by France, French nationality was not specifically mentioned by the youth (Shi'a nor Christian) as one they wished to acquire.

Interestingly, despite Lebanon's long history of sectarian strife, the youth understood 'religious tolerance' to be one of the key signifiers of Lebanon's pluralism. As one male youth explained,

> Lebanon is the connection point between East and West. We respect other religions and sects. Lebanon is a lesson in cohesion among faiths. Lebanese have freedom to believe in God as we like. We are the only country in the Arab world that has a Christian president. (MM19)

While the youth framed much of their discussion about Lebanon in relation to 'East' and 'West', the lived experience of several of the youth who had grown up in African countries[9] (Nigeria, Ghana, Cote d'Ivoire) served to destabilise this simplistic 'East/West' dichotomy.

Although nations are 'imagined' communities with boundaries that are continually being redrawn through discursive shifts, modern nation-states are anchored within physical spaces with fixed political borders. For Shi'a youth, Lebanon's cultural boundaries may be fluid and permeable, yet its physical borders with Israel (its neighbour to the south) are static, and Lebanon's territorial integrity is to be respected and preserved at all times and at all costs. One experience which unifies all Lebanese, regardless of religious sect, is the history of conflict between Lebanon and Israel. This is particularly true for Lebanese living within the south of the country, who lived under Israeli occupation until May 2000 and have experienced recurrent conflicts with Israel ever since. As one male youth stated,

> Lebanese history is distinctive. We rejected the Israeli enemy and we saved our country. Everyone has sacrificed something for this country. My cousin is a shaheed (martyr). He shed his precious blood for his country. We have the duty to defend Lebanon and resist the Israeli enemy. (MM16)

In other words, it is the experience of collective 'suffering' at the hands of (and 'victory' against) the Israeli 'other' within living memory that has helped the youth in South Lebanon to construct a shared notion of 'Lebanese-ness'. The comment above is indicative of the 'conflict narrative' that permeated much of the discussion with the youth around what it meant to be 'Lebanese'. For example, when asked to define the most important events in Lebanese history, virtually all youth (Shi'a and Christian) mentioned the 2000 expulsion of the occupying Israeli forces from South Lebanon, with the Shi'a youth emphasising the 2006 war between Hezbollah and Israel (and Hezbollah's 'victory' in that conflict). Moreover, the Lebanese army was mentioned by both groups of youth as being the only unifying institution across sectarian lines in Lebanon (the majority of schools being private and denominational).

7.4 Religion, Ethnicity and External Others

As discussed above, in the context of Lebanon's geographical positioning, its historical role as a crossroads of civilisations and its uniquely complex sectarian composition, Lebanese youth are constructing notions of a distinctive 'Lebanese' identity based on the shared narratives of cultural pluralism and a history of suffering (at the hands of the Israeli 'other'). However, identity is:

> [...fragmented and fractured; never singular but multiply constructed across different, often intersecting and antagonistic discourses, practices and positions] (Hall 1996: 17).

In the Lebanese context, a complex and historical internal cultural segmentation cuts through Lebanese identity around discourses of religion. While these discourses serve to unite religious communities within (and across) national borders, they also serve to challenge the notion of a culturally unified Lebanon and a distinct 'Lebanese' identity.

In the context of the contemporary Middle East, religion is one of the most important cultural spaces that individuals inhabit, and it serves as an important signifier of identity. For many Shi'a youth, Islam is important in their lives as a personal faith. As one female youth remarked,

> I love Shi'a. I read about all religions, and I read the Qu'ran. I find the Qu'ran summarises all other religions, and it is the most logical. (MF20)

Within this are constructions of the true and 'authentic' Shi'a believer. When asked to name 'good' (exemplary) Shi'a (*mithal yuh'tatha*), the youth primarily drew on historical narratives of suffering, martyrdom and military victory and referenced male historical figures, such as Imam Ali[10] or Imam Hussein,[11] who exhibited the traits of honesty, bravery and sacrifice to spread and defend Shi'a Islam throughout '1400 years of oppression'. These narratives were particularly taken up by youth attending Shi'a politically affiliated and religious schools, where symbolic resources (such as shrines to 'martyrs') were used to keep historical 'wounds' against the Shi'a community open and fresh, and inscribe 'memories' of Shi'a collective suffering (largely at the hands of Sunnis) in the consciousness of young people.

However, what was noticeable was that these historical narratives offered youth very few examples of accomplished contemporary Shi'a to emulate beyond male military and political figures. This is significant as, mentioned earlier, the MENA region currently has the world's highest youth unemployment rate, and Lebanon's youth unemployment (22.1%) is the highest of the country contexts discussed in this book (Table 3.1). Moreover, the Shi'a have traditionally been the most economically disenfranchised population in the country. By contrast, when asked to name examples of good Christian role models, Christian youth were able to draw on male and female historical and contemporary figures across the fields of politics, science, sports, art, music and literature, such as Khalil Gibran (author and poet), Fairooz (singer) and Maxime Shaaya (mountaineer who climbed Everest).

Despite the important role of religion in the lives of young Shi'a, not all youth are devout, and two youth respondents went so far as to self-identify as secular/atheist in belief while maintaining Shi'a community affiliation and attachment. This helps to illustrate that although religion is important as a personal belief, it is also important in many other ways. For example, religion often provides individuals with ontological security in the context of chronic conflict, such as the territorial insecurity in South Lebanon. Within this context, religion can be seen as a 'birth rite' which is more 'stable' and 'secure' than national identity because it does not require land, and it cannot be taken away through military force (Stewart 2009). Moreover, for the youth, 'Muslim' is understood to be a subject position which is 'innate' and 'fixed'. In other words, adherence to Islam is not a choice to be taken or an idea to be negotiated, and conversion to another faith is not possible, unlike national identities (and some religious affiliations in other contexts), which may be both acquired and relinquished. As this female youth stated,

> If my Shi'a identity is gone, what is left for me? If my Lebanese identity is gone, what is left for me is my Shi'a identity. We are not able to choose. (MF21)

Religion can also provide individuals with a framework for interpreting nationalist struggles and function as an important rallying point for community mobilisation and political action. Although the Shi'a community has historically been both politically and economically marginalised in Lebanon, ongoing conflict with Israel and their self-appointed role as 'defenders of the nation' have provided Shi'a with a strong sense of belonging, honour and respect in the country in ways that affirm their sense of Lebanese national belonging. Moreover, it has given them a sense of purpose within the Lebanese nationalist project. As one male youth explained,

> Lebanon is the source of the Islamic Resistance (Hezbollah). The Shi'a have responsibility for Lebanon and the world. We defend our rights and the rights of the oppressed. In spite of all the wars in Lebanon, we are still standing and we defeated the strongest army in the world (Israel). We did not run away to another country. In spite of all the international pressure on Shi'a from some countries (America) and organisations such as Da'ash[12] (so-called Islamic State), we are still stronger than them. We are the source of military power in Lebanon. The Shi'a resistance is the strength for Lebanon. We will not be weakened and we will never surrender. (MM18)

The Shi'a self-positioning as 'defenders of the nation' is reflected in the youths' understanding of what it means to be a good Lebanese patriot. When asked the question 'who is a good Lebanese?', the three figures most commonly mentioned by both male and female Shi'a youth respondents were Hassan Nasrallah (leader of Hezbollah), Musa Sadr (founder of Amal Movement[13]) and Nabih Berri (leader of Amal Movement). What all three of these individuals have in common is that they are male, Lebanese leaders of Shi'a political/paramilitary organisations. In other words, Shi'a subjects are recruited within specific representations of the community.

However, the relationship between nation, religion and ethnicity is very complex for Shi'a youth in South Lebanon. For example, when asked to identify 'good Shi'a', many examples provided by the youth were neither Lebanese nor Arab. Rather, male Iranian political figures and religious leaders were often cited, such as Ayatollah Khomenei[14] and Ayatollah Khamenei.[15] Moreover, 'Iran' was most frequently mentioned by the youth (both male and female) attending Shi'a politically affiliated and religious schools when they were asked what country they would like to live in if residence in Lebanon was not open to them. This was despite the fact that virtually none of the youth had been to Iran before. One male youth explained it this way,

> They are similar to us. We understand their minds and are the same in terms of living and dressing. We have a common enemy—Israel. Iran helped the Shi'a in Lebanon with weapons and money. (MM16)

By contrast, Christian youth generally felt that their 'way of thinking' was similar to that of Americans.

This comment above illustrates how a 'supra-national' Shi'a identity has been constructed, which transcends national borders and discursively unites Shi'a across ethnic communities, offering strength in numbers. It also illustrates how the relationship between religion and ethnicity has been a complex one for the Shi'a in Lebanon. On the one hand, Lebanese Shi'a are ethnically Arab and share much culturally, linguistically and economically with other Arabs in Lebanon and the neighbouring Arab countries of the Levant. On the other hand, most Arabs are Sunni (the dominant sect in Islam), while there is a significant Christian minority in Lebanon. Within this context, the Shi'a are simultaneously positioned as members of the Muslim majority in Lebanon and the wider region, yet constructed as 'Muslim others' in relation to the Sunni subject in the Arab world.

As religious identities are constructed in essentialist terms, the youth cannot be members of both Sunni and Shi'a communities. In other words, inclusion within one community results in exclusion from another. For Shi'a youth in South Lebanon, this sense of exclusion (which is reinforced in schools and through popular media) has resulted in feelings of mistrust and fear towards the 'Sunni other'. As one female youth explained,

> I love Christians a lot. They are beautiful and sweet. We share their happiness and sadness. We are more free with Christians than with Sunni.

> Christians accept us more than other religions. Our conflict is with the Sunni. They hate us. Some Sunni say Shi'a are kafir (infidels) and it is their responsibility to kill us. (MF23)

Ironically, during the Lebanese Civil War, sectarianism was largely framed as a conflict between Muslim and Christian communities, and Shi'a youth recounted how their parents were unable to visit Christian areas in Lebanon during this historical period. That the nexus of conflict has now shifted to Sunni/Shi'a relations (although it has long historical roots) illustrates how identity positions and relations are contingent, and culture is dynamic and always in a state of flux.

Through their adherence to an 'unorthodox' and 'suspect' version of Islam, and by their very existence, the Shi'a challenge the presumed homogeneity, unity and unbroken historiography of the Muslim *ummah*.[16] It is for this reason that the Shi'a are viewed by some as an unresolved 'problem' within Islam (Fuller and Francke 2000). In contemporary times, the identity construct of Sunni/Shi'a tension is mediated through politics between the regional superpowers of (Shi'a) Iran and (Sunni) Saudi Arabia, with Iran being positioned as the spiritual homeland and champion of the Shi'a and Saudi Arabia (and to a lesser extent, Qatar) as the patron and defender of the Sunni. This political association has helped the youth in South Lebanon to conflate 'Sunni' with Saudi (and Qatari) foreign policy and influence in the region. Moreover, it has helped the youth to frame the conflict between Sunni and Shi'a as a moral battle of 'righteousness' in which Shi'a are hegemonically positioned above the Sunni. For example, when asked what the difference was between Sunni and Shi'a, one male youth remarked,

> We are better believers. We stick to the original meaning of the Qu'ran. Other Muslims have changed it. Sunnis don't acknowledge the 12 imams. They don't follow the complete Islam. Shi'a have fatwas (religious decrees) from well-educated and established ayatollahs,[17] but for the Sunni, any street boy can study for two years and they start giving fatwas in shedding people's blood. If I were a Sunni, I would live in Saudi Arabia, be an extremist and follow Sunni politicians despite their corruption. Their weak leaders (such as Saad Hariri[18]) take a 'selfie' (photo) and spread their

message. Hassan Nasrallah (leader of Hezbollah) would never do that. They have no honour. They are ignorant and primitive. Saudi is a backward country full of terrorists. (MM19)

Although the Shi'a youth went to great lengths to discursively construct 'difference' between themselves and Sunnis, most youth admitted that their lives in Lebanon would not be significantly different if they were Sunni due to a shared lifestyle among Muslims and a shared position of relative political and economic disadvantage in relation to Christians in Lebanon. As one female youth explained,

> Christians achieve higher positions in Lebanon. They can work wherever they want. Good jobs are usually reserved for Christians in the government. It's easier for a woman who doesn't wear a hijab (Sunni or Shi'a) to get a job. A woman who wears a hijab cannot enter the army or work in a bank or work as a flight attendant. (MF24)

Interestingly, despite Shi'a youth perceiving there to be vast differences between Muslim sects and expressing closer affinity with Christians than Sunnis in Lebanon,[19] when asked what the difference was between Sunnis and Shi'a, the Christian youth responded that there was no difference and that Muslims were 'all the same'. Moreover, a couple of Christian youth indicated that they felt more comfortable remaining within the Christian quarter of the city.

Despite these contradictions, conflict between Sunni and Shi'a communities has become very tangible for youth in Lebanon within the contemporary context of war in neighbouring Syria, with Lebanese Shi'a Hezbollah fighters (backed by Iran) fighting on the side of Syrian president Bashar Al Asa'ad, and Lebanese Sunni rebels (backed by Saudi Arabia) fighting to topple the Alawi[20]-led Syrian government. As all Lebanese are not Shi'a, and a significant number of Lebanese are Sunni, Lebanese youth have been confronted with conflicting loyalties between nation and religion. Within a 'pan-Shi'a' discourse, it is the duty of all Shi'a to defend other co-religionists. It is within this context that several male Shi'a youth taking part in this study indicated that they had gone to fight in Syria with Hezbollah against 'the Sunni terrorists' (and 'other' Lebanese) as a kind of 'sacred duty'.

On the other hand, as the neighbouring conflict in Syria has spilt over into Lebanon, it has resulted in increasing tension and mistrust between communities and reinforcement of existing 'sub-national' identities within Lebanon based on religious sect. As one male youth stated,

> Sunnis are afraid to go to some places in Lebanon, but Shi'a will have their throats cut if they go to other places. (MM19)

Fear of the Sunni 'other' among Shi'a youth has also helped to exacerbate existing wariness towards, and social exclusion of, Palestinians resident in camps and gatherings in Lebanon (who are overwhelmingly Sunni). Several Shi'a youth spoke of how they believed that Palestinians were sympathetic to *Da'ash* (so-called Islamic State) and that they were harbouring *Da'ash* fighters in the camps due to a (perceived) shared religious affiliation.

Interestingly, it is clear from Shi'a youths' narratives that many of their impressions and understandings of 'others' are based on their consumption of media images (for example through *Al Manar* TV[21]) rather than through direct personal contact with individuals from those communities. This has resulted in the portrayal of 'others' in a kind of over-exaggerated and essentialised caricature. As one female youth explained,

> We don't see Shi'a kill anyone because of differences of opinion like we see Sunnis do on TV. (MF17)

However, identity constructions are open to contestation, and some Shi'a youth did challenge essentialist notions of 'us' and 'them' by making the distinction between religious extremists and the general Sunni population (and Israeli Zionists and the general Jewish population). These youth tended to attend religiously 'mixed' schools and had the opportunity to travel abroad where they interacted with people from outside of their own religious community. Some youth also credited social media as being a medium through which they learned to communicate with other youth across sectarian lines. As one female youth stated,

> I think it (social media) changed the way we think about other people. In the past, the sects did not interact, but now we communicate with each other from other parts of Lebanon. I made a few friends from other sects and from other places, for example from Tripoli (northern Lebanese city which has a Sunni majority). We used to think that all Sunni don't like Shi'a, but now we see that some of them like us. I communicated with Israelis who are against Zionism on social media. I also communicated with some American people who agreed with the [military] intervention in (Shi'a majority) Iraq but changed their minds after I communicated with them. Sometimes social media makes relations closer. It helps us to understand other people's opinions. (MF24)

On the other hand, some youth felt that engagement with social media was intruding on family time and eroding traditional culture and values, thus challenging the notion of a distinctive 'Shi'a' identity for youth in Lebanon.

Essentialist notions of 'us' and 'them' were also blurred for Shi'a youth as they acknowledged variations in Shi'a devotional practice and performance around the world. Although the youth generally imagined the Shi'a to be a monolithic and politically unified community, their speech revealed ruptures in this narrative. As one female youth put it,

> Iran is more conservative than Lebanon. The most conservative communities are in Iran and Iraq. Shi'a in Europe don't pray or follow the rules. Shi'a in South Lebanon are different than those in Beirut. We are more committed. Families in Beqa'a Valley are more conservative than others. (MF17)

In other words, the youths' speech revealed Shi'a youth identities to be highly context-dependent and mediated through other discourses, such as location, culture, ethnicity and politics (see Chap. 2, Geographies of Identity). In this way, shared life experiences with 'other' young people in Lebanon often became more significant for the youth than shared religious affiliation with Shi'a abroad. As one male youth put it,

> There is no difference between people. We are all Lebanese. (MM23)

7.5 Gender and External Others

One of the key discourses through which identities are constructed and performed is 'gender'. Gender does not produce categories of people in uniform ways. Rather, it mediates the articulations and performance of other discourses, such as nation, ethnicity and religion. For the Shi'a in South Lebanon, gender intersects with other discourses to construct new configurations of identity and to call subjects into specific forms of representation of the community.

As discussed earlier, 'pluralism' is a key narrative through which Lebanese identities have been constructed. Just as there is no clear, unifying and 'authentic' nationalist narrative of what it means to be a 'Lebanese', so there is no particular way of understanding 'Lebanese masculinity' or 'Lebanese femininity'. Rather, as the complex internal cultural segmentation that cuts through Lebanese society is framed around religion, it is largely through discourses of religion, which are mediated through culture, that gender identities in Lebanon are constructed. As one female youth explained,

> In Lebanon, women can wear what they want and get an education, but the problem is the society. She is forced to fit into societal norms and traditions. (CFT18)

As Lebanese are generally homogenous[22] in terms of ethnicity, Arabic culture plays an important role in mediating religious discourse and in the construction of gendered identities in Lebanon. Julie Peteet (2006:107) argues that 'Arab masculinity' is,

> [...acquired, verified and played out in the brave deed, in risk-taking, and in expressions of fearlessness and assertiveness. It is attained by constant vigilance and willingness to defend honour (sharaf), face (wajh), kin and community from external aggression and to uphold and protect cultural definitions of gender-specific propriety.]

In other words, the defining characteristic of 'Arab masculinity' is its oppositional status relative to 'Arab femininity'. Therefore, tremendous emphasis is placed on preserving difference between men and women in Lebanese society. This involves maintaining a separation between the 'public sphere', where men are responsible for earning the household income and protecting the family, and the 'private sphere', where women are charged with maintaining the household, bearing and raising the children and protecting the family's 'honour'. These cultural values provide gender 'scripts' for both males and females, shaping and constraining their movements, activities, hopes and aspirations. As one female youth explained,

> The woman has endurance, patience and she sacrifices a lot, preferring to die for her children. But she is also discontent and demanding. She doesn't accept a man who doesn't have proper status. The man has to have high status, such as a house, car and money. (MF19)

Moreover, these cultural values are largely adhered to across religious communities in Lebanon. As one female Christian youth put it,

> Men become independent before women. Men can work and travel alone. Even if women are educated, we are expected to stay home and take care of the children. (CF19)

In this way, the performance of Arab cultural scripts ensures that women's personal, educational and professional goals are subordinated to compulsory heterosexuality, marriage and childbearing. Moreover, the 'innate' differences between males and females constructed through this discourse are used to construct and regulate inequalities between them in terms of decision-making and participation in political, social and economic life. As one male youth explained,

> Men participate in politics, not women. No woman achieved anything in politics because the man is the supreme ruler. Women are more emotional. They don't think logically. When women drive, they get confused and cause accidents. (MM16)

In other words, women's limited economic and political participation in Lebanon is the 'natural' consequence of their 'weak' and 'unstable' bodies. Within this discourse, Lebanese girls and women are encouraged to perform roles which fall within their 'natural capabilities' as 'females'. In this way, discourses of gender and ethnicity intersect to shape the aspirations of Lebanese females, as well as restrict their opportunities to actively participate in public life. This helps to explain why both male and female youth had difficulty in thinking of any 'good' Lebanese women. When pressed, the youth often mentioned the wives, sisters and daughters of famous Lebanese men who had demonstrated the appropriately 'feminine' values of 'compassion' and 'charity' by caring for orphans and disabled people, or women who had patiently endured the deaths of husbands or sons to 'martyrdom' in battle. As one female youth reflected,

> Women don't play an important role in Lebanon. They don't have value in this society. (MF18)

When traditional Arab cultural norms intersect with religious discourse, new gendered identities are constructed. For Shi'a women, this involves performing (Shi'a) Islamic scripts within the context of Arabic culture. As one female youth put it,

> Women have to leave her work and raise the children to make God happy. (MF17)

Within religious discourse, Shi'a Lebanese women are called upon to become 'metaphors' and 'gatekeepers' for the community and inscribe the collectivity on their physical bodies by following the Islamic dress code,[23] wearing the *hijab*[24] and conducting themselves with utmost propriety in public spaces (Yuval-Davis 1997) (see Chap. 2, Geographies of Identity). For the youth, these signifiers work to demarcate boundaries between 'Muslims' and 'others'. One female youth explained it this way,

> Muslim women dress modestly. We wear hijab and loose clothes. She doesn't do things that attract attention to her such as laughing and talking

in a loud voice in the presence of men. We must be discreet. Women have to abide by religious doctrines more than men. (MF18)

In other words, women bear the burden of representation for the collective identity and are made to embody 'Shi'a ideals' such as 'tradition', 'culture' and 'honour' through the regulation of their dress, movements and behaviour. Integral to this is a regulation of women's biological reproduction, regulating when, how many and whose children women will bear. In order to prevent Shi'a women from marrying 'outside the faith',[25] and to ensure that any offspring produced from a marital union will be raised 'Shi'a', women's sexuality before marriage is tightly controlled to ensure the 'purity' of the community (Yuval-Davis 1997).

Religious signifiers, such as the *hijab* do more than just mark out 'Muslims' from 'others'. They are also used to construct 'difference' between different kinds of Muslims and between members of the Sunni and Shi'a communities. For example, when asked how Sunni females could be differentiated from Shi'a females, one female youth explained it this way,

> We (Shi'a) tie our hijab differently. Most Sunnis wear white hijab. Some of us wear black chadour.[26] Every Shi'a will wear black for the first ten days of Ashura.[27] We also have different names.[28] (MF16)

Moreover, in their 'role' as 'defenders of culture and traditional values', Shi'a women are called upon to construct 'difference' and to erect 'boundaries' between their community and 'others' through the sanctity of their bodies. Within the context of South Lebanon, this involves Shi'a women differentiating themselves from Sunni women through marked performances of piety. As one female youth remarked,

> We don't shake hands (with men) like Sunni women. They love money and showing off. Their hijab is pushed back on their head and they are not committed. (MF17)

Although it is immediately evident if a devout Lebanese Muslim woman is Sunni or Shi'a from her appearance, it is not obvious if a Lebanese man is Sunni or Shi'a or even Muslim. Although Shi'a men can choose to adorn their bodies with jewellery embossed with Shi'a symbols, such as the 'sword of Ali', and they may adorn a short beard (in contrast to the long beard worn by some devout Sunnis), these signifiers of the Shi'a collectivity are optional for men.

Gendered identities are also shaped through conflict. As mentioned earlier, South Lebanon has experienced considerable conflict in the last century. For the Shi'a community in particular, conflict has been particularly influential in shaping identities. After a long period of relative economic and political disenfranchisement in Lebanon, the Shi'a rose to prominence through engagement with armed resistance against Israel. This provided many Shi'a with a strong sense of belonging, honour and respect in the country, as well as a sense of purpose within the Lebanese nationalist project. In this way, myths of wars, survival and heroic endeavours have been integral to the Shi'a experience and central to the construction of gendered Shi'a identities in South Lebanon. It is within this context that hegemonic Shi'a masculinities are produced, with males being constructed as 'protectors' and 'defenders' of the collectivity (both Lebanese and Shi'a). As one male youth explained,

> The man has the duty to defend the Shi'a community, such as by going to fight in Syria. (MM17)

However, as explained earlier, identities of nation, ethnicity and religion often come into conflict for Shi'a in Lebanon. For example, within the contemporary context of war in neighbouring Syria, Shi'a men are being called upon to defend their co-religionists (other Shi'a) against fellow Arabs, as well as their Lebanese compatriots. In this way, religion is working to fracture both ethnic and nation affiliations for Shi'a men in Lebanon.

It is also within the context of conflict that men's power over women is emphasised in the recall of traditional masculinities. Interestingly, gender 'roles' and women's compulsory compliance with the 'honour and shame'[29] paradigm have been constructed as 'religious duties' through religious discourse. As these gender scripts are inscribed with the divine, they are not easily contested. One male youth explained it this way,

> Shi'a men dominate their wives and daughters. He has power over the woman. The man is the head of the house and responsible for it. He protects his daughters and his wife. He enforces the code of honour on the wife and daughters. He keeps the code to protect his honour. (MM17)

Masculinities are also used to construct 'difference' between different kinds of Muslims and between Sunni and Shi'a. For Shi'a youth, 'Muslim masculinities' are hegemonically ranked, with 'Shi'a masculinity' being positioned above 'Sunni masculinity' in relation to the 'Lebanese' values of moderation and tolerance. As one male youth put it,

> Sunni men are more dominating than Shi'a men. Sunni women have less freedom. Shi'a men respect women. We are more open-minded. Shi'a women can inherit from her father, but Sunni women have to share their inheritance with their living male relatives. In Saudi Arabia, women have no rights. They cover their faces and can't drive. (MM18)

In this way, Shi'a males become constructed as good Lebanese patriots (in contrast to Sunni males). Moreover, Shi'a females come to feel fortunate that they are not subjected to 'Sunni misogyny', while at the same time willingly subjecting themselves to the status quo within their own religious community.

However, far from being coerced into Islamic subject positions, many Shi'a female youth in South Lebanon take them up voluntarily. In some cases, this is because Islam provides them with comfort and clarity in the often uncertain context of South Lebanon. Through Islam, Shi'a females are offered a guiding purpose, explicit rules for living, a framework for understanding the world and a social network of 'sisters' who share the same values. This is very appealing for many Shi'a girls and women who live their lives in the context of chronic conflict and economic hardship in South Lebanon.

Moreover, some Shi'a females feel empowered through Islamic discourse and believe that it is through Islam that they can claim their rights. Interestingly, some female youth feel that they would be better placed to claim their rights by living under an Islamic theocracy, as in Iran. As one female youth explained,

> Women and Shi'a never comes into conflict. Women have more rights in Iran. In Iran, Shi'a women can do any job because it is an Islamic Republic. In Iran, a woman can be a fighter jet pilot, but here it is the man who drives the car. In Lebanon, Shi'a are the minority and don't have the opportunity to practice their complete faith. Lebanon would be better as an Islamic country to give women their rights. (MF20)

In other words, it is the 'dilution' of Shi'a Islam within the context of a multicultural and pluralistic society like Lebanon, rather than Islamic discourse itself, which is the cause of women's inability to live lives that they aspire to. This youth's desire to voluntarily take up an Islamic subject position to achieve her goals and to attain a better life illustrates how identity is strategic and positional, and individuals form attachments to specific subject positions based on the positions of perceived advantage. It also illustrates how religious discourse is often implicated in the construction of romanticised ideals and utopian politics (i.e. the perceived advantages of theocracy).

While attachment to Islam gives some female Shi'a youth a sense of belonging and purpose, others experience tensions between being a 'good Muslim' and achieving their own personal goals and aspirations. For example, one female youth lamented,

> The Islamic religion oppresses women in some matters. Sometimes I wish I had no religion. Women have to stay within the boundaries of her house. The man takes his decision without referring to anyone, but the woman always has to refer to the man. The man's testimony is equal to two women. Inheritance for women is half that of a man. It bothers us, but women are not fighting for more rights. (MF21)

As the comment above indicates, there is tremendous pressure on young Shi'a women to acquiesce towards the established social-symbolic order. However, contestations are possible, and a few female youth have found possibilities to act out within the system in ways that are subversive and transformative to form new 'hybrid' identities. As one female youth said,

> We don't wear hijab or keep the dress code, and we listen to music (which is traditionally forbidden). But we pray and fast and do Ashura. We are Shi'a on our own terms. (MF18)

This comment powerfully illustrates the importance of agency. Although the dominant culture may try to dictate what can be thought and what can be done through a sustaining of the certainties associated with history and historical practices, it does not stand uncontested. Rather, emergent culture in the form of new values, meanings and practices puts pressure on the existing dominant culture while guiding its future directions. In this way, Shi'a youth identities are constantly being transformed through the processes of contestation, negotiation and accommodation.

7.6 Conclusion

The discussion above has highlighted the ways that Shi'a youth in South Lebanon construct and negotiate their identities of nation, religion, ethnicity and gender within the local context of Lebanon's complex sectarian balance and within the broader context of contemporary regional conflicts.

In the context of Lebanon's geographical positioning along the Eastern Mediterranean, its historical role as a crossroads of civilisations and its uniquely complex sectarian composition, the absence of a clear, unifying and 'authentic' nationalist narrative has long been at the heart of the country's political fragility and social strife. Yet, the resulting ontological uncertainty, complexity and 'messiness' have opened up spaces for the youth to draw on cultural narratives from both 'East' and 'West' to construct notions of a distinct Lebanese identity based on 'pluralism'. Moreover, Lebanon's long history of conflict with Israel has helped the youth to construct a strong nationalist narrative based on the discourses of shared 'suffering' from a common 'enemy'. In this way, the youths' lived experiences of conflict with the Israeli 'other' have helped to construct a specifically 'Lebanese' identity that unites individuals across religious sects.

However, 'the nation' is not constructed through a singular or linear narrative, and a complex and historical internal cultural segmentation cuts through Lebanese identity around discourses of religion. For the Shi'a in South Lebanon, historical narratives of suffering, sacrifice, martyrdom and military victory are used to construct 'sameness' with other co-religionists (as well as 'difference' from 'other' religious communities) and to recruit subjects within specific representations of the nation, both shaping and limiting the experiences and life choices of Shi'a youth. This is often accomplished through formal educational processes, particularly in schools that are politically or religiously affiliated. While these discourses serve to unite Shi'a communities both within and across national borders, they also problematise the relationship between nation and religion for the youth in Lebanon. As religion is implicated in the construction of both 'supra-national' and 'sub-national' identities within this context, it serves to challenge the nation, as well as the notion of a distinct 'Lebanese' identity. On the other hand, as Shi'a identities are highly context-dependent and mediated through other discourses, such as location, culture, ethnicity and politics, shared life experience in South Lebanon with 'other' Lebanese often becomes more significant for the youth.

The relationship between religion and ethnicity is also problematised for Shi'a youth in Lebanon. On the one hand, Lebanese Shi'a are ethnically Arab and share much culturally, linguistically and economically with other Arabs in Lebanon and neighbouring Arab countries of the Levant. However, most Arabs are Sunni (the dominant sect in Islam), whereas globally most Shi'a are not Arab. Within this context, the Shi'a are simultaneously positioned as members of the Muslim majority in Lebanon and the wider region, yet constructed as 'Muslim others' in relation to the Sunni subject. This has been challenging for the youth, as the war in neighbouring Syria has meant that Shi'a men are being called upon to defend their co-religionists against fellow (Sunni) Arabs, as well as their (Sunni) Lebanese compatriots. While the current national and regional nexus of conflict is focused on Sunni/Shi'a relations, historical tensions between Muslim and Christian communities in Lebanon illustrate how identity positions and relations are contingent, and culture is dynamic and always in a state of flux.

One of the key discourses through which Shi'a youth identities are constructed and performed is gender. Gender intersects with other discourses to construct new identities and to call subjects into specific forms of representation. In the context of Shi'a communities in South Lebanon, it is largely through discourses of religion, which are mediated through Arab culture, that gender identities are constructed. The cultural values that are produced through these narratives provide gender 'scripts' for both male and female youth, shaping and constraining their movements, activities, hopes and aspirations. These scripts largely position Lebanese Shi'a men as household breadwinners, defenders and protectors of the family and Lebanese Shi'a women as wives, mothers and protectors of the family's 'honour'. Gendered identities are also shaped through conflict, and armed resistance against the Israeli and Sunni 'others' has positioned Shi'a males as 'protectors' and 'defenders' of the collectivity (both national and religious). Within this narrative, men's power over women has been emphasised in the recall of traditional masculinities. Moreover, gender 'roles' and women's compulsory compliance with the 'honour and shame' paradigm have been constructed as 'religious duties' through religious discourse. The appeal to religion makes contestation difficult, as it is a claim by the earthly to godly authority to sustain inequalities.

Although Shi'a youth identities are constrained by multiple and intersecting discursive formations of nation, religion, ethnicity and gender, they are not determined by them, nor do these identities stand uncontested. Rather, Shi'a youth (female and male) in South Lebanon strategically negotiate their identity positions in order to gain positions of perceived advantage within any given context. This may include a strategic embrace of particular identities at particular times to achieve a specific purpose. In this way, Shi'a youth always have the possibility to exercise agency and to act out within the system in ways that are subversive and transformative to construct new identities.

Notes

1. Christian Lebanese sometimes reject the label 'Arab' because of its perceived association with Islam.
2. The 18 officially recognised religious groups include four Muslim sects, 12 Christian sects, the Druze sect and Judaism.
3. The Shi'a represent the second largest sect of Islam globally. They are followers of the Prophet Mohamed's son-in-law and cousin, Ali, who they believe to be Mohamed's successor to the Caliphate and the first Imam. Modern Shi'a Islam has been divided into three main groupings (Twelvers, Ismailis and Zaidis), who make up the majority in Iran, Iraq, Azerbaijan and Bahrain and significant minorities in Lebanon, Yemen and Kuwait.
4. Although only an estimated 15% of Pakistanis are Shi'a, this Shi'a minority forms the world's second largest Shi'a population and is larger than the Shi'a majority in Iraq.
5. For a map of Lebanon please see http://www.nationsonline.org/oneworld/map/lebanon_map.htm.
6. One of the largest Eastern-rite communities of the Roman Catholic Church especially prominent in modern Lebanon. The Maronites trace their origins back to St. Maron, a Syrian hermit of the late fourth and early fifth centuries.
7. Jos 19:29, 2 Sm 5:11, 1 Chr 22:4, Jer 27 3–11, Ez 26/27/28, Mk 3:8, Lk 6:17, Mt 15:21–28, Mk 7:24–31, Mt 11: 21–24, Acts 21: 3–7.
8. United Nations Relief and Works Agency for Palestinians in the Near East.
9. Approximately 250,000 Lebanese live in West Africa, the largest non-African group in the region. Some settled there to escape the Lebanese Civil War, whereas others have been drawn by increased economic opportunities.
10. The cousin and son-in-law of the Prophet Mohamed, who ruled over the Islamic Caliphate from 656 to 661.
11. The son of Imam Ali (Ali ibn Abi Talib), the first Imam of Shi'a Islam. He was killed and beheaded in the Battle of Karbala in 680, along with most of his family and companions. The annual commemoration for him, his family and his companions is called 'Ashura' (tenth day of Muharram) and is a day of mourning for Shi'a Muslims.

12. A contemporary Sunni Islamist political movement attempting to 'recover' an 'authentic' past identity when Sunni Muslim Caliphates ruled a large geographical area in the modern Middle East. The Ottoman Caliphate, under the Ottoman dynasty of the Ottoman Empire, was the last Sunni Islamic Caliphate.
13. A Lebanese political party associated with the Shi'a community. It was founded as the 'Movement of the Dispossessed' in 1974. Amal Movement is currently in an alliance with Hezbollah, the Free Patriotic Movement and the Progressive Socialist Party.
14. An Iranian religious leader, revolutionary, politician and leader of the 1979 Iranian Revolution which saw the overthrow of Mohammad Reza Pahlavi, the Shah of Iran. Following the revolution, Khomeini became the country's Supreme Leader, the highest-ranking political and religious authority in the country.
15. The second and current Supreme Leader of Iran and a Shi'a cleric.
16. Totality of the international Muslim community.
17. A high-ranking Shi'a cleric considered to be an expert in Islamic studies, such as jurisprudence, ethics and philosophy.
18. Lebanese Prime Minister from 2009 to 2011 and son of former Lebanese Prime Minister, Rafik Hariri.
19. At the time of writing, Free Patriotic Movement leader (and Maronite Christian), Michel Aoun, was in political alliance with Hezbollah leader, Hassan Nasrallah. Nasrallah was backing Aoun's candidacy for the Lebanese presidency.
20. A Sect of Shi'a Islam.
21. Hezbollah-operated TV channel based in Lebanon.
22. Armenians make up approximately 4% of the population of Lebanon. There is also significant intermarriage, with Lebanese men (and sometimes women) often taking spouses from abroad.
23. Revealing only face, hands and feet in the presence of men outside of their immediate families.
24. A veil that covers the head and chest, which is worn by some Muslim women beyond the age of puberty in the presence of adult males outside of their immediate families.
25. Shi'a men may marry Christian or Jewish women ('people of the Book') as long as the women convert to Islam and agree to raise any forthcoming children Muslim.

26. A full-body-length black semicircle of fabric that is worn as an outer garment by many Shi'a women.
27. Marks the anniversary of the Battle of Karbala when Imam Hussein ibn Ali, the grandson of the Prophet Mohamed, and a Shi'a Imam, was killed by the forces of the second Umayyad Caliph Yazid I at Karbala (present day Iraq).
28. Some names have a sectarian marker. 'Sunni names' include the male names of Omar, Othman, Abu Bakr, Moawiya, Shimir and Yazid and the female name of Aisha. A Shi'a will almost never have one of these names.
29. Where the 'honour' of the husband and family rests on the propriety of female family members.

References

Al Jazeera World. (2011). *A lesson in history: Does the absence of a common history textbook reflect broader divisions in Lebanon?* Retrieved April 10, 2016, from http://www.aljazeera.com/programmes/general/2010/04/20104673737483233.htm.

Alexander, C. (2002). Beyond black: Rethinking the colour/culture divide. *Ethnic and Racial Studies, 25*(4), 552–571.

Anderson, B. (1991). *Imagined communities: Reflections on the origin and spread of nationalism.* London: Verso.

Appiah, K. A. (2006). *Cosmopolitanism. Ethics in a world of strangers.* London: Penguin.

BBC. (2009). *Safavid empire (1501–1722).* Retrieved May 17, 2016, from http://www.bbc.co.uk/religion/religions/islam/history/safavidempire_1.shtml.

BBC. (2015). *Lebanon profile—Timeline.* Retrieved May 10, 2016, from http://www.bbc.co.uk/news/world-middle-east-14649284.

BBC. (2016). *Sunnis and Shia: Islam's ancient schism.* Retrieved May 10, 2016, from http://www.bbc.co.uk/news/world-middle-east-16047709.

Bhabha, H. K. (2004). *The location of culture.* London and New York: Routledge.

Fisk, R. (2001). *Pity the nation: Lebanon at war.* Oxford: Oxford Paperbacks.

Frayha, N. (2009). *The negative face of Lebanese education.* Retrieved May 16, 2016, from http://www.lebanonrenaissance.org/assets/Uploads/0-The-negative-face-of-the-Lebanese-education-system-by-Nmer-Frayha-2009.pdf.

Fuller, G., & Francke, R. R. (2000). *The Arab Shi'a: The forgotten Muslims*. London: Palgrave Macmillan.

Hakim, C. (2013). *The origins of the Lebanese national idea, 1840–1920*. Berkeley: University of California Press.

Hall, S. (1996). Introduction: who needs identity? In S. Hall & P. du Gay (Eds.), *Questions of cultural identity* (pp. 1–17). London: SAGE Publications.

Harik, J. P. (2004). *Hezbollah: The changing face of terrorism*. London: IB Taurus & Co Ltd.

International Labour Organisation (ILO). (2015). *Global employment trends for youth 2015: Scaling up investments in decent jobs for youth*. Geneva: ILO.

International Monetary Fund (IMF). (2012). *Youth unemployment in the MENA region: Determinants and challenges*. Retrieved May 17, 2016, from https://www.imf.org/external/np/vc/2012/061312.htm.

Kaufman, A. (2006). Between Palestine and Lebanon: Seven Shi'i villages as a case study of boundaries, identities, and conflict. *Middle East Journal, 60*(4), 685–706.

Peteet, J. (2006). Male gender and rituals of resistance in the palestinian intifada: A cultural politics of violence. In M. Ghoussoub & E. Sinclair-Webb (Eds.), *Imagined masculinities: Male identity and culture in the modern Middle East* (pp. 103–126). London: Saqi.

Rarrbo, K. (2009). Studies on youth policies in the mediterranean partner countries—Lebanon. *EuroMed*. Retrieved May 19, 2016, from http://www.youthpolicy.org/national/Lebanon_2009_Youth_Policy_Report.pdf.

Saad-Ghorayeb, A. (2002). *Hizbu'llah: Politics and religion (critical studies on Islam)*. London: Pluto Press.

Shuayb, M., Makkouk, N., & Tuttunji, S. (2014). Widening access to quality education for Syrian refugees: The role of private and NGO sectors in Lebanon. Centre for Lebanese Studies. Retrieved May 18, 2016, from http://lebanesestudies.com/wp-content/uploads/2014/09/Widening-Access-to-QualityEducation-for-Syrian-Refugees-the-role-private-and-NGO-sectors-in-Lebanon-.pdf.

Stewart, F. (2009). Religion versus Ethnicity as a source of mobilisation: Are there differences? Micro con: A micro level analysis of violent conflict. *Institute of Development Studies*. Retrieved May 10, 2016, from http://www.microconflict.eu/publications/RWP18_FS.pdf.

Tabet, G. (2005). Women in personal status laws: Iraq, Jordan, Lebanon, Palestine, Syria. SHS papers in women's studies/gender research, No. 4.

Gender equality and development section, division of human rights, social and human sciences sector. *UNESCO*. Retrieved May 10, 2016, from http://www.unesco.org/new/fileadmin/MULTIMEDIA/HQ/SHS/pdf/Women_in_Personal_Status_Laws.pdf.

UNESCO. (2014). *EFA global monitoring report. Teaching and learning: Achieving quality for all*. Paris: UNESCO.

UNESCO. (2016). *Global education monitoring report*. Paris. Retrieved May 10, 2016, from http://en.unesco.org/gem-report/node/6.

UNHCR. (2015). *LCRP sector response plan*. Retrieved May 18, 2016, from http://data.unhcr.org/syrianrefugees/working_group.php?Page=Country&LocationId=122&Id=21#.

USAID. (2015). *Education—Lebanon*. Retrieved May 17, 2016, from https://www.usaid.gov/lebanon/education.

Winter, S. (2010). *The Shi'ites of Lebanon under Ottoman rule, 1516–1788*. Cambridge: Cambridge University Press.

Yuval-Davis, N. (1997). *Gender and nationhood*. London: Sage.

8

Conclusions: Intersecting Nation, Religion and Gender

Abstract This chapter draws together the main conclusions of our analyses of four country case studies that set out to 'trouble' Muslim youth identities. Our cases, Pakistan, Senegal, Nigeria and Lebanon, all in the Global South, provided contrasting contexts in which to explore how youth constructed and performed their identities along the intersecting axes of nation, religion and gender. We begin by revisiting the key arguments and theorisations that provided the basis for the empirical work on youth identities. We elaborate our theorisation of identity as a fluid, dynamic and discursive process of becoming, constituted within local places and replete with reference to particular histories and cultures. This identity work involves the constant reiteration of the inclusions of 'us' as well as the difference and distinction from 'others'. Our theorisations resist and trouble homogenised and essentialised understandings of identity and attend to the intersections and sutures of different identity discourses in a located way. This provides the theoretical backdrop for our synthesis of the four country case studies. Our analyses illustrate the complexities of youth identity narratives and the ways these are infused by historical and contemporary discourses of belonging. Importantly, these provide nuanced explorations that challenge the dominant constructions of nation, religion and gender of the West. While acknowledging the limitations of our research, our analysis confirms the centrality of women to imaginaries of nation and religion. Nevertheless, we highlight gender as a site of struggle and draw attention to the particular tensions this produces for the achievement of gender equality within postcolonial nation-states.

8.1 Introduction

In this final chapter, we draw on the analyses of our four country case studies to set out the main conclusions of this research that set out to 'trouble' Muslim youth identities. Our cases, all from the Global South, provide contrasting contexts in which to explore how youth construct and perform their identities along the intersecting axes of the nation, religion and gender. It is on the basis of this empirical work and analysis that we have 'troubled' stereotypes and homogenised accounts of Muslim youth. This book is timely given the heightened concern in the West about youth, Muslims and the seemingly intractable religious-based conflicts and resultant national fragility in many parts of the globe. In advance of our discussion of the main conclusions, we return briefly to the key arguments and theorisations that we set out in Chap. 2, Geographies of Identity.

8.2 Identities

Our theorisation of identity sees it as fluid and involves dynamic, discursive processes of becoming (Hall 1996). This is a critical shift away from fixed, essentialised, unitary understandings of 'the self' through which youth identities in the Global South all too often are represented. As we described in our introductory chapter, the discourses through which our identities are constituted are replete with umbilical referents to particular histories of place and culture. These provide the symbolic and affective attachments (Ahmed 2004) through which the

8 Conclusions: Intersecting Nation, Religion and Gender

identity claims of belonging and distinction can be made. This identity work involves a constant reiteration of the inclusions and particularities of 'us', as well as the exclusion, distancing and often the denigration of the 'other'. In other words, identities are constructed through difference and through processes that are neither singular nor absolute but accomplished across multiple intersecting and sometimes contradictory boundaries of belonging.

A conceptualisation of identity work as fluid and performative resists and troubles polarisation. In Chap. 2, we exemplified the implications for gender by troubling a binary understanding of gender through the poles of male and female. Instead, we stressed how gender is performative, rather than a natural biological 'fact'. It is constantly brought into being, in ways that *constitute* the very categories that otherwise may be regarded as a natural consequence of biology (Butler 1990). Gender identities are performed within cultural milieu and are contingent on the particularities of each context. As gender is only one axis of identity, our theorisation means that we also attend to the intersections and sutures of different identity discourses in a located way, rather than looking to the signifiers of belonging as if they held any essential or 'universal' meaning.

Within our increasingly interconnected contemporary world, discourses within the local are also interpenetrated by those in global circulation. Of particular relevance to our research are discourses of human rights, as well as those of different world religions, including Islam (Beck and Levy 2013). These global flows have been enhanced in our contemporary era of mass communications, ICTs and new media, opening up new possibilities to see and observe practices elsewhere. As we show in our previous chapters, these have allowed youth to make associations with and differentiations from others across space and distance—whether this is in respect to other nations or similar or alternative religions or sects.

Notwithstanding these intersections of the global and the local, our analysis resolutely privileges the local. In other words, rather than seeing the intersections and sutures between the global and the local in youth narratives as productive of new 'cosmopolitan' universalisms, we have tried to illuminate the constant play between the local and the global and the identity work that is done through invocations of any such 'universalisms', particularly in relation to religion. In other words, we see how youth call upon the 'global' to claim special and unique identities is always being related to how they are incorporated or excluded in their particular contexts and the different symbolic referents available to them through which to claim distinction.

To illustrate this briefly, our analysis of Northern Nigerian youth's invocation of their 'pure' form of Islamic practice highlights how this serves to mark out distinctions between Northern and Southern or Yoruba Muslims. This recruitment of more 'universal' religious practices transcends national boundaries and so could be equated with more 'cosmopolitan' or post-national forms of citizenship (Calhoun 2008; Eliassi 2014). However, this identity work is inseparable from the construction of the internal 'others' of the nation and integral to its reimagining (Beck and Levy 2013). In relation to Shi'a youth in Lebanon, comparisons of different forms of Islam and the positioning of one over the other in terms of their godly authority and moral righteousness are similarly seen from a located, situated perspective, that is to say as a way of claiming distinctiveness by youth in a relatively disadvantaged political and economic situation. The construction of a shared Lebanese identity based on the narratives of pluralism and 'cosmopolitanism' seems bound up with modern sensibilities that have always privileged the universal. These are coupled, however, with the particular contextual difficulties in the construction of a shared and 'authentic' narrative of national identity.

After this brief review of our discursive understanding of identities, and our concomitant insistence in our analysis on a resolute attention to the local, we now turn to the key concluding points from our analysis of the four country cases, addressing, in turn, our three main axes of differentiation—nation, religion and gender.

8.3 Troubling the Nation—Muslim Youth's National Belongings

In Chap. 2, Geographies of Identity, we commented on the ways globalisation had posed challenges for the nation-state and how alternative post-national, cosmopolitan or global forms of citizenship have been

8 Conclusions: Intersecting Nation, Religion and Gender

posited as being more relevant within contemporary society. However, our different cases all suggest that a national imaginary remains important to youth and to Muslim youth. Indeed, nationality often seemed to have the status of a 'naturalised facticity' (Butler 1990), as inherent with a 'national identity' as an entirely normal consequence of having been born in a particular location. At one level this brings an entitlement to rights, such as the right to education. At another level, as youth narratives indicated, it involved an ongoing production of recognisable and affectively charged national imaginaries, reiterated in claims to national distinction and uniqueness that demonstrated deep affective attachments.

This does not mean that these narratives were unitary or without contradictions. Across all of our country cases, youth narratives illuminated how their national identities were recruited from and against a wide range of structures of feeling in ways that demonstrated selective and shifting alliances. Variously implicated in this were markers of ethnicity, region and religion, inflected through collective histories in which (neo)colonial traces could be recruited to mark distinction from an internal 'other' or to signal the differentiation of the nation against the (neo)colonial external 'other'. This is illustrated in the Senegal case where references to 'Frenchness' were recruited at different times either as a positive to claim higher status and superiority over internal others or as a negative to claim a postcolonial national distinctiveness. In other cases, symbols of the nation that were claimed cited as unique were shared by groups well beyond the boundaries of the nation-state. In the case of Lebanon for example, such claims embraced wider regional histories, Arabic language, Arab ethnicity and cuisine to once again illustrate that 'national' belongings were not necessarily contiguous with nation-state boundaries but may refer to wider and more historic connectivity.

All case studies demonstrated that the respective histories of their nation-state formation remain significant to youth's imagining of the nation. National leaders at the time of state emergence from its colonial past were often identified as exemplary figures in the national imaginary. Lebanon was a possible exception, where, in the proximity to ongoing conflict, youth foregrounded contemporary military (and religious) leaders rather than historical figures. The formal structures of government and of the constitution, developed in the formation of the nation-state, were intrinsic to the axes of difference in the national imaginary. As elaborated in each of the case studies, these constitutional structures as well as the lands within the national boundaries are themselves products of their histories that were shaped by earlier eras of colonial and/or imperial rule. As demonstrated in Chap. 7, the three regions brought together in the formation of Nigeria as a nation-state, at the end of the British colonial administration, remains significant. These regional fault lines still reverberate vividly in the identity narratives of the Muslim youth in Northern Nigeria and are used to accumulate multiple internal distinctions around religion, ethnicity and language. Similarly, Lebanon demonstrates how the sedimentation of religious differences within its confessional constitution has sustained the historical subordination of the Shi'a which they have endured over centuries under different forms of imperial and colonial rule. As in Nigeria, we can also see how a sense of otherness within the nation can contribute to supra-national religious allegiances, particularly when oppression can be associated with a wider 'global' or neo-colonial other.

We stated above that youth narratives showed deep affective ties to a national imaginary, which suggests the continuing relevance of the nation to for them as a structure of belonging. As we have explained in the preceding chapters, each of our case study countries sought to institute a form of modern constitutional democracy as they emerged as independent nation-states. Youth also demonstrated their awareness of the principles of modern democracy, but they were equally aware of the failures of politicians in realising these principles. Across the cases, Muslim youth frequently critiqued those in government and other public offices for corruption and cited this as an aspect of their nation of which they were not proud. The youth were aware of ideals of democracy, but they were disenchanted by the workings of their nation-state. In the case of Nigeria for example, they recognised and resisted how politicians manipulated religious divisions for political purposes. Youth were not being served by their political leaders; democracy was instead being subverted by partisanship and clientelism. Different writers have pointed to the sedimentation of social divisions during the different

8 Conclusions: Intersecting Nation, Religion and Gender   269

periods of colonial rule suffered by our case countries. They further highlight the ways that this allowed the sustenance of patrimonial relations of kinship and clientelism after their emergence as independent nation-states (Joseph 1999; Kabeer 2002; Mamdani 1996). Overall, youth's narratives vividly demonstrate their frustration with such partisan relations and practices and concomitantly their commitment to democratic ideals.

The previous two points have both highlighted the entanglement of religion with youth's national imaginaries. This is consistent with our critique of the secular in the discourses of the West that we offered in Chap. 2. We drew on Butler (2011) and Asad (2003) to refute the West's claim to make a sharp separation of religion and the state and to argue that religion was 'already inside' the states that proclaimed their 'secular' character. Similarly, religious affiliations have remained central to youth's national imaginaries in each of the country contexts, with Pakistan providing a clear and elaborated example of this conjunction. Given this, we find it useful instead to consider our different cases as involving different 'formations of the secular' (Burchardt and Wohlrab-Sahr 2013). This concept allows us to attend to the 'shifting symbolic meanings' of the secular in particular historical contexts (607). We return to this below when discussing youth's religious affiliations.

We conclude this section by considering the nexus of nation and gender in youth's identities. We discussed above how our participants' narratives of national belongings often assumed 'the nation' as if a 'naturalised facticity' (Butler 1990). Essentialised gender positions and gender hierarchies were deeply embedded in this 'facticity' within each of our country contexts. These were assumed, naturalised and thoroughly normalised. The gendered frames of the imagined nation were readily re-cited by female and male youth alike and by both Muslim and Christian. Gender was largely represented as being wholly unproblematic and often involved the fusion of traditional customs with a national imaginary. The ways the concept of 'teranga' was invoked in Senegal is one such example, where the burden of this hospitality fell on and was assumed by women in ways that both essentialised and subordinated. Again focusing on Senegal, we saw how national equality legislation giving women the right to paid maternity leave was resisted by a

Christian male, in favour of respecting her as a mother. As Chatterjee (1993) suggests, the differentiation of the modern postcolonial nation against the spectre of Western modernity redoubles the requirement to preserve local markers of cultural differentiation—which falls primarily on women. In a general way, women were bearers of national cultures, charged with the reproduction of its values and its progeny, they were scrutinised for their propriety and morality, and readily subject to opprobrium or worse if found wanting.

Our composition of sex-segregated focus groups, except for two mixed groups in Lebanon, was intended to create space for youth critique of gender relations; their power was such, however, that this strategy was occasionally but not always productive. Where contestation of such norms did arise, however, it was mainly from women, for example female students in higher education who were resisting masculine hegemonies to claim a space in the public sphere. We take up the complex intersections of such relations with religion below.

8.4 Troubling Religion?

We have already raised the importance of religion in youth's national imaginaries. More broadly, it was the most significant axis of identity for our participants across all cases. It was also striking that Islam was consistently described by our participants in all of our research contexts as a religion of peace and tolerance. Our youth participants were aware of but strongly resisted contemporary constructions of Muslims as 'jihadist' and the association of Islam with terrorism. For youth in Senegal, for example, those who 'killed for religion' were not 'proper' Muslims; Shi'a youth in Lebanon similarly disowned associations with terrorism, constructing this as a sectarian issue. With some exceptions, our participants' insistence on Islam being a religion of peace and tolerance led them to identify more strongly with youth of other religions in their own context than with youth of the same religion in other contexts.

Alongside this dominant, shared understanding of Islam as a religion of peace, and youth's openness to local social relations that transcended

8 Conclusions: Intersecting Nation, Religion and Gender

religious differences, our cases also point to the multiplicities of the Islamic practices and affiliations of our participants across our different contexts. These multiplicities stand in stark contradiction to the homogenised and unitary depictions of Islam that are stereotypically found in the discourses of the West. What Islam is and means to youth had some overarching similarities as identified above, but in addition to spanning Sunni, Shi'a and Sufi forms of Islam, our cases show how youth's religious identifications intersected with local cultures, blending with ethnic and regional practices, and in Africa in particular, leading to syncretic fusions with traditional (animist) religions. In all its diverse forms, Islam's local particularities across each of our cases clearly had long and embedded histories, which related not only to the relatively recent emergence of their respective nation-state formations, but also to the pre-state social formations.

Our analysis shows—as is also implied by the above—that discourses of religious belonging are never solely about religious ideology. They intersect with other axes of belonging, which are always contextually located and embedded in collective histories that shape time and space. Islam is inevitably expressed through political particularities within local contexts, whether through markers of ethnicity, region, religious sect or religious brotherhoods as well as through the different ways that the state has incorporated different religions or different versions of Islam. In other words, following Mouffe (2005), these religious belongings are deeply imbricated in both politics and the political. The positioning of the Shi'a youth in Lebanon vividly illustrates the complex intersections of nation, ethnicity and religion. Lebanese Shi'a live in a multi-religious but Muslim-majority nation-state. However, on the one hand, the Shi'a are ethnically Arabs and share much culturally, linguistically and economically with other Arabs in Lebanon and neighbouring Arab countries. On the other hand, they are a minority among Arabs who are predominantly Sunni Muslims. Within this context, the Shi'a as Muslims are simultaneously positioned as members of the Muslim majority in Lebanon and the region, yet constructed as 'Muslim others' in relation to the Sunni majority in the Arab world.

When put under pressure, these intersections can produce a deep suturing of different axes of identity, so that nation, ethnicity and religion become tightly bound up. A clear illustration of this can be found in the narratives of the Sunni Muslim youth in Pakistan, where the discursive construction of multiple antagonistic non-Muslim 'others' and the contemporary violence of their daily lived experiences tended to solidify Islam as a boundary between 'us' and 'them'. In this particular case, Pakhtun ethnicity further reinforced an imagination of the nation through Islam, so that discourses of the nation, *Pakhtunwali*, and Islam were sutured tightly together in concerted opposition to the external other. The pressures of a conflict situation are also highly germane to the situation of the Shi'a youth in Lebanon. While the Shi'a community has historically been both politically and economically marginalised in Lebanon, ongoing conflict with Israel and their self-appointed role as 'defenders of the nation' have provided Shi'a youth with a strong sense of belonging, honour and respect in ways that affirm their sense of Lebanese national belonging.

Youth sometimes showed their awareness of the instrumentalisation of religious affiliations by their political leaders and their resistance to this. As shown in the case of Senegal, youth could also make sweeping generalisations that sutured together the nation, ethnicity, different forms of religious belongings, in association with and rejection of 'extremist' forms of Islam. In such articulations, we see Islam being deployed strategically to construct allegiances and differences in the consolidation of local political positioning. 'Strategically' may overestimate the level of intentionality that inform such articulations. It is perhaps better instead to think of the range of discourses which are available for youth to assert their identities and to claim distinction. We emphasise again how this is contingent upon local social relations.

In this respect, our analysis shows how religious certainty can work as a particularly powerful discourse through which distinction can be claimed. In other words, it is a central pillar through which argument can be closed down, particularly within Islam, where challenges to godly authority can be constructed as absolutely 'other' (Krämer 2013). There were, of course, interesting variations across our cases about what 'proper' Islam was, which demonstrated its social locatedness. However, the invocation of this moral, religious binary of right versus wrong is extremely powerful. It serves to essentialise and solidify differences, and

8 Conclusions: Intersecting Nation, Religion and Gender

is used to assert claims to the distinction that reverberate with masculinist certainty and authority. It is thoroughly gendered in other words. This is well illustrated in the ways Muslim males in Nigeria proclaimed a competitive, absolutist version of Islam, aligning themselves with what was constructed as 'proper' Islam, and so claiming religious authority that positioned them above impure and illegitimate Islam, in particular the Islam of other Nigerians in the South. Our analysis suggests how youth's claim to this position of superiority was bound up with their wider economic and educational marginalisation in the Nigerian federal state. In other words, in every claim to the external authority of a 'proper' Islam, or the global *ummah*, we see the discursive 'othering' of some religious communities, marking them as inferior or illegitimate.

If this identity work involves recruiting the authority of the global *ummah* against an internal other, Islam was also central in the construction of difference against external others, often in ways that sutured the nation and religion together. We see this in the cases of both Pakistan and Senegal. In both contexts Islam was historically central as a modernising and secular influence in their struggles for independence. This echoes Badran's (2009) discussion with respect to different Middle Eastern contexts. Our analysis also shows how youth's Islamic ideals could sit compatibly with the ideals of modern democracy. As shown in Chap. 4 in relation to Pakistan, youth readily deployed discourses of secular democracy and citizenship in the construction of the nation. Specific references to secularism and to modernity were also made by Senegalese youth, and the secular character of their democracy was proclaimed as a marker of distinction.

We have highlighted in the previous section the importance of the particular histories of each of our nation-states in leading to their particular formations of the secular. However, this is also conjoined with their positioning within contemporary civilisational encounters, such as the 'War on Terror', or the contemporary crises in the Middle East, which are bound up with religious affiliations. Our analysis has shown how the injustices of colonial eras or the sense of 'Islam under siege' as experienced in Pakistan fosters resistance and opposition to an external other that can be mapped against the '*West*', or in the Senegal case against '*les blancs*' or against '*the modernity European people had a tendency to instil in us*'. Youth are not necessarily showing resistance in these cases to the 'modern' or 'the secular' but to the imposition of particular formations of the modern and the secular by an external other who is associated with the perpetration of injustices, historically and contemporaneously. Our analysis suggests the importance of being open to different cultural understandings of the 'secular', including formations of the secular which can accommodate different forms of religious expression (Burchardt and Wohlrab-Sahr 2013). Here, it is very clear from youth's narratives that the recent articulations of the 'War on Terror' voiced by the 'secular' West inserts a binary that provokes reiterations of 'Islam under siege'. Our cases illustrate how this has the power to foster resistance and deepen the rifts between religious others as well external other nations—and indeed, given its association with a Western other, against the notion of the secular itself.

8.5 Gender Untroubled?

From the above, it is clear that the gender resonates powerfully through the data from all our country contexts, often pointing to patriarchal relations and the subordination of women. From the outset of this section, we seek to alert the reader both to the ways in which our analysis nevertheless disrupts naïve assumptions that Muslim women are passive and lack agency, and also to the limitations of our research approach, and what this allowed us to know of women's agency.

Taking the methodological point first, we recognise the limitations of our research approach and our reliance on focus group data. Our intention was to create a space in which participants engaged with one another directly and in this process performed their identities. However, we invited them to participate in a very public space in which they were subject to the regulatory gaze of their peers, which often encouraged conformity and uniformity. It is important to recognise the imperative of demonstrating one's religious observance, for example in terms of showing respect for the words of Mohammed. An illustration of this can be found in Sect. 5.6 on Senegal. We recognise that a more nuanced understanding of the complexities of participants' positioning and its agonisms would only have been possible through an ethnographic approach as, for example, in Mahmood's (2012) research into the 'women of the mosque'.

Turning to the theoretical point, we also resist any reading of the performance of the Muslim identities of our female respondents as demonstrating their 'passivity' or lack of agency. From a poststructural perspective, identities are always discursively constructed through difference, so that our critique is never of 'individuals', but of the dominant discourses and their power relations, through which subjects become legible. Like Mahmood (2012), our poststructural analysis is questioning of liberal associations of agency with individual emancipation and freedom. Instead, agency is discursive rather than individual. As we have pointed out in Chap. 2, the discursive production of identities depends on conflictual relations of difference which are haunted by otherness. Because difference inheres in the production of the social constantly leaves open the possibilities for the resignification and reconstruction of social norms (Butler 1997). Mahmood (2012) also alerts us, however, to the different modes of subjectivation through which identities can be constructed, which can involve quite different 'architectures of the self' (p. 31) from those that are privileged within modern, liberal understandings. Her analysis draws on Foucault to show how submission to forms of external authority was intrinsic to the processes of subjectivation of the women of the mosque—indeed, it is only through such submission that they could realise their ideal as a Muslim subject. Her analysis demands, therefore, a redoubled awareness of the limitations of modern understandings of the self and its restricted and overly individualised understandings of agency and freedom.

With these caveats, we now move to our concluding remarks on gender. As we noted above gender has already been implicated in the hierarchical marking of identities with respect to both nation and religion. Gender hierarchies were also very obvious in relation to ethnicity. For example, our analysis of the bio-data sheets in the contexts where respondents were of diverse ethnicities (Nigeria and Senegal especially) showed that with very few exceptions, ethnicity was claimed through the paternal line.

In all of our case study contexts, gender identities were essentialised within a male/female binary, in which the subordination of females was assumed. Females were associated with the home, the family and domestic labour. This positioning was strongly bound up in projections of the national imaginary, as demonstrated on a Dakar billboard poster advertising the forthcoming summit of the Francophonie, which described Senegal as the '*country of teranga*' and portrayed two young and smiling females with their arms outstretched in welcome. The prime female responsibility for the family and the reproduction of the nation was re-cited by males and females, both Muslim and Christian across our different case studies. This was opposed to males who were cast as breadwinners, heads of households and as active in the public sphere. While there was an acknowledgement of women becoming more educated and entering professional fields, this did not disrupt the expectation that eventually they would privilege their primary positioning as a mother.

In all of our cases, we see how the construction of women as the defenders of national culture and traditional community and family values was redoubled when this positioning was overlaid with religious imperatives. Reference to religious authority was used by both male and female youth to justify the social restriction of Muslim women to the home and more generally as innately inferior to men. There were a few isolated occasions when Islamic texts were quoted in support of gender equality, see for example the Pakistan case study. However, as Velayati (2016) commented, while submission to God's will is an obligation for all good Muslims, in the case of women, this could often readily be interpreted as requiring submission to male authority. We have seen in the Nigerian case how Muslim males could invoke religious authority in masculinist ways that quashed all arguments. The invocation of religious authority to justify gender hierarchies was equally difficult to refute. As we noted in the Senegalese case, Muslim females in higher education who were actively contesting gender norms pointed out how the conflation of religion with the subordination of women meant that their arguments could readily be constructed as anti-religious—indeed, one female cautioned another about taking the words of the Prophet in vain during a focus group discussion about women's place in Islam.

Overall, we can conclude that, with rare exceptions, masculinist positions in the discourses of both nation and religion reciprocally drew on the subordinated position of women to construct and assert authority. Males often drew on an assumed certainty of religion and its prescriptive codes as a means to articulate an absolute and justified dominance. However, as the example above demonstrates, females were also complicit and agentive in the invocation of religious authority and in the construction and performance of these hierarchies. The claim to proper religious practice was an exemplary means by which to claim superiority and to silence discussion or hesitation on gender inequalities and patriarchy. At the same time, we return to the methodological limitations of our research and recognise that we cannot know how the women used their agency to negotiate their positioning within other contexts.

Across our focus groups, there was a considerable level of consensus about the respective positioning of males and females. Gender was left relatively *untroubled*. Where contestation occurred, it was predominantly voiced by women in higher education. The case of Nigeria, for example, included a group of women who discussed the local difficulties in practicing proper Islam. They pointed directly to the ways that Muslim males with their greater freedoms did not always fulfil their concomitant responsibilities, in particular with respect to marriage and their obligation to support their wives and families. It is important to note that in questioning local gender relations, these women did not invoke national equality policies but referred rather to principles of Islamic practice (Mahmood 2012). However, as already noted, although gender norms were being challenged by some Muslim females, they could easily find themselves thwarted by the invocation of masculinist religious authority. The examples already provided above also show how gender equality could be constructed as an alien other to local cultures, an imposition from the West and part of a wider project of reform that was incompatible with Muslim norms (Krämer 2013; Badran 2009).

Overall then, gender was used as a site of struggle in relation to both external and internal others, confirming the centrality of women to imaginaries of nation and reproduction. Similarly, patriarchy was pivotal within youth's religious sensibilities and was conjoined with the production of distinction against the formations of modernity associated with the colonial past, as well as contemporary neo-colonial imperatives. However, it is important to point to the ways that female youth were constantly agentive in both the production of their own identities and in contesting their positioning within local social relations. As we have pointed out before, our research approach through FGDs demanded a public and collective discussion in ways that encouraged performances of conformity. At the same time, as we acknowledge this limitation in our research, we also recall the arguments of Mahmood (2012), who in her ethnography illustrated how Muslim women, even in positions of ostensible subordination, continually exercised agency within and against dominant social formations.

In the final paragraph of this book, we highlight the complex social and political scenarios within which youth struggle to make sense of themselves and their world. We underline this as a dynamic process of becoming within increasingly porous local contexts that are shot through with historical narratives of position, place and belonging and cut across by more emergent globalised discourses made available by communication technologies. This produces a very complex interplay of the local and the global which are the contexts of inclusion, exclusion and difference within which youth shape themselves as citizens of the future. In this research, we sought to move beyond antagonistic binaries of 'us' and 'them' and the comforts of easily available stereotypes to trouble such fixity and its facile depictions of 'others'. Instead, we have provided in-depth analyses of youth voices to develop more nuanced understandings of how youth identities are configured and performed through often complicated interweaving of the multiple locally available discourses of identity. We offer this book as a beginning, there is evidently much more work to be done.

References

Ahmed, S. (2004). *The cultural politics of emotion*. Edinburgh: Edinburgh University Press.

Asad, T. (2003). *Formations of the secular. Christianity, Islam, modernity*. Stanford: Stanford University Press.

Badran, M. (2009). *Feminism in Islam. Secular and religious convergences.* Oxford: Oneworld Publications.

Beck, U., & Levy, D. (2013). Cosmopolitanized nations: Re-imagining collectivity in world risk society. *Theory, Culture & Society, 30*(2), 3–31.

Burchardt, M., & Wohlrab-Sahr, M. (2013). Multiple secularities: Religion and modernity in the global age—Introduction. *International Sociology, 28*(6), 605–611.

Butler, J. (1990). *Gender trouble. Feminism and the subversion of identity.* Routledge: London.

Butler, J. (1997). *Excitable speech. A politics of the performative.* Routledge: London.

Butler, J. (2011). Is Judaism Zionism? In J. Butler, J. Habermas, C. Taylor, & C. West (Eds.), *The power of religion in the public sphere* (pp. 70–92). New York: Columbia University Press.

Calhoun, C. (2008). Cosmopolitanism in the modern social imaginary. *Daedalus, 137*(3), 105–114.

Chatterjee, P. (1993). *The nation and its fragments. Colonial and postcolonial histories.* Chichester: Princeton University Press.

Eliassi, B. (2014). Nationalism, cosmopolitanism and statelessness: An interview with Craig Calhoun. *Kurdish Studies, 2*(1), 61–74.

Hall, S. (1996). Introduction: Who needs 'identity'? In S. Hall & P. du Gay (Eds.), *Questions of cultural identity* (pp. 1–17). London: Sage.

Joseph, S. (1999). Descent of the nation: Kinship and citizenship in Lebanon. *Citizenship Studies, 3*(3), 295–318.

Kabeer, N. (2002). Citizenship and the boundaries of the acknowledged community: Identity, affiliation and exclusion. *IDS Working Paper 171.* Falmer: Institute of Development Studies.

Krämer, G. (2013). Modern but not secular: Religion, identity and the *ordre public* in the Arab Middle East. *International Sociology, 28*(6), 629–644.

Mahmood, S. (2012). *Politics of piety: The Islamic revival and the feminist subject.* Princeton, NJ and Oxford: Princeton University Press.

Mamdani, M. (1996). *Citizen and subject. Contemporary Africa and the legacy of late colonialism.* Princeton, NJ: Princeton University Press.

Mouffe, C. (2005). *On the political.* London and New York: Routledge.

Velayati, M. (2016). Gender and Muslim families. *The Wiley Blackwell encyclopedia of family studies* (pp. 1–5). London: Wiley Blackwell.

Appendix A
Generic Bio-data Sheet

Name (nickname/initials)
How many years have you studied for?
Gender
Age
Your nationality(ies)
Your religion
Father's religion
Mother's religion
Home State
Your ethnicity
Father's ethnicity
Mother's ethnicity
Main home language(s)
Other languages

Appendix B
Generic Focus Group Discussion Pro-forma

Introduction

- You as the researcher.
- The research project.

–How young people understand, construct and enact their identities.
–Has taken place with groups of young people in other countries.

- Confidentiality within FGD and afterwards.
- Permission to tape and freedom to leave the group at any time.

Questions

1. Who are you?
   On the back of bio-data sheet write 3–6 words to describe yourself.
2. What does it mean to be a [national]?
3. What do you do that shows that you are a [national]?
4. What are the characteristics of a [national] woman? man?
5. How are [nationals] different from other [national] people?
6. What makes you proud to be a [national]?

7. Is there anything that does NOT make you proud to be a [national]?
8. What are the most important historical events of your [nation]?
9. Which [national] do you most admire? Why? Ask for an example of the other gender.
10. If you were not a [national] which nationality would you <u>most</u> like to be? Why?
11. If you were not a [national] which nationality would <u>least</u> like to be? Why?
12. Now to religion—what does it mean to be a [Muslim/Christian]?
13. How do you show that you are a [Muslim/Christian]?
14. How is it different to be a [Muslim/Christian] man compared to a [Muslim/Christian] woman?
15. Is being a [Muslim/Christian] different for people who live in different parts of [nation]? How?
16. Is being a [Muslim/Christian] different for people who are from different ethnic groups in [nation]?
17. If you had to belong to another ethnic group which would you <u>most</u> like to be? Why?
18. If you had to belong to another ethnic group which would you <u>least</u> like to be? Why?
19. Which [Muslim/Christian] do you most admire? (what was their ethnicity?) Give an example of the other gender (what was their ethnicity?)
20. How do [national] Muslims compare to other Muslims in the world?
21. In what ways is being a [national] Muslim different from being a [national] Christian? Muslim/Christian man? Muslim/Christian n?
22. Do you feel closer to [national] Christians or Muslims from other countries?
23. Do you think a sense of [national] identity is getting stronger or weaker among young people? [religious/ethnic/gender]. Explain.
24. Does your identity as a [national] ever come into conflict with your identity as a Muslim/ Christian? [<u>gender/ethnic</u>]
25. Which identity is most important to you? Why? How has ICT influenced your sense of identity?
26. Do you think your identity is different from your parents?

Author Biographies

Máiréad Dunne is a Professor of the Sociology of Education and former Director of the Centre for International Education at the University of Sussex http://www.sussex.ac.uk/education/cie/. Her research has attended to the links between educational and social inequalities in the Global South. In particular, she has focused on gender and sexuality; identities and difference; youth and citizenship in contexts of poverty, inequality and conflict. Máiréad has used a range of theoretical and methodological approaches from sociology, cultural studies and education to explore the experiences, perspectives and livelihoods of young people within different local and national contexts. She has worked alongside teams of local researchers and practitioners in contextually located, multi-dimensional explorations of policy, institutions and practices. These studies have realised several highly rated research projects, research reports and academic publications. Her writing has attracted several excellence awards.

Dr Naureen Durrani is a Senior Lecturer in International Education and Development at the Centre for International Education, University of Sussex where she convenes the internationally reputed

MA in International Education and Development and teaches on PhD, postgraduate and undergraduate courses. Naureen's research addresses the links between identity construction and education and the ways these impact on social relations, social cohesion and conflict. Her theoretical framing focuses on the intersection of identities, in particular, gender, religion (Islam), ethnicity and age (youth). Her research projects have explored education policy, curriculum, teacher education, citizenship identities and youth in diverse contexts including Pakistan, Nigeria, Rwanda, South Africa and the UK. Her research has been funded by DFID, ESRC, UNICEF, Oxfam Novib, SIDA and AusAid. Naureen is a Fellow of the Higher Education Academy, UK and has held research/academic positions at Northumbria University, University of Central Lancashire and University of Peshawar.

Dr Kathleen Fincham is a Senior Lecturer in Education and Social Science at St Mary's University (Twickenham). Working at the nexus of development and humanitarian scholarship, policy and practice, Kathleen's professional experience has been wide-ranging and varied, including research, teaching, training, programme and project management, policy analysis, partner coordination and advocacy with education institutions, governments, bilaterals, multi-laterals and INGOs in Canada, the UK, Asia, Africa and the Middle East (including extended research projects in Lebanon). Kathleen's research interests centre around the sociology and politics of education and learning, particularly within the contexts of developing countries and societies affected by conflict and forced migration (refugees). Specific themes of interest include: identities, inequalities, social exclusion, social cohesion, social mobility, citizenship, inter/intra community relations and institutional power. Kathleen's research has been funded by UNHCR, UNICEF, the European Union, SIDA and the British Council.

Dr Barbara Crossouard is a Reader in Education at the University of Sussex, UK and an active researcher working within the gender, identities and citizenship strand of the Centre for International Education (CIE). Barbara's previous research has spanned many different education contexts and sectors, including schooling and higher education. It reflects an enduring concern for education and social justice, and has had a central focus on the ways education can work to reproduce or disrupt structures of inequality such as gender and social class. She is especially interested in drawing upon post-structural and postcolonial theories to produce nuanced understandings of the ways educational policies and practices contribute to the production of identities. Much of her recent research has focused on youth citizenship identities and gender in different African contexts. Before joining the University of Sussex, Barbara lived and worked for 20 years in different countries in the Middle East, North Africa and Europe, experiences which were formative in contributing to her interest in education in the Global South.

Index

A

Adamawa 180, 184, 186–188
Affect 4, 9, 12, 28, 30, 43, 46, 48, 68, 95, 97, 105, 114, 118, 194, 210
Afghanistan 20, 84, 86
Agency 21, 22, 51, 52, 177, 216, 219, 257
Age relations 17, 131
Ali Bhutto, Zulfikar 83
Ali Jinnah, Muhammad 97
Arab Spring 20, 47

B

Belonging 2, 4, 9, 11, 13, 16, 29, 31, 39, 45, 46, 53, 62, 67, 103, 111, 117, 140, 170, 195, 210, 217. *See also* Affect
Biafran War 178, 201

Body 22, 28, 49, 51, 81, 161, 201, 211, 234. *See also* Embodiment
Boko Haram 9, 20, 178, 181, 203, 217
Borno 185
Buhari, Mohammadu 178

C

Child 18, 98, 134, 195, 203, 213, 229
  child-trafficking 195
Christianity 9, 10, 25, 38, 39, 44, 47, 67, 69–71, 90–92, 97, 104-106, 109, 117, 118, 133, 136, 146, 151, 152, 156, 158-160, 164, 167, 168, 178, 180, 184-186, 188, 189, 198, 200, 202,

204, 207, 209, 217, 219, 220, 226–229, 234, 235, 237, 241, 243, 245, 249, 257, 276
Catholic 90, 92, 143, 151, 202
Christian missionaries 232
Protestant 40, 44, 202
Citizenship 5, 7, 16, 24, 32, 36, 37, 45, 48, 52, 63, 72, 93, 94, 103, 116, 131, 134, 147, 196, 217, 236, 237, 266. *See also* Democracy
citizen 4, 16, 31, 36, 87, 95
Clientelism 34, 194, 195, 269
Colonial 6, 8–10, 12, 16, 22, 28, 30, 32–34, 37, 40, 42, 51, 53, 54, 62, 65, 67, 85, 106, 119, 130, 143, 148, 151, 158, 159, 165, 180, 195, 228, 238, 267, 269, 273
colonialism 22, 51, 80, 176, 177, 189
colonial rule 34, 65, 67, 79, 132, 143, 168, 268
indirect rule 34, 130, 135, 195
Conflict 4, 11, 20, 37, 43, 47, 67, 86, 87, 97, 105, 118, 159, 177, 178, 181, 199, 206, 226, 239, 241, 252, 255. *See also* War
ethnic conflict 199, 217
regional conflict 11, 255
religious conflict 43, 87, 105
Corruption 96, 131, 141, 152, 193, 207, 210, 217, 244, 268
Cosmopolitanism 17, 36, 38, 43, 45–48, 100, 170, 237
Muslim cosmopolitanism 17, 38, 46, 112

Cultural practices 13, 200, 204
Customary law 135, 181
Customs 8, 44, 51, 169, 201

D

Dakar 7, 30, 136, 137, 162, 276
Democracy 7, 8, 20, 22, 24, 31, 33, 38–40, 53, 62, 65, 67, 85, 93, 97, 101, 116, 130, 131, 134, 147, 149, 155, 170, 178, 179, 208, 226, 268, 269, 273
democratic election 131, 178
elections 83, 95, 145, 146
liberal democracy 22, 30, 33, 38, 39
Desire 27, 45, 64, 84, 106, 107, 254
Difference 2, 7, 8, 11, 12, 25, 28, 30, 36, 41, 50, 52, 63, 69, 71, 73, 74, 86, 95, 97, 99, 101, 111, 130, 136, 153, 158, 164, 191, 206, 213, 217, 228, 229, 236, 238, 240, 244, 246, 249, 265, 266, 272, 274, 275, 278
ethnic difference 8, 11, 157, 177, 179, 187, 200
gender difference 159, 190, 212
regional difference 182, 202, 204, 205, 209
religious difference 34, 67, 86, 228, 268, 271
Discourse 10, 22, 25, 26, 29, 33, 41, 43, 52, 64, 85, 86, 93, 94, 99, 107, 119, 143, 170, 191, 197, 219, 240, 245, 247, 252, 253, 265, 278
dominant discourse 3, 118, 168

E

Early marriage 88, 183
Education 3, 8, 19, 20, 23, 62, 65, 69, 70, 79, 88, 100, 109, 133, 134, 136, 137, 139, 151, 159, 161, 169, 181, 186, 187, 231, 232, 249, 256, 267, 277
   curriculum 89, 183
   Education Development Index 182
   higher education 8, 69, 79, 137, 139, 167, 169, 231, 233, 270, 276
   Integrated Qur'anic Tsangaya Education 183
   private education 134, 151
   Qur'anic education 183
   Western education 181, 183
Election 83, 95, 193
Embodiment 216
   dress 20, 51, 94, 97, 99, 106, 108, 160, 191, 250; hijab 20, 29, 41, 211, 251, 255; veil 157, 212
Ethnicity 2, 3, 6, 8, 12, 23, 27, 63, 67, 70, 81, 83, 86, 91, 92, 102, 103, 106, 109, 116, 118, 128, 137, 147, 169, 180, 196, 200, 202, 207, 209, 216, 226, 234–236, 242, 247, 255, 257, 267, 271, 272, 275
   Arab 11, 20, 47, 52, 156, 159, 245, 257, 267, 271
   Baloch 81, 83, 84, 86
   Bengali 83
   Diola 142, 157, 165
   ethnic conflict 178, 217
   ethnic identity 6, 133, 199, 204
   Fulani 133, 178, 187, 201, 202
   Hausa 179, 185, 187, 201, 212
   Igbo 178, 201–203
   Lébou 133, 138, 157
   Mohajir 87
   Pakhtun 91, 92, 98, 100, 102, 105, 107, 109, 110, 112, 114, 116, 118
   Peul 142, 147
   Punjabi 82, 91, 102
   Sindhi 81
   Wolof 72, 132, 133, 137–139, 142, 151, 158, 161, 162
   Yoruba 179, 202, 205, 206, 209, 210, 212, 218, 266
Europe 19, 33, 35, 45, 50, 166, 247, 273
Eurocentrism 99

F

Family 2, 11, 23, 42, 50, 70, 95, 98, 108–110, 135, 158, 161, 165, 167, 192, 200, 203, 214, 229, 237, 247, 249, 257, 276
   family law 135
Femininity 7, 10, 51, 159, 211, 219, 248. *See also* Gender
Focus group 6–8, 49, 63, 68, 69, 72, 136, 137, 139, 149, 151, 157, 159, 161, 164, 165, 169, 184, 186, 191, 219, 234, 270, 274, 276
Fragile state 20, 87

G

Gender 2, 3, 5, 6, 8, 11, 13, 16, 17, 19, 21, 24, 26, 29, 35, 49, 51–54, 63, 64, 71, 74, 86, 87, 92, 95, 106, 108–111, 113, 117–119, 130, 134, 136, 138, 139, 149, 159, 176, 182, 184, 186, 189, 197, 199, 206, 211, 214, 226, 231, 235, 248, 252, 255, 274–276
  domestic labour 276
  gender equality 10, 13, 168, 215, 277
  gender gap 65, 89, 134, 182
  gender identity 7, 26, 106, 211
  gender inequality 21, 64
  gender norm 49, 169, 216
  gender parity 89, 164, 165, 231
  gender violence 88
  patriarchy 50, 199, 211, 277
  women's subordination 164, 169
Generation 18, 94, 108, 183, 228, 236
Globalization 143

H

Heterosexuality 27, 108, 160, 249
Honour 11, 50, 84, 88, 93, 242, 245, 272
Human Development Index (HDI) 82

I

ICTs 9, 167, 204, 210, 218
  social media 154, 246

Identity 2, 3, 5, 6, 8, 9, 11, 13, 16, 21, 25, 26, 28, 29, 34, 37, 46, 49, 53, 54, 62, 64, 68, 71, 74, 79, 80, 85, 86, 88, 92, 93, 95–97, 102, 103, 105–107, 111–113, 115, 117, 118, 128, 138, 143, 148, 150, 160, 166, 168, 188, 190, 196, 199, 202, 203, 205, 207, 209, 217, 218, 232, 236, 238, 240, 241, 243, 250, 254, 255, 257, 264, 265, 270, 271
  ethnic identity 6, 199, 204
  gender identity 7, 26, 116, 211
  intersectionality 3, 17, 27, 29, 46, 47, 53, 64, 71, 119, 128, 139, 149, 166, 263
  national identity 6, 63, 87, 94, 99, 102, 106, 112, 114, 116, 117, 143, 160, 166, 189, 207, 209, 217, 232, 236, 241, 267
  regional identity 203
  religious identity 9, 13, 101, 105, 146, 188, 197, 204, 218
  youth identity 3, 5, 10, 12, 53, 63, 64, 199
Imagined community 4, 16, 28, 31, 34, 160. *See also* Nation
Independence 7, 34, 39, 42, 54, 84, 85, 101, 119, 128, 132, 135, 143, 155, 158, 177, 180, 201, 202, 228, 233
India 6, 41, 46, 54, 67, 79, 80, 82, 83, 94, 112, 113
  partition 6, 67, 83, 105, 112
Individualism 24, 25, 36, 40

Iran 78, 84, 156, 227, 242, 254
Islam 2, 3, 5, 6, 8, 13, 16, 19, 29, 38, 40–42, 44, 45, 47, 49, 51, 54, 65, 86, 87, 94, 96, 101–103, 105–107, 109, 111–119, 128, 132, 147, 148, 150, 153, 154, 156, 158, 163, 164, 166, 168, 170, 179, 185, 196, 204, 206, 210, 214–217, 219, 226, 228, 237, 240, 242, 244, 250, 253, 265, 270–273, 277
- Hezbollah 230, 231, 239, 242, 245
- Imam 240, 244
- jihad 41, 44, 87, 153, 155, 170, 270
- Layenne 44, 132, 136, 138, 154
- Mouride 132, 135, 138, 146, 148, 151, 153
- political Islam 41, 45
    - Shi'a 10, 11, 13, 67, 90, 92, 138, 153, 220, 226, 229, 231, 234, 235, 237, 239–241, 243, 245, 246, 248, 250, 251, 253, 254, 256, 257, 266, 270, 271; Ismaili 90
- Sufi 87, 130–132, 135, 138, 271
- Sufi brotherhoods 131, 132, 135
- Sunni 6, 8, 10, 11, 44, 67, 87, 92, 97, 99, 138, 153, 179, 220, 226, 229, 231, 243, 245, 246, 251, 256, 271
- *ummah* 5, 43, 45, 49, 118, 181, 244

J
Jonathan, Goodluck 178, 181, 185

K
Khan, Ghaffar 85
Khan, Imran 95, 96
Koran. *See* Qu'ran

L
Language 31, 36, 40, 51, 67, 70, 81, 94, 95, 97, 133, 139, 144, 149, 151, 157, 159, 163, 178, 199, 201, 231, 235, 236, 238, 268
- linguistic diversity 8, 81, 219
- official language 133, 178

M
Marriage 88, 109, 138, 160, 167, 183, 199, 215, 219, 237, 249, 251, 277
Masculinity 7, 10, 11, 13, 44, 49–51, 85, 88, 159, 160, 162, 168, 199, 205, 210, 217, 218, 248, 252, 257, 273, 276, 277
Media 20, 47, 93, 99, 112, 131, 163, 167, 243, 246, 265
Middle East 3, 8, 10, 18, 20, 42, 43, 45, 63, 78, 148, 159, 169, 226, 227, 240
Migration 31, 47, 81, 138, 180, 200
Military 67, 86, 96, 113, 128, 141, 178, 202, 229, 230, 234, 240, 241, 256, 267
Modernisation 39, 40, 42, 54, 189

Modernity 5, 16, 21, 22, 24, 33–35, 37–39, 41–44, 47, 54, 106, 149, 166, 169, 197, 237, 270, 273, 277
  modern self 12, 25, 40
Muhammadu, Buhari 181
Muslim youth 2, 3, 5, 8, 9, 12, 13, 21, 52, 63, 72, 79, 97, 99, 101, 109, 117, 143, 147, 150, 152, 158, 166, 184, 196–198, 202, 204, 205, 209, 210, 215, 217, 218, 264, 267, 268

N

Nation 2–4, 6, 8, 9, 12, 16, 17, 22, 24, 28–32, 34, 35, 37, 41, 43, 49, 51–53, 62, 65, 74, 81, 86, 92, 96, 97, 113, 128, 129, 132, 134, 139, 140, 147, 149, 153, 155, 156, 158, 161, 165, 168, 184, 187, 192, 195, 196, 202, 205, 206, 208, 209, 215, 216, 218, 219, 226, 234–236, 238, 239, 245, 248, 252, 255, 256, 265, 268, 273, 277
National constitution 64, 104, 177
Nationalism 35, 42, 43, 50, 51, 79, 106
Nationality 27, 41, 53, 64, 70, 93, 94, 97, 103, 140, 147, 151, 156, 162, 164, 188, 190, 208, 238, 267
National unity 6, 86, 99, 105, 147, 197–199, 202, 209

Nation-state 8, 12, 16, 32, 36–38, 169, 177, 202, 207, 217, 267, 268
Neo-colonialism 35, 143

O

Obasanjo, Olusegun 180
Orientalism 33, 37, 53, 115
Other 21, 25, 44, 53, 54, 142, 182, 194, 267
  external other 8, 53, 54, 97, 149, 156, 187
  internal other 13, 54, 155, 156, 196, 199, 202, 205, 267

P

Pakhtunwali 84, 103
Parental relations 138, 187, 201
Performativity 5, 12, 16, 26, 31, 48, 159, 205
Policy 5, 17, 21, 79, 164, 215, 216, 244
Politics 5, 9, 11, 16, 24, 34, 36, 38, 51, 80, 96, 131, 141, 146, 152, 199, 207, 215, 236, 241, 244, 249, 256, 271
  political leadership 7, 96, 128
Postcolonial 2, 4, 5, 160, 218, 270
Poststructural 2, 26, 27, 275
Poverty 19, 24, 37, 130, 177, 181, 183, 206

R

Religion 2, 3, 5, 6, 8, 9, 11, 12, 16, 19, 22, 27, 29, 30, 34, 36, 38–40, 42, 49, 51, 52, 54, 62, 67, 70, 72, 74, 79, 87,

92, 97, 100, 105, 110, 128, 132, 136, 138, 139, 145, 150, 152, 153, 155, 157, 159, 163, 165, 168, 179, 184, 192, 195, 197, 199, 200, 202, 204, 206, 208, 209, 211, 215, 216, 218, 219, 227, 234–236, 238, 245, 248, 252, 254–256, 264, 267, 271, 273, 275, 276. *See also* Christianity, Islam
  fundamentalism 19, 41, 62
  syncreticism 8, 9, 38, 44, 49, 132, 169, 204, 205, 207, 271
Republic 6, 41, 67, 97, 128, 135, 138, 143, 145, 149, 169, 177, 228, 254
  secular republic 7, 35, 46, 67, 130, 135, 138
Rural 46, 89, 109, 118, 134, 138, 167, 182, 183, 231

S

Sall, Macky 131
Secularism 13, 20, 38–41, 44, 52, 135, 140, 149, 169, 179
Senghor, Leopold 130, 143, 144
Sharif, Nawaz 95
Siddiqui, Aafia 113, 121
Subordination 8, 164, 169, 211, 216, 268, 274, 276

T

Teranga 141, 162, 269, 276
Terrorism 9, 29, 37, 42, 62, 92, 95, 99, 114, 156, 195, 198, 217, 270

U

Urban 7, 82, 83, 134, 138, 167, 182, 200

V

Violence 28, 31, 33, 40, 41, 47, 88, 96, 112, 133, 148, 181, 184, 185, 188, 228, 272

W

Wade, Abdoulaye 131, 165
War 11, 35, 42, 170, 228–232, 239, 242, 244, 245, 252, 256, 274
War on Terror 7, 24, 95, 112, 113, 273

Y

Youth bulge 19, 20, 88
Youth identity 3, 5, 10, 53, 63, 65, 199
Youth radicalisation 5, 62, 90
Youth researcher 6, 63, 64, 70, 72, 92

Printed by Printforce, the Netherlands